THE CYCLE OF AMERICAN LITERATURE

THE MACMILLAN COMPANY
NEW YORK · CHICAGO
DALLAS · ATLANTA · SAN FRANCISCO
LONDON · MANILA

**THE MACMILLAN COMPANY
OF CANADA, LIMITED**
TORONTO

THE CYCLE

OF

AMERICAN LITERATURE

An Essay in Historical Criticism

by

ROBERT E. SPILLER

NEW YORK
THE MACMILLAN COMPANY
1955

CONTENTS

CONTENTS

The eye is the first circle; the horizon which it forms is the second; and throughout nature this primary figure is repeated without end. It is the highest emblem in the cipher of the world.

—EMERSON

PREFACE

THERE seems now to be little doubt in the minds of critics at home and abroad that the United States has produced, during the twentieth century, a distinctive literature, worthy to take its place with the great literatures of other times and other peoples. There is no similar agreement on the reasons for this, or for the apparently sudden cultural maturity of a people which, throughout nearly two centuries of political independence, has thought of itself as heterogeneous and derivative in its racial and cultural make-up. American writings of the past quarter-century give evidence of a literary renaissance which could come only from a long tradition and a unified culture. This literary renaissance, the second to occur in the United States, must have both a history and a pattern of relationships within itself. As yet it has not been clearly defined or understood, because literary historians have failed to comprehend it as an organic whole.

The theory of literary history which was most generally held during the nineteenth century proposed that, because almost all of the literature produced by citizens of the United States was written in the English language, and because literature is expression and can presumably be best described by the language in which it is expressed, American literature is, and always will be, a branch of English literature. The consequence of this theory was that undue emphasis was placed on the Colonial period, on that part of the United States which most successfully preserved its British characteristics, New England, and on those authors, like Irving, Longfellow, Lowell, and Howells, who discovered ways of using American "materials" without greatly violating British proprieties. Writers like Walt Whitman, Herman Melville, Mark Twain, and Theodore Dreiser, who were more deeply American than any of the other group, were dismissed either as evidences of a cruder stage in cultural development or as curiosities. Thus an American romantic movement could be clearly distinguished as evolving from the imitative beginnings of Irving, Cooper, and Bryant, and culminating in the poetry of the bearded sages of the Cambridge group. Thereafter came the "Gilded Age," a deterioration into "realism" and "pessimism," and a literature in the twentieth century that was described as close to degenerate in both inspiration and form. Literary histories which are firmly rooted in this theory are still produced and sold by the thousands of copies in the United States and elsewhere.

The first successful challenge to this theory—not counting the pioneer work of Moses Coit Tyler—came in 1927 with V. L. Parrington's *Main Currents in American Thought*, the literary historian's version of a widespread movement in historical writing which was then attempting to retell the record of the past in terms of economic and other forms of environmental determinism. The literary historian of this school owed his ultimate debt to Taine, Hegel, and Marx, but as an American and a democrat he recognized the social philosophies of none of these masters, taking from them only the method of relating literary expression directly and simply to the life which it expressed. American schools began to use "Literature and Life" readers instead of the old "Belles-Lettres" varieties, while scholars in the universities and journalists outside began a process of reevaluation of both major and minor American authors and their works. The result was a new pattern of American literary history that succeeded in rediscovering such writers as Freneau, Thoreau, and Melville; in giving more sympathetic recognition to Whitman and Mark Twain; in showing just what was American in such writers as Henry James; and in arousing widespread interest in humor, local color, realism, folk ballads and legends, and in minor authors who were faithful to their materials and reflected the ideas and moods of their times. Under this dispensation the literature of the late nineteenth century and of the years that followed could at least be regarded without prejudice, and awarded laurels for its vigor and its authenticity, even though at times it seemed to lose its character as art.

The pendulum had again swung too far. So great was the value assigned, under this theory, to accuracy of record that the best literature seemed to be merely that which struck closest to the facts. Imagination was crowded aside by political and social data, and American literary history threatened to become no more than a history of documentation; often, as even in the case of Parrington, the documentation of a specific theory of social and political development. Ironically, major authors like Poe, Dickinson, and Henry James, who in one way or another were above or outside the obvious data of American life, seemed irrelevant and alien, at the same time that others, like Cooper, Melville, and Mark Twain, were gaining a new dimension. Although this theory made possible an *American* literary history, it threatened to make *literary* history as such an anomaly. In its most extreme form it even accepted the Marxian formula and imposed a schematic dogma that was not too different from the "socialist realism" of the dictatorships.

An escape into pure aesthetic analysis, which many critics then proposed, was not the resolution of this dilemma. It was rather an acknowledgment of failure by the literary historian, a confession that he had lost faith in the continuity of life and the organic principle of its expression in art. There was no good reason why, with the old prejudices cleared away and the relationship between American literature and American life clearly established, the real literary history of the United States could not begin to take shape.

The writer of this new history must first recognize that the major author, even though he becomes major by rising above his times or otherwise alienating himself from his society, is nevertheless the specific product of his times and of his society, and probably their most profound expression. Literature, therefore, has a relationship to social and intellectual history, not as documentation, but as symbolic illumination. Valid literary history must concern itself chiefly with major authors, but it must deal with them, both directly and indirectly, in provable context. Therefore the first task of the new American literary historian was to discover which were or are the major American authors, and not to be misled by the fact that some of them denied their country and became expatriates, others lashed out against it with satire or overt denunciation, or escaped from it into dreams and fantasies. These are merely varying forms of relationship between the writer and his materials.

The rational view of history, which deals only with logical sequences of cause and effect, is inadequate to deal with relationships such as these. If there is one idea that most major American authors have in common, it is the belief that life is organic; and the American literary historian can do no better than to adopt for his study an organic view of history. The individual organism follows the circular pattern of life; it has a beginning, a life cycle, and an end. This simple principle may be discovered in the structure of a poem, in the biography of an author, in the rise and fall of a local or particular cultural movement, or in the over-all evolution of a national literature. The historian's task is to discover the cycle, or cycles, by which his literature is determined both in general scheme and in detail. American literature, when reviewed in terms of its major authors and from the vantage point of the period of its greatest achievement, the twentieth century, reveals such a cyclic rhythm.

The basic theme for this rhythm is also the central historical fact of the American experiment: the removal of a mature and sophisticated civilization—that of Western Europe —to a primitive continent ideally suited to its needs and virtually unexploited of its apparently infinite natural resources. The American expansion to the West, and the impact in turn of the newly formed civilization on its parent, set the circular pattern for the whole story. On the level of symbolic illumination, the literary historian must disclose the vast and intricate pattern of this unfolding cycle, perhaps not yet completed, but firmly defined by its varied recurrences through four centuries.

When applied to the story of American literature as a whole, this cyclic theory discloses not only a single organic movement, but at least two secondary cycles as well: the literary movement which developed from the Eastern seaboard as a center, and culminated with the great romantic writers of the mid-nineteenth century; and that which grew out of the conquest of the continent and is now rounding its full cycle in the twentieth century. When applied to the individual work, the same theory supplies a formula for measuring the aesthetic distance of a poem or play or novel from its origins in some phase of American experience. The letter home comes first, then the debate on religion or philosophy, then the imitative work of art, and finally the original and organic expression of the new life. Thus the process of cultural growth into art is endlessly repeated as a civilization moves forward in time.

The historian of this process, on the other hand, takes his position in the present and looks backward over the past. His is the task of reorganizing experience so that its larger meanings are revealed, rather than that of repeating history in all its details. He must select, omit, and reorganize from the great mass of available data so that a coherent view of the total literary culture can emerge. The broad contours of a landscape and the organic pattern of its hills and valleys can be seen only from a height at which some details are obscured and others take on meaningful relationships because of the angle of vision of the observer. The writing of history, like other forms of art, requires aesthetic distance before it can claim perspective.

This book is an essay toward such a singleness of vision. It is also and inescapably a by-product of the shared experience of editing the *Literary History of the United States*. Ideas and methods which in that project could be used only as implements of organization can here take full control because one person alone is responsible for them. The editors and contributors of that ambitious work need not be implicated in the methods and conclusions of this lesser one by a simple acknowledgment of so long and intimate an association. That several of them cared enough to read this manuscript with keen and helpful advice—in particular, Willard Thorp, Thomas H. Johnson, and Sculley Bradley—does not lessen the debt. The manuscript also owes much to the scrutiny of my wife, Mary S. Spiller, and of Thomas J. Johnston, Sigmund Skard and other friends who read all or parts of it.

SWARTHMORE, PA.
March 15, 1955

THE CYCLE OF AMERICAN LITERATURE

THE

FIRST FRONTIER

MOST of the literature of the United States is written in the English language, much of it by men and women whose forebears came from the British Isles; yet the first man from Western Europe to write home about his adventures in the New World was not an Englishman, nor was the land he discovered a part of the continental United States. Even so, the famous Columbus *Letter* (1493) sets the form and the point of view of the earliest American literature. In a far country, man's immediate impulse is to tell his distant friends of what he finds and how he fares. Columbus, a Genoese in the service of the

Spanish King Ferdinand, wrote to the Royal Treasurer, "Because my undertakings have attained success, I know that it will be pleasing to you." Here was the beginning of the written record of the American adventure.

It has been said that the settlement of America was a by-product of the unsettlement of Europe, for both events took place during the sixteenth and seventeenth centuries. Then it was that the great mercantile powers of Spain, France, Holland, and Britain emerged from the combinations of feudal baronies that had kept the Middle Ages in a state of local and constant warfare; that Protestant reformers like Martin Luther and John Calvin finally broke the authority of the medieval church-state that had dominated Europe since the fall of Rome; that the spirit of inquiry and enjoyment of the senses aroused man to his greatest age of art and learning. By 1600 Italy had its paintings and sculpture, Holland its learned skeptics and scholars, and England the great plays of Shakespeare. The horizons of the spirit and of the known geographical world expanded together. Shakespeare, the man of thought, and Columbus, the man of action—there is a parallel in the contrasting gifts of these two pioneers. The civilization of Western Europe virtually exploded of its own inner energy in the century 1500–1600, and one wave from that explosion swept over the undiscovered seas and lands to the west.

Other "letters home" reported most of the subsequent voyages of the explorers who followed during this and the next century. The empires of Spain and Portugal followed the course charted by the Genoese sailor, skirting the Gulf coast and the Caribbean Sea, centering in Mexico, and fanning out along the California coast, over the great plains to the north, and southward into Brazil and Peru. France's explorers and

priests followed the course of the St. Lawrence River and the
Great Lakes, and then went down the Mississippi River to
cross the Spanish routes at New Orleans. British, Dutch, and
Swedes came finally to settle on the fertile Atlantic coastal
plain, and, held back by the mountain wall, to build the most
stable of all colonial societies. In these two hundred years
American literature, though little more than the report of
Western European culture on the move, was as cosmopolitan
as it was ever to be again.

Except for a few sturdy volumes like William Bradford's
Of Plimoth Plantation (undertaken in 1630, first published in
1856), much of the writing left by these early explorers and
settlers makes rather dreary reading today for anyone not interested in the history of probably the greatest single migration
of civilization on record. Writers sought mainly to justify
their own enterprises, to take possession of the new lands,
riches, and peoples for the monarchs who had sponsored their
undertakings, and to describe geographic and economic conditions in order to help those who were to follow them. The
temptation to belittle hardships and to overstate the possibilities of the future was great. The Spanish Conquistador
Coronado, the French Father Hennepin, and the British ad-
venturer Captain John Smith told much the same story of lands
rich in natural resources and peopled by strange and primitive
tribes.

Forests many hundreds of years old greeted these men
from Europe upon their arrival, and the elaborate trappings of
their own warriors or priests contrasted sharply with the na-
kedness of the "savages" they met. But these apparently primitive natives, in spite of their childlike gullibility, were the outer
fringes of the ancient civilization that included the Mayas,

Aztecs, and Incas, centered far to the south and west in Mexico and Peru. The people whom the white man called Indians because he thought that the land he had reached was ancient India were the nomadic descendants of rich and powerful Mongoloid races which had migrated many centuries earlier from Asia. They had probably come by way of the Bering Strait, but they had long since built their major cities and temples in the more hospitable regions nearer the Equator and had then spread out over two continents.

These men of the forest were equally unprepared for the impatient idealism that sought to convert them to Christianity and for the greed that clutched hungrily at their gold and their land. Because they were pushed back, despoiled, and exploited for three hundred years, their part in American literature is more a hint of what might have been than a record of what actually was. It seems to be a law of nature that any species will rapidly become extinct when confronted with a sudden change in environment or with a new foe whose ways it does not understand. The fact that the American Indian retreated and suffered is not necessarily an evidence of his inferiority. He left an indelible stamp upon the imagination of his conqueror. The Indian was an individualist not because he was in revolt but because he had accepted his place in the physical universe, and with it his place in his own limited society. To the white invaders he was an obstacle to be removed, but to their imaginations he often symbolized the nobility man could achieve by living openly with nature.

In describing him, the Europeans used only black or white, with no shading; and little is left of the Indian's own account of life because his poetry and prose existed only in oral tradition. He had no written record other than pictographs, and his conqueror was not usually interested, at the time, in writing down his thoughts and feelings for him. The stoic calm of his few reported speeches and poems gives only a hint of the rich culture that was so soon forgotten.

Early descriptions of the Indian and his life by the white man are on the whole favorable, with the exception of some of the narratives of captivity. Columbus speaks of the gentleness and timidity of those he encountered on the island of San Salvador, and John Smith makes King Powhatan and his daughter Pocahontas into reasoning human beings. The French friars and the Spanish conquistadors report friendly relations except where the explorers were drawn into the internecine wars of the natives. Puritan, Moravian, and Quaker missionaries of a slightly later date were inclined to take sides in such differences, and in this way helped to cultivate the myth of the very good and the very bad Indians who found their way into later romances. Usually the Europeans were not as much interested in studying the Indian and his civilization as they were in converting him to Christianity or in using him for their own ends, and they were likely to read into his character the traits they wished to find. It was the Indian of the white man's imagination rather than the Indian of historical fact who finally became an important part of the usable past of American literature.

During the seventeenth century the Spanish and French spread out over the entire American west from the ice fields to the Equator, while the British firmly established themselves on the thin strip of the Atlantic coast. This small area of fertile land was left relatively unmolested for two centuries to develop a new civilization composed of almost all the elements thrown off by a seething Europe. French, Dutch, Scots-Irish, Welsh, and Swedes were gradually absorbed into the dominant British group. Anglicans and Roman Catholics mingled with the dissenting sects whom they had caused to emigrate, and they thus brought to the New World the full spectrum of religious beliefs and practices they had known in the Old. The solid mercantile and farming middle classes of England and Northern Europe comprised the bulk of the migrants, but there were also lords and indentured servants, Dutch patroons and Negro slaves.

One of the miracles of history is that, by 1700, this new land had become so solid and homogeneous an association of colonies, owing fealty to the British king, mainly Protestant in religion, agricultural in economy, and English in speech. Differences from this pattern of culture, where they continued to exist, were subordinated. Former aristocrats joined with the enterprising bourgeoisie to establish a half dozen and more thriving seaport towns, to lay out acres of fertile farms, and to build the ships that were to circle the globe. Diversity within unity was from the start the shaping characteristic of the new people, their land, and ultimately their literature. Man's hunger, divided to serve both his physical and his spiritual needs, created on the continent of North America a civilization that was similarly divided because it offered tempting satisfactions on both the higher and the lower levels. The chance to create a new order that would reflect divine goodness was made to seem possible by an infinity of material resources which could as well feed the lowest desires. Perhaps in the beginning of American civilization can be found a clue to the incongruous mixture of naïve idealism and crude materialism that produced in later years a literature of beauty, irony, affirmation, and despair. The violence of twentieth century American literature owes much to the energy and the contrasts in its cultural origins.

CHAPTER I

ARCHITECTS OF CULTURE
Edwards, Franklin, Jefferson

THE discovery and settlement of the Western continent is only the first part of the American story; America was also a new world of the mind and spirit. The breakdown of the Middle Ages released a flood of energy out of which the modern idea of the free individual was constructed. "I went to the woods," wrote Thoreau many years later, "because I wished to live deliberately, to front only the essential facts of life, and see if I could not learn what it had to teach, and not, when I came to die, discover that I had not lived." The joy that comes from acceptance of this simple faith or the despair that comes from its denial are the two main streams of the American tradition. Americans from the start have gone to the woods to live deliberately, and their literature is the record of their successes and failures. From the religious and political debates on how life should be lived and how a society should be constructed were fashioned a nation and a way of life.

In the creation of this new world of the mind, America became, in the seventeenth and eighteenth centuries, a vast laboratory in which ideas formed in England and Western Europe could develop into action without being hampered by the laws, customs, and traditions of an obsolete feudal society. The difference in those years between America and Europe was that the things which could be only talked about in Europe, in America could be actually done. The great religious, political, and intellectual revolution that moved from the Renaissance and the Reformation into the Enlightenment and the Age of Reason became, in the colonies of the Atlantic seaboard, the pattern of everyday life. For its first two hundred years, American writing reflected this sense of the present importance of ultimate things.

As Luther defined it by his "theses" of 1517, the Protestant Reformation was a political as well as a religious movement, a break away from the temporal as well as the ecclesiastical authority of the Church of Rome. In England that break was almost wholly political when the separation of the Church of England was declared by King Henry VIII for his own personal reasons; but the wars of theological doctrine that had originated in France, Germany, Holland, and Switzerland had, by the seventeenth century, crossed the Channel and become central in British political and religious life. The fall and restoration of the Stuart dynasty and the rise and fall of the Puritan Commonwealth determined in large part the characters of the first American colonies, for members of all parties sought refuge in their turn in the fertile lands to the West. Thus Puritanism settled New England, Pennsylvania took its character from the Quakers and Deists, Virginia was predominantly Anglican, and Maryland was at least in part Roman Catholic.

Of the early colonies, Massachusetts—together with its offshoots, Connecticut, Rhode Island, and later the settlements to the north—was most consecrated to the ideals of the Protestant Reformation. Although the shore had first been scouted by the irreligious Captain John Smith of Virginia, it was soon settled by men devoted to the cause of freedom of conscience and to the religious way of life. Both the "Pilgrims" who settled Plymouth in 1620 and the "Puritans" who settled Massachusetts Bay ten years later accepted religion as law, custom, and daily care because they had been denied and persecuted at home. The Plymouth colonists, as they prepared to disembark from the *Mayflower* under the leadership of William Bradford, drew up a covenant in which they combined themselves "into a civill body politick" for the "glorie of God, and the advancement of the Christian faith." The Bay colonists were even more devout, while to the south in Connecticut and Rhode Island the fiery Roger Williams and other dissenters from Puritan orthodoxy used the language of religion for ideas that anticipated the revolutionary theory of the rights of man.

Much has been written to prove that in their first century the New England colonists were as much concerned with the things of this world as with those of the next, but their own writing was sober. These were plain men and women, devoted to the arduous task of creating a civilization in a wilderness, and their sense of responsibility generally outweighed their sense of humor. Many had university training, but none were of the court where much of Elizabethan literature had been made. Their poetry and prose have the variety if not quite the finish of the religious writers of seventeenth century Britain, from the stark directness of the journals of Bradford and Winthrop to the rhetoric and symbolism of Cotton Mather's massive history, the *Magnalia Christi Americana* (1702), and the subtle and exquisite metaphysical poetry of Edward Taylor.

It was in the sermons and tracts of Jonathan Edwards (1703–1758), the last and greatest of the Puritan divines, that this intensity of spirit found its most enduring expression. In his church at Northampton, Massachusetts, this spare and devout man, of thin lips and quiet eyes, for twenty years fanned the dying fires of Calvinism to a white heat—and then retired, an exile from his people, and a missionary to the Indians in a remote village in the Berkshire Hills.

Although his recent biographers are careful to point out that the philosophical idealism of his college writings, the emotional abandon of his mid-life sermons, and the dogmatic logic of his later tracts are but three parts of the same substance, it is easier to understand this complex and powerful nature if they are also regarded as three periods in his life. And to understand him is essential if it is admitted, as his most learned biographer insists, that he is one of America's five or six major artists—one who happened to work with ideas rather than with poems or novels, and one who, like Franklin and Jefferson, succeeded in generalizing his personal experience into the meaning of America.

In his earliest phase Edwards seemed to be the liberal who would bring sweet reason to the dogmatic rule of the Puritan oligarchy. Born of a cultured family which was to become famous for the many gifted minds it produced, as a boy he early gave evidence of genius in his essay on "flying" spiders, written at the age of twelve. His sensitive and scientific curiosity and his rejection of the materialism of his day led him, when he entered Yale College the next year, to a greedy study of John Locke and that philosophy which sought the reality of ideas rather than of objects. His college essays laid the foundations of a rationalistic idealism in America and prepared the way for Emerson and the great literary and intellectual movement of the next century. At the same time he became convinced of the Calvinistic doctrines of absolute divine sovereignty and human depravity, and he began his long task of rebuilding the structure of dogma which the Arminians and other freethinkers had nearly destroyed. His idealism became confined to these self-imposed limits, and, working in the methods of the medieval scholastics, he put the most advanced psychological knowledge of his day to the services of theological architecture. His system was a massive and brilliant structure of emotion and intellect to which modern man, in his present sense of loss and confusion, is likely to turn with admiration and no little longing.

Edwards has recorded his early seeking in a "personal narrative" in which he tells how he discovered for himself the innate sinfulness of mortal man and the sweet content of submission to the inevitable will of God in Christ. His prose poem on Sarah Pierrepont who was later to become his wife has the same note of calm: "They say there is a young lady in [New Haven] who is beloved of that Great Being, who made and rules the world. . . . She is of a wonderful sweetness, calmness and universal benevolence of mind . . . and seems to have someone invisible always conversing with her."

After taking up his life work, first with his grandfather, Solomon Stoddard, in Northampton, and then as minister in his own right, he became oppressed by the worldliness of his parishioners, and undertook to arouse them to a realization of their sins. The "Great Awakening" which resulted was a part of an evangelical movement then sweeping through Western Europe, England, and America. The agony of spirit that is prompted by the fear of Hell becomes converted in this ex-

perience into a complete passivity and peace when the absolute
authority of God is fully realized. It was the mission of Edwards to distinguish between the genuine achievement of union
with God and the spurious mysticism which to him was a mere
form of trance in which the Devil had open access to the un-
suspecting soul. His sermons, in their kind, particularly that on
"Sinners in the Hands of an Angry God," have probably
never been equaled for passionate strength and for beauty of
form.

Such power over his fellows was not meant for any one
man, and Edwards was rejected by his people when the wave
of emotion had passed. At his lonely retreat in the Berkshire
Hills, he set himself the task of reformulating a doctrine which
would, he hoped, stand for his own day and for the future
against weakness of the spirit. As he had triumphed in emotion,
he now became supreme in logic. With relentless analytical
power, his tracts on the freedom of the will, the nature of true
virtue, and the doctrine of original sin even today drive through
to an empty victory over his forgotten adversaries. Failing in
his immediate mission of restoring the rule of his God on
earth, he succeeded in building, if only for himself, perhaps
the most perfect structure of thought and feeling yet erected
in this land. It is the philosophical system with which the history of American philosophy starts; but it is also the house of
tragedy, in which the sense of guilt and agony survives, the
release into the peace of submission fails. It is the structure of
tragic realization which was repeated in the work of Poe,
Hawthorne, and Melville; O'Neill, Eliot, and Faulkner.

– 2 –

In the Middle Atlantic Colonies and the South, no such
theological edifice was erected because life in this world was

generally accepted as something to be lived on its own terms. The richness and beauty of the land found by the early explorers stimulated interest in agriculture and botany rather than in religion. Excellent harbors developed cities with mercantile and commercial interests. The remark that Benjamin Franklin was born in Philadelphia at the age of seventeen is not all whimsy, for when he migrated from his native Boston in 1723 he found a provincial town already preparing to become the cultural as well as the political capital of the colonies. The worldly industriousness of its safe harbor harmonized with the spiritual toleration of its Quaker founders, for in the followers of George Fox there was combined an acute personal sense of the inner life with the common sense that was unafraid of man and his sins. Akin to the Arminians and other radical New England groups in their emphasis on individual revelation, the members of the Society of Friends recognized no authority other than their own "inner light." Thus the physical world of Newton and the mental world of Locke provided, in the Middle Colonies and the South, where no single religious faith dominated, a frame of reference for the new civilization which was open to variety in its parts but single in its direction. The worldly materialism of a Southern planter like William Byrd, the special conscience of a mystic like John Woolman, the love of nature of a botanist like John or William Bartram, and the common sense of an opportunist like Franklin conspired to create a free man in an open society. This was the nation, in the making, which was to break from the Old World on a near tomorrow.

Benjamin Franklin (1706–1790), more than any other man, opened his mind to the full range of experimental possibilities of eighteenth century America. As Jonathan Edwards was the symbol of the religious fervor of Puritanism at its purest, so

Franklin became the symbol of the Enlightenment in America —the Age of Reason. When, just turned fifty, this portly but still spry tradesman-philosopher set sail for London as the agent of the people of Pennsylvania, he left behind him the normal lifetime span of activity in shaping the new civilization. He also had provided a testament of his guiding principles in "The Way to Wealth," the Preface to *Poor Richard's Almanack* for 1758, through which he had been advising and admonishing his contemporaries for a quarter of a century. Why waste time in complaining of taxes, he asked, when by our idleness and our sloth we are continually taxing ourselves? Why wish for better times when with industry we can make such times as we wish? Why be poor and in debt when thrift will purchase all our necessities? Here—tongue in cheek, perhaps— the self-made spokesman of the "middling people" offered his sage counsel.

Behind this apparently worldly advice lay a deeply considered philosophy which had started to form in *A Dissertation on Liberty and Necessity, Pleasure and Pain* (1725), written at the age of nineteen as an exercise in thinking and typesetting. In trying to refute the heresy of a rational Deistic God in this essay, he convinced himself of its logic. A wide reader with an insatiable curiosity, Franklin early aligned himself with this liberal school of thought, choosing to believe, in contrast to Edwards, that God in his goodness allows each man to come to his own terms with nature rather than requiring that he submit to divine dictation. When he had thus reasoned himself out of the doctrines inculcated early with Cotton Mather's "Essays to Do Good," his mind was opened to the skepticism of the age, and he found himself on the side of natural rights rather than that of divine prerogatives. Hastily leaving formal religion to others, he devoted his ingenuity to making his own world a better place to live in. A pragmatist long before William James defined the term, he believed that whatever works is true because it demonstrates a natural law. This belief followed him through all his many and ascending activities.

It is as a printer and author in Boston that we first see the boy, setting with his own hand the type of those rascally essays by "Dame Silence Dogood" in his brother's pioneer paper the *New England Courant*, and it was a printer's apprentice who broke his indentures and set out for Philadelphia to make his own way. By 1727 he was gathering the young tradesmen of the provincial city into a club for self-improvement, and from that year to 1748, when he retired and turned his print shop over to his partner, he was the mainspring of civic life. Like all printers of the day, he had his own bookshop too; but, unlike most printers of any day, he founded a college, a circulating library, and an international scientific society. The story of these years is told in the *Autobiography*, written long after and speaking an old man's reflections on the successes and failures of his past, but one of the frankest and freest of all personal records. Unhappily, perhaps, it is this Franklin most of us know even when we forget that he is smiling through his octagonal glasses at his own follies and ironically pointing the moral at himself. Read with a touch of the comic spirit, the *Autobiography* is one of the classics of its kind.

Franklin retired in order to become a scientist and philosopher, but the times made him a politician and statesman. His experiment with a kite and a thunderstorm confirmed one of the fundamental hypotheses about static electricity. He invented the smokeless chimney, the Franklin stove, the lightning rod, but behind each device is a principle which the inventor found out for himself and then applied to a human need or comfort. When he went to London in 1770 to speak for all the colonies and to debate their cause at the bar of the House of Commons, and when he became, in 1778 in France, the first American minister to a foreign court, he was received primarily as a philosopher and scientist.

Through all these experiences, his writing kept pace with his activities. His tracts on science were read in the learned gatherings of London and Paris as well as at home, and his satires on the follies of the British colonial policy rank, for wit and innuendo, with the political satires of Swift and Voltaire. At the same time he wrote serious letters to Joseph Priestley, Lord Kames, and David Hartley, and charming notes of flirtatious but fatherly advice to young ladies on both sides of the Atlantic. This lighter side of the aging Franklin is perhaps the most engaging of all, especially when it appears in those letter-essays the "Bagatelles": "Dialogue Between Franklin and the Gout," "The Whistle," "The Ephemera," whose lighthearted banter has too often been lost by the textbook moralist. Here irony is distilled into whimsy, and a comic delight in life is made the source of deep wisdom.

Franklin brought the era of colonial America to a close when he won his Socratic victory for the cause of the colonies in the House of Commons. He was soon helping to create the new nation as a participant in the Second Continental Congress. But the wise philosopher of nature who left a written record of all he thought and felt and did is the Franklin who takes his place with Edwards as one of the first really great writers in the new literature. His progeny will be found among the realists and doers like Cooper and Mark Twain, Howells and

Dreiser, and all the thousands of lesser men who have told a living story of the American experiment.

– 3 –

The period 1760–1790 was perhaps the darkest in the history of the United States, but in the struggles of those days the political and economic life of the new nation was formed by a small group of philosopher-statesmen, of whom Thomas Jefferson (1743–1826) was the acknowledged leader.

The American Revolution was, in a sense, a private war between the Atlantic seaboard colonies and the parent British nation; but it was also a crusade for human liberty. The theoretical issue of whether or not man can break away from all civil authority and rely upon natural law alone to guide his conduct would not in itself have caused a clash of arms had there not been a more immediate difference. But once the colonies had decided that British tyranny was insufferable, independence could be declared in the most exalted of general terms. The fervor of the small group of revolutionary leaders came not so much from anger at Britain as from the conviction that they were fighting for human rights. The concept of the sovereignty of the people, formulated in the intellectual battles of Locke, Hobbes, Shaftesbury, and Hume on British soil, was transformed into a challenge of British rule.

The Declaration of Independence was not the first pronouncement on human rights and plan for colonial unity to be formulated in America. The Mayflower Compact of 1620 had contained the principle of government by the consent of the governed, as did the Hartford Constitution of 1639, drawn up by the followers of Thomas Hooker: Well knowing "that to mayntayne the peace and union of such a people there should be an orderly and decent Government established according to God, . . . [we] doe therefore assotiate and conioyne our selves to be as one Publicke State or Commonwelth." And a plan for colonial union under one Grand Council responsive to the will of the several signers was presented by the practical Franklin to the Albany Convention of 1754. By 1776 there was no novelty in the idea of union based on the voluntary relinquishment by the several colonies of individual rights.

The declarations of human rights which were passed by the First Continental Congress in Philadelphia (1774) and by the Virginia Convention (1776) preceded the classic Declaration of Independence and, like it, opened with general statements of the natural rights of which man cannot ever deprive himself or his posterity: "namely [in the Virginia statement], the enjoyment of life and liberty, with the means of acquiring and possessing property, and pursuing and obtaining happiness and safety."

This is the basic American principle; all else in the American tradition leads up to it or away from it or is otherwise related to it. But from the earliest days of settlement there was also its contrary, the principle of submission to external authority. The Calvinists, with their belief in the sovereignty of God and the depravity of man, had a very different notion of human liberty, as expressed in the "little speech" by Governor John Winthrop of the Massachusetts Bay Colony in 1645: "If you will be satisfied to enjoy such civil and lawful liberties, such as Christ allows you, then will you quietly and cheerfully submit unto that authority which is set over you, in all the administration of it, for your good." From there, the conservative tradition can be traced without too much difficulty through Increase Mather and Jonathan Edwards to the Anglican Jonathan Boucher who defended the Loyalist cause in the Revolutionary War on the grounds that civil liberty "is a severe and restrained thing; implies, in the notion of it, settled subordination, subjection, and obedience." Even the exiling of the Loyalists did not end the matter, for the more reactionary Federalists of the next generation made use of the same argument in a milder form when they called for a strong central government above the rights of the states. The part of the argument that is deeply American is the constant concern for human liberty; but there has always been a party of the extreme "right," and one of the extreme "left," as well as a wide middle ground between them in the process of defining and redefining the nature and sanction of that liberty.

As the hour of crisis approached after 1770, the battle of words was taken up by the pamphleteers, men like Joseph Galloway for the Loyalists and Tom Paine for the Rebels, and the issues were narrowed to those of the immediate situation. In the twenty years between 1763 and 1783, some nine thousand of these "little books," hastily written and printed for the hour, were issued from the American presses. This was a time for tracts calling for action in the unequivocal terms of Paine's *Common Sense* (1776) rather than for philosophy or poetry.

The most violent, yet also the most carefully considered, tract of the times was the Declaration of Independence which was adopted by the Continental Congress on July 4, 1776. Its principal author, Thomas Jefferson, was the most learned of the scholar-statesmen who provided leadership when the revolutionary issue moved into the stage of crisis. By 1776 indignation at British "tyranny" had become so intense that most partisans of the American cause forgot their philosophy and answered Paine's call to action. Jefferson was remarkable for his ability to maintain perspective at the same time that he shared the popular protest. He wrote into this first "official" document of the Republic the intellectual foundations of the political and social system of a democracy founded upon independence.

The committee of five appointed to draft the Declaration consisted of Adams, Franklin, Sherman, and Livingston as well, but Jefferson did the writing because, as Adams later declared, he could write ten times better than Adams. The "Rough Draft" was revised, mostly for details of style, by the committee and then somewhat softened in tone by the Congress, but the final form was essentially what Jefferson had written.

The importance of this document lies not in its defiance of the British king, but in its statement of the principles of human liberty in general: that men are created free and equal; that they inherit inalienable rights to life, liberty, and the pursuit of happiness; that government must be by consent of the governed; and that the people retain the right to throw off a government which attempts to use arbitrary power in defiance of their will. Familiar to those who know the history of colonial ideas of religious and political freedom, these few principles had never been so clearly and succinctly expressed. Upon them Jefferson built the system of democracy which ranks him with Edwards and Franklin as the third great Architect of the American mind.

Next to Franklin, Jefferson was the most versatile of the colonial leaders; but, unlike Franklin, he was temperamentally more a man of thought than a man of action. A Virginia gentleman, born to the land in 1743, he was trained in the law, studied at the College of William and Mary, served in the Virginia House of Burgesses, and went from there to the Second

Continental Congress. Temperamentally retiring and meditative, he would doubtless have preferred to spend his life with
his acres and his books at Monticello, but the times called him
to be Governor, Minister to France, Secretary of State, and
third President of the young Republic.

A lifetime of study made him at home in the law, government, history, mathematics, architecture, education, music,
philosophy, and all the branches of natural science, yet he
published only one real book, *Notes on the State of Virginia*
(1784), an answer to a set of queries posed by the secretary to
the French legation at Philadelphia as to the real character of
the American people and their land. Deceptively simple, this
little study is perhaps the best picture that has survived of
American civilization in its early and unproven days. The rest
of his writing, as he himself notes in a letter of 1809, consists
mostly of "a class of papers not calculated for popular reading": state papers, personal letters, and reports on economic
and technical matters. He was a master of English style, and
his words ring with conviction and sincerity even though they
lack the whimsy and variety of the more devious Franklin.

The essence of Jefferson's thought lies in his faith in the
integrity of the individual man. On this foundation he built
his structure of government and society with a minimum of
arbitrary controls. His purpose was to make the experiment
of free government so successful that it would be an example to
the rest of the world and a moral force in the destiny of mankind. The principles of decentralization of authority, agrarian
economy, public education, and flexible laws were all by-
products of the central doctrine of perfectibility.

Against this doctrine Alexander Hamilton and the other
founders of the Federalist party offered a political version of

Winthrop's theory of liberty. Because he did not share Jefferson's faith in human integrity, Hamilton argued for a liberty which comes through submission to authority, in this case a clear and firm system of civil law derived from nature by experience but virtually rigid when once formulated. Centralized government, an economy determined by financial and manufacturing rather than by agrarian interests, and firm laws strictly enforced were, in Hamilton's thinking, the logical conclusions from a skepticism of man's basic goodness. The full force of this philosophy was brought to a focus in *The Federalist* (1787–1788), a series of eighty-five tracts prepared by Hamilton, Madison, and Jay in defense of the Constitution and in exposition of the Federalist system of government. In these clear and finely reasoned papers, the fundamental doctrines of cohesion and orderliness were added to Jefferson's ideal of liberty to make a system of government and of society that was full of both compromises and vitality. Perhaps it is the very existence of conflicting ideals within a single practical frame of operation which makes the American system so relatively immune to shock and change. Man is not consistent in design or action, and the Constitution of the United States, with its added "Bill of Rights," by reflecting two such opposite views as those of Jefferson and Hamilton, probably comes as near to being a description of basic human nature as any document that lawmakers have framed.

Except for an implicit agreement that man in the New World had perhaps his best chance to redeem the errors of his past and to create a society pleasing at once to himself and to his God, the ideas of these three shapers of American culture—Edwards, Franklin, and Jefferson—form no consistent pattern. The extremes of idealism and materialism, of convention and revolt, are represented in one or another of their writings; but even in the most reactionary of their moods they shared the conviction of a new day in human history. With an unexplored continent spread before him, and the mistakes of his past clearly revealed, why should man fail to create a new society, worthy of his hopes, and plans, and dreams?

CHAPTER II

THE MAN OF LETTERS
Irving, Bryant, Cooper

ONE proof that there was a new nation in the making would be the appearance of a new and characteristic literature. No sooner was political independence from the Old World assured than the hue and cry for an independent literature set in. The problem was a simple one; the answer not easy. Here, far from the sophistication and corruption of Europe, were unspoiled nature waiting to be described and regenerated man eager to express his ideas. The materials of a new civilization and a new literature were at hand; but art is form, and new form does not suddenly appear. The colonists from long habit looked to British poetry, fiction, drama, and essay for their standards of literary expression. The eighteenth century had been a time of formal art. Somehow the new wine must be put into old bottles. Somehow American literature must equal or surpass its British models in perfection of expression and at the same time be faithful to its native ideas and experience. Caught between the urge of youth to break all ties with the past and the need of art for a tradition and a model by which to bend the raw materials of life to formal expression, our earliest men of letters were at once naïve, experimental, conformist, self-conscious, and imitative.

The first need was for the instruments of culture: the institutions and the equipment for creating and producing books and for training writers to write them and a public to read them. This process was well advanced by 1760, when the public attention was first drawn to the disturbing issues of the Revolution; it was somewhat delayed by the war itself; and it was greatly stimulated by the peace.

By 1764 seven colleges, of student age level not much above that of the modern high school, were established in the colonies. All but Pennsylvania were sectarian in their foundations, and religious training took its place with Latin, Greek, philosophy, mathematics, and other branches of learning. There was little study of English or modern literatures, almost none of history or geography, and comparatively little of natural science. But these struggling little colleges brought inquiring young minds together to read and think and talk, and education followed. In the 1790's the literary groups of Boston, Hartford, New York, and Philadelphia were composed chiefly of college students.

These young men turned to the circulating libraries for their books. The libraries of Harvard and Yale were large enough to issue catalogues by the middle of the century, but much richer collections were to be found in the library societies of Philadelphia, Newport, Charleston, and New York, the first of which was founded in 1731. Theological, political, historical, and scientific books predominated in these collections, but they also offered a generous selection of English and Continental authors, both classic and contemporary, and, as the century progressed, more and more books by American writers. As women gained leisure and influence, novels increased in numbers, as did poetry and drama.

Perhaps the most serious handicap that our early writers had to contend with was the lack of regular publishers. Colonial books by Americans were usually issued in London, although Franklin was printing books by 1740. Other provincial printers did the same thing, but most of these books were by British authors because of the absence or inequality of the American copyright laws. Usually an American author had to pay the costs of his own work and publish it through a local bookseller. The copyright law of 1790 made it illegal to reprint a book by a native American author, whereas foreign books had no such protection.

The first newspaper, published in Boston in 1690, was suppressed, but by 1800 most of the seaboard towns had at least one paper each; and in addition to news most of them printed an occasional poem or essay. Between 1741 and the end of the century, eighty magazines had been started, but only a few survived one or two issues. As we turn the pages of these earlier journals, we may wonder how they could have encouraged literature. Even in their own day, the small type in double columns and the lack of vitality in their borrowed contents must have done little to stimulate reading.

The American theater had a slightly later but parallel growth. Plays had been written or acted in the colonies, chiefly by college students, before 1767, when Thomas Godfrey's sanguinary and conventional tragedy *The Prince of Parthia* was offered by "the American Company at the New Theatre in Southwark," Philadelphia, on the twenty-fourth of April. The "American" company was composed of British actors and had been producing British and Continental plays in American towns since 1752 in such makeshift halls as it could command. The real history of the American drama began in 1787, when a reorganized American Company presented Royall Tyler's *The Contrast*, a study of New York society which was the first dramatic treatment of an American subject by an American writer.

When the Peace of 1783 put a premium on native writing, a small group of young men was ready to answer the call. Most of them planned to go into law, politics, or the ministry, but many would have preferred a career in literature. Only a few, like Joseph Dennie, Charles Brockden Brown, Royall Tyler, and Philip Freneau, had anything resembling a literary career.

The accepted way of declaring literary independence of Britain was to write something on an American theme as nearly as possible in the manner of a favorite British author. Joel Barlow sang the eternal glories of Columbia in the measured couplets of Pope; Royall Tyler's "piece, which we may fairly call our own," had an American theme, but most of the characters and the situation suggested a comedy of Sheridan; Brockden Brown wrote Gothic novels that transplanted Horace Walpole's horrors from crumbling castles and dark dungeons to the haunted minds and the open forests of his imagination; and Philip Freneau had to pay lyric homage to the death of death before celebrating American heroism and the beauties of nature. It was too soon to have an American way of writing as well as American things to say.

Fortunately for American enthusiasm, British writing was by then becoming more and more romantic. In the distant background were the masters of the past, notably Shakespeare, Milton, and Dryden. In the near distance were the masters of the formal essay and poem, of criticism and satire, Defoe, Pope, Addison, and Swift. Among elder contemporaries were Samuel Johnson and Goldsmith, the novelists Richardson, Fielding, and Sterne, and the bluestocking ladies. The romantic impulse had already been felt in the poetry of Thomson, Gray, and Cowper, and was becoming more pronounced in that of Blake, Burns, Wordsworth, and Coleridge. In the novel, just barely established as a reputable literary form, new experiments were already being tried in the Gothic horror of Walpole and Lewis, and in the ironic domestic comedy of manners of the gentle company of Jane Austen, while the short story was just beginning to emerge from emphasis on character rather than incident in the periodical essay. The era of Byron, Shelley, Scott, Lamb, and Bulwer was yet to come.

In spite of the growing spirit of nationalism, competition with British literature was too acute for the American writers. By 1800 most of the first group had turned from the frivolities of literature to more serious pursuits, and no new group had appeared to take their places. Brown, Freneau, and many others had turned to journalism; and Irving, Bryant, and Cooper did not publish their most characteristic work until about 1821. There were books published in the interval, but the contrast is sufficiently striking to draw a sharp line between the two generations. The first impulse had failed.

Most of the reasons for this failure are obscure, but two are fairly obvious. The first generation had overreached itself in its effort to create both a literature and an audience. It was forced ultimately to follow Freneau's advice: "Graft your authorship upon some other calling as the helpless ivy takes hold of the vigorous oak." The printers, the booksellers, the reviewers, the librarians, and the readers would require time to create the necessary conditions for a grass-roots literary movement; and the romantic movement in Western

European literature, which was to give the United States its first real literary impulse, was still in its infancy in 1800.

The essence of romanticism is the ability to wonder and to reflect. In searching the meaning of the known, the human spirit reaches for the unknown; in trying to understand the present, it looks to the past and to the future. Faith and hope lead to a positive romanticism, fear and doubt to a negative; but when both reason and authority have failed, man has a further refuge in the larger emotions which are always his. Only when these are fully awakened is a really great literature born. Shakespeare lived in one such era, Goethe in another.

In Europe, at the close of the eighteenth century, the revolt against political and religious authority was followed by a revolt against reason, and the romantic movement swept through its peoples. Coming to the United States at the moment of an awakening national consciousness, it assumed an even more ardent nationalism than it had in the older countries abroad. This attitude was expressed in the denial of tradition and of the European cultural inheritance, a delight in the grand scale and the infinite mysteries of nature on the unexplored western continent, and a pride in the "American ideas" which had so successfully created the Republic. Later it was to move into the abstractions of philosophy, but for the present the creation of an American myth out of the new materials was its first and greatest task.

In this task, the American writers Washington Irving, William Cullen Bryant, and James Fenimore Cooper had an advantage over their European contemporaries, for they had almost nothing to revolt against. Like them, European writers were also straining at traditions and conventions and seeking in nature and in forgotten corners of the past, and the far-away, for the "originality" which was the mark of the romantic temper, but the Americans had novelty at their doorstep. It was fortunate for them that the Old World was also going through a period of literary experimentation just at the moment when American writers most needed flexibility in the models they must use for their art. Irving still looked to Goldsmith, but Bryant had Wordsworth as well as Cowper, and Cooper had Walter Scott.

– 2 –

The genial personality of Washington Irving (1783–1859) made him a natural center for the literary group that developed in the thriving little town at the mouth of the Hudson in the early years of the nineteenth century. New York City, with its historical blending of Dutch and English ways, was already beginning to acquire the cosmopolitan personality of its great harbor. European and even more distant trade was moving from nearby ports into New York's hospitable waters, and better roads and a navigable river were attracting the commerce of the interior away from Boston, Philadelphia, Baltimore, and Charleston. With wealth and population came the means and the patronage of culture. Writers could live and write elsewhere, but by 1820 most of the leading booksellers and printers were in Manhattan.

The "Knickerbockers," named after Irving's own quaint historian Diedrich Knickerbocker, were the young men of Manhattan in the early years of the century, of mixed Dutch and English stock and of the mercantile and landed families that could so easily mix in the freedom of New World society. More interested in having a good time than in reforming mankind, they succeeded where the earlier generation had failed in making literature an accredited profession in America. Among them were two of Irving's brothers, William and Peter, who joined the youngest of the family in early literary experiments; James Kirke Paulding, essayist and novelist; Fitz-Greene Halleck and Joseph Rodman Drake, poets; John Howard Payne, actor and dramatist; and many a lesser name—not to mention those who were attracted to New York, as were Bryant and Cooper, by its growing literary interest and opportunity.

The struggle of the young Irving to make a profession of writing epitomized the problem of the emerging national literature. Born at the moment when peace and independence were assured, the youngest son of Deacon William Irving, merchant, was named for the hero of the day. His four elder brothers made sallies into law, medicine, and literature but were soon absorbed into the family hardware business; and Washington barely escaped. All evidences point to a bad case of pampering; the assigned task of reading for the law was frequently interrupted by the pleasanter activities of dancing, scribbling, and roving. The life-long bachelor Irving was as well known to the belles of Philadelphia and Baltimore as to those of New York; and his closest friends were the actors, painters, and writers who were beginning to appear in ever increasing numbers.

A trip up the Hudson to Montreal in 1803 was followed by two years abroad. In Rome he met Allston and flirted with the idea of becoming a painter; in Paris and London he haunted the theater; everywhere he went he made friends of the road, mostly Americans traveling, like himself, without other purpose than their own amusement. All of this went into the vellum notebook which was always his companion, to supply the career for which he was instinctively preparing himself.

Meanwhile he had already tried his hand at essays on the pattern of Addison's *Spectator* and, soon after his return, the *Salmagundi* papers began to appear. Launcelot Langstaff and his friends of the crazy "Cockloft Hall" on the Hudson were so successful in their announced aim "to instruct the young, reform the old, correct the town, and castigate the age" that they became minor terrors in the social and business circles of New York.

In this first phase of his writing, Irving accepted all the canons of the London coffeehouse. Goldsmith was his immediate model, together with the whole offspring of Addison, for style and mood, but his whimsical comment on society and politics smacked little of Fleet Street, and even his sentimental essays had the verve of a young man in love with life rather than the sophistication of a London dandy. The same mood carried over into *A History of New York from the Beginning of the World to the End of the Dutch Dynasty* (1809; revised 1812), by Diedrich Knickerbocker, announced in the New York press by a series of notices supposedly from the landlord of the Independent Columbian Hotel on Mulberry Street. It would seem that a mysterious little scholar in cocked hat and old black coat had registered there and departed, leaving a bulky manuscript. Begun as a burlesque of the pompous style of the day, Irving's book was soon carried away by the gusto of its author and became a genial and witty satire on the Dutch and their ways as well as an informed account of the history of the city.

Perhaps it was the death of his dark-eyed Matilda Hoffman, or the financial difficulties of his brothers, that drew him back to the family business. For a decade he wrote nothing, and then bankruptcy called his hand. Now he must prove that he could make writing a paying profession or forever give it up. Literary worth alone could not have done it, but the business-man in Irving now came to the support of his real ambition. In London as his brothers' agent, he made arrangements for pub-lication of *The Sketch Book* (1819–1820) so as to take advan-tage of the differences in copyrights between the two coun-tries, and by having the right social and literary friends he managed to produce an international best seller. American literature was finally launched in its first successful professional man of letters.

"Geoffrey Crayon, Gent.," the author, was first cousin to Launcelot Langstaff except for his addiction to travel. "My native country was full of youthful promise," he explained; "Europe was rich in the accumulated treasures of age." He rambled first in the one, then in the other; but the real author had rambled most of all in the libraries of his friends Henry Brevoort of New York and Walter Scott of Abbotsford. To his eighteenth century wit and his American vivacity he now added the nostalgia of the romantic British essays then popular.

The Sketch Book was unique in its day, although often imitated since. Composed of essays, character sketches, de-scriptions, and short stories, it mixes bits from books with bits from life, fresh observation with childhood memories. Whole passages virtually translated from the German are passed off as original creations, while things observed actually at the moment are given the flavor of the past. The tale of "Rip Van Winkle"—perhaps the first short story in the modern manner —was composed at white heat, and the sketch of "Roscoe" was painfully reworked from the notebooks; other essays, written long before, were now rescued from oblivion for filler. There is no continuity of subject matter, no central purpose, no unity other than that of tone; but the mellow friendliness of the book had a universal and enduring charm.

Irving's reading had brought him into the stream of melancholy which was the first phase of the romantic movement in Germany and England. The year 1812 had seen the first two cantos of Byron's *Childe Harold*, 1814 Scott's *Waverley*, 1816 Shelley's *Alastor*. The literary climate had changed since the days of *Salmagundi*. British writers were reading German horror tales with their scenes laid in medieval castles, and were fleeing to Italy for its sun, its freedom, and its relics of the past. Irving was caught up in the current, but the romantic past to which he fled was something the British writers could not recognize because it was so familiar—the past of England itself, a past that never was, with synthetic country houses and squires, story-book rural customs, ancient abbeys, and country churchyards. Suddenly the commonplace present was shrouded in the same melancholy mist that gives glamour to far-away places. The smells and sights and voices of Old England were all about, made suddenly vivid by this appreciative American.

With the success of *The Sketch Book* Irving's spirits were revived, and he immediately set to work on a sequel, developing the delightful Christmas sketches of his first romantic visit to an English country house. *Bracebridge Hall* (1822) had much of the old charm, but it was too attenuated; already the vein which had seemed so rich had begun to run thin. For the rest of his life he would strive to recapture the mood of his classic of indolence, first in Germany with *Tales of a Traveller* (1824), then in Spain with *The Alhambra* (1832), and finally at home in Tarrytown on the Hudson. In Paris he tried none too successfully to collaborate in playwriting with his friend John Howard Payne; in Dresden he fell in love with an American girl, Emily Foster; and in Spain he took up his residence in a Moorish palace and lost himself in its archives.

Irving's reputation rests on his trivial work, while his more ambitious undertakings, like his five-volume life of Washington, lie heavily on the shelves. Lacking the sustaining qualities of a great imagination, his sensitive versatility made him an ideal moderator of differences between past and present, Europe and America. Because his undoubted genius fitted so exactly the role he was called upon to play, he became the first purely cultural ambassador from the New World to the Old, the first American man of letters to gain international fame.

– 3 –

As Irving set the romantic pattern for the American short story and essay, William Cullen Bryant (1794–1878) led American poetry out of the stiff restraints of the Augustan mode into a simplicity and delight which accurately reflected the new frontiers of mind and spirit. When this young country lawyer, of quiet dignity and earnest gaze, stood before the members of the New York Athenaeum in April, 1825, to discuss poetry, he was already recognized as America's most distinguished writer of verse and of criticism. In an essay in the *North American Review* (1818) he had analyzed the state of American poetry and pointed to the need for a more courageous originality. Now, in the four New York lectures, he was faithful to his own challenge; and his analysis of the nature and meaning of his art served both major and minor poets for many years as a gauge of what poetry should be and do. Longfellow and Lowell, among others, followed his prescriptions, and his influence extended down the century to form the main stream of American verse.

Bryant's position was a blending of the impulses and ideas of the British romantic movement with his own conservative New England political and religious views. The story of his life is the story of a gradual breaking away from an inherited Calvinism in religion and Federalism in politics to a position of leadership of the Unitarians and the Jacksonian Democrats. Deeply grounded in the literary ideals of Pope, Johnson, and the more formal of the British poets of nature, he learned from Byron, Wordsworth, and Coleridge to throw his heart open to the life about him. In his quiet way he wrote a truly personal kind of poetry, and taught three generations of poets to do likewise.

It is hard now to realize that it was only 1825 when Bryant told his audience to beware the current idea that science and reason had driven poetry out. Poetry, he argued, is a suggestive art and, by using symbols rather than by direct imitation of life, it stimulates the imagination of the reader and takes strong hold of his feelings, arousing him to passionate action. It also appeals to the understanding, and is therefore capable of conveying "direct lessons of wisdom." Thus it places upon the poet a moral obligation to deal only in the most noble of ideas and feelings and to leave to prose the trivial and the commonplace. It is also distinguished from prose by its use of "metrical harmony." In its special role it is needed in an age of reason to supply release for the emotions, and in a country where the beauties of nature are available alike to everyone, there is all the more reason why poetry should be produced. Obviously America was the place and the year 1825 the time for a poetic revival.

The moral justification for art was deep in this poet's bloodstream. The little mountain town in western Massachusetts where he was born was still, in 1794, a typically devout and conservative community, holding to the Calvinistic faith of its founders and voting the Federalist ticket. Bryant's family was of the earliest New England stock; his schooling was under local ministers. In his father's library he found the pastoral English poets of the classical school, while he saw about him the cleared mowings and the heavy forests of the Berkshire Hills. When he began to write his own poetry, it was only natural for him, on the one hand, to attack in heroic couplets the wickedness of the Jeffersonian administration and, on the other, to celebrate, with Thomas Gray of the "Elegy," the meditative calm of death. His greatest poem, "Thanatopsis," was among his earliest, written in its first form when the poet was only seventeen but frequently revised thereafter:

> "To him who in the love of Nature holds
> Communion with her visible forms, she speaks
> A various language."

The "direct lesson of wisdom" in this elegy upon the abstract idea of death, clothed as it is in the simple dignity of blank verse, seems harmless enough until one realizes that no God is mentioned, no afterlife promised; merely there is a returning to the antique majesty of nature where all the sons of man must go, "to mix forever with the elements." Already Bryant had come far from the teachings of his Puritan forebears—further even than he was to remain, for he later deserted this purer form of naturalism for one blended with the Unitarian creed. With quiet faith in the religion of Nature, he threw himself into the world about him. The fields, the streams, the woods, and the flowers became, almost totally unadorned, the substance of his poems, written as he prepared himself for the law, married the "fairest of the rural maids," and settled in nearby Great Barrington to practice.

The most memorable of Bryant's poems come from these earlier years. In 1825 he went down to New York to become a journalist, and by 1829 he was editor and part owner of the New York *Evening Post*, a position he held until his death in 1878. Abruptly his role in American letters had changed. As the leading liberal editor of the day, he defended free trade, abolition, free speech, and other causes, helped to found the Republican party, and took a prominent share in the cultural life of his city and of his country. His frequent trips to Europe were recounted in travel letters that were among the most widely read at a time when travel letters were the fashion; his eulogies at the deaths of his distinguished contemporaries— Cooper, Irving, Halleck, and Thomas Cole, the painter—made him seem almost like the voice of eternity. At the last he turned his failing poetic talents into translations of the *Iliad* and the *Odyssey*. By now the gentle young nature poet of Cummington was lost in the dignified and bearded sage, the Solon of his times.

It seems the destiny of the United States to produce in its literature ironic paradoxes rather than logical sequences. The violent and passionate young nation had cried out for a poet to express its spirit, and then it had forgotten the fiery Freneau for the restrained spokesman of the ideal and ancient verities. With Bryant's poetry the first separation of literature and American life took place; his theory that the poet should deal only with noble materials, and should teach as well as reveal, closed his quiet spirit to the rugged vulgarities from which Walt Whitman was later to hew a more vital American verse, as well as to the dark horrors out of which Poe was to exhume a universal beauty. Yet the "visible forms" and the passion which Bryant made available to the native poet opened a way which he himself was too restrained to follow. Like Irving, he had learned freedom from his romantic contemporaries abroad and he had led the movement at home from imitation to originality. He remains a singularly authentic but minor voice in the awakening national literature.

– 4 –

Irving's grace of mind and Bryant's lyric gentleness tended to slur the difficulties that confronted the artist in America, but Cooper's blunt honesty and sharp temper made them all too understandable. That he overcame them, for his own purposes at least, and produced a distinctively American shelf of books, known and loved throughout the world, is a tribute to his dogged perseverance rather than to his tact. After a single false step with *Precaution,* an imitative novel of British life, he had only one answer to what an American novelist should write about: he should use his art to acquaint all mankind with American facts and American ideas. Luckily a broader love of nature, of people, and of adventure was deep in his singing blood, and he could not help writing romances of action and excitement. For these the readiest model was that old Tory Scott, but one need not accept an author's politics in order to learn from him how to write. In fact, the best way to correct an author's political errors is to do his job all over again for him, but in corrected political perspective. This is essentially what Cooper tried to do; his was to be the democratic historical novel.

Because he was the first American novelist to exploit successfully the colorful life of the naked red Indian deep in the

American forest, James Fenimore Cooper (1789–1851) was thought of in his own time as a kind of frontiersman with gun, leather buskins, and beaver cap like his own Natty Bumppo. Even though he was actually the son of a landed gentleman, with aspirations for social acceptance like Irving's in the most exclusive of European circles, this portrait has perhaps a kind of truth in it because in spite of himself Cooper's heart was in the upstate New York frontier which was passing when he was a boy, and which he reconstructed from the writings of the missionary Heckewelder and other pioneers of earlier days. In 1790, at the age of one, he was taken to the still unsettled Cooperstown by that true pioneer, his father, Judge William Cooper. The Indian wars were already history, for the Iroquois had left their hunting grounds to the white conquerors and had pushed up into Canada and on to the West. James (he added his mother's family name, Fenimore, later) was reared in the imposing Hall that his father had built of native timber at the foot of Otsego Lake. Judge Cooper owned everything within walking distance, but he tells us, in his *Guide in the Wilderness* (1810), that his aim was to subdue nature and to introduce settlement and commerce. The children had the best education he could devise: a local school of his own making, tutoring for college with respectable clergymen, and then Yale or Princeton. The older brothers presented no problems, but James had too much spirit for an academic life, and spent the next five years (1806–1811), on and off, at sea, in the merchant service or in the Navy. At the end of his roving, he knew the forest and the sea, and he had stored up enough education to provide the perspective necessary to the writer. The social habits of a Federalist squire, the love of mankind of a Jeffersonian democrat, and the urge to adventure of a boy who would never grow up, conspired to turn Cooper, at the age of thirty, into a writer of New World romances. By then he was himself a country gentleman, married to Susan Augusta of the Loyalist De Lancey family, and settled in Westchester County, New York, with a cluster of daughters, plenty of land, and a not too distant view of the blue waters of Long Island Sound.

The immediate occasion was the reading of a recently imported British novel of the domestic school that Cooper had picked up on one of his frequent trips to New York City, where he was the center of a literary and sociable group of young men. In the evenings he delighted to read to his wife while she spun or sewed or knit. This time he threw the book down in disgust. "I could write you a better book than that myself." The result was a pseudo-British domestic tale, *Precaution* (1820), whose chief virtue was its lesson to Cooper that he should attempt hereafter only native material. His next, *The Spy* (1821), was a brilliant effort to correct his error. An adventure tale of the neutral ground about New York City during the British occupation, it is still one of the best romances of the Revolution.

Without a native literary tradition, the novelist of that day had no "usable past" on which he could draw for material. The Revolutionary War was an obvious beginning, but it was still very recent. Cooper never did better at a straight historical novel than *The Spy*, even though he extended his range of material. The frontier wars later proved useful because of the Indians, and the War of 1812 because of the sea and the opportunity to describe the vivid action of naval engagements. Finally, the patterns of colonial Dutch and English society which Irving had burlesqued in his *History of New York* were used by Cooper mainly for serious illustration of social principles and manners, but they served their literary purpose by adding color to otherwise unexciting material.

The problem of what to write about was solved for Cooper when he decided to use only the recent past which he could blend with his own memories and describe against a background which he knew and loved. The Indian and sea tales, with their repeated plot of the long chase and capture, their free use of coincidence, even their bookish style and wooden characters which were to Cooper merely aspects of the conventions of romance, provided him with the ideal ingredients for his ready-made art. Cooper discovered realism in that incomparable tale of the border of his youth *The Pioneers* (1823), and in *The Pilot* (1823) and *The Last of the Mohicans* (1826) he made it the very stuff of romance. Naïve as these tales are, Cooper never again equaled them for verve and vividness. Like many an American, he reached his artistic peak almost at once, and then tended to decline through the rest of his life.

The Leatherstocking Tales—*The Deerslayer* (1841), *The Last of the Mohicans* (1826), *The Pathfinder* (1840), *The Pioneers* (1823), and *The Prairie* (1827), in that order—tell the tale of their central character Natty Bumppo, backwoodsman and wilderness scout, homespun philosopher and deadshot, personification of the democrat's ideal of the democratic man. "A character of fiction," pleads Cooper, "has a fair right to the aid which can be obtained from a poetical view of the subject." Natty is a fictional character, based on certain originals remembered from the author's boyhood, who "possessed little of civilization but its highest principles, as they are exhibited in the uneducated, and all of savage life that is not incompatible with these great rules of conduct." Here, embodied in a clear-cut romantic type, is the American moral ideal. All of Cooper's social criticism derives from this norm, which was, like that of the earlier American thinking, both religious and political in inspiration.

No one character or group in his other tales performs quite the same function, but Long Tom Coffin of *The Pilot* and Andries Coejemans of *The Chainbearer*, to cite two, have the same primitive honesty and strength. To find its source, one must go back to Jefferson, Franklin, and the early liberal thinkers; to find its imitators one need only turn to the romantic novels and motion pictures of the frontier from Cooper's day onward.

Cooper's social criticism was integral with his conception of romance. His seven years in Europe, his friendship with Lafayette during the old man's last fight for democracy in the French Chamber of Deputies in 1830–1832, as well as the attack which his own outspoken novels and essays brought from American and European critics alike, tended after 1830 to separate his ideal of democracy from his fictional art. With age, his temper became more irascible and his social and political philosophy more like the Federalism of his father—a growing sense of the right of property and a fear of the equalizing tendencies of the Jacksonian-Whig era. The paradox of a landed gentleman who believes in absolute human equality before God and absolute property rights on earth had been present but not too troublesome in the thinking of Jefferson and his contemporaries; with the opening of the West, and the reshuffling of American society that resulted in the 1820's, the paradox became critical in Cooper's. A Democrat by party affiliation, he battled with the Whigs and defended what amounted to a forgotten Federalism. A partisanship that had no party left him embittered, fighting with back to the wall, and at the same time pouring out novel after novel with the old zeal and almost the old imaginative power.

His other prose, including *A Letter to His Countrymen* (1834), the five volumes of travel letters beginning with *Gleanings in Europe* (1837), *The American Democrat* (1838), and *The History of the Navy of the United States of America* (1839), forms an impressive shelf of now almost unread books. They contain Cooper's inventory of America's achievements and problems, his analysis of the incongruity of the democratic ideal in an America that was in danger of being absorbed by material values and the aristocratic ideal in a Europe that was unable to give up the corruption imbedded in its traditions. As answer, Cooper supplied moral indignation rather than logic, and poured his ire onto Old World culture in *The Bravo* (1831), a story of the Venice of the Doges, and onto New World crudity in *Home as Found* (1838), a story of the America he found on his return. Better novels than these have been written, but few with so violent a passion for human values and so bitter a dismay at what seemed to their author a light that was in danger of failing.

Cooper's sudden determination to give up fiction in middle life could not resist the urgency that drove him on to new creative effort in 1840. With a new Indian tale, *The Pathfinder*, in that year and with one of his best sea tales, *The Two Admirals*, in 1842, he tried to regain his old uncritical audience, but it was now too late; he had become too much a storm center of American life. To the criticism brought against him and his novels, chiefly by political enemies, he replied with libel suits that helped, by his active participation in trial after trial, to shape the law on that question; against attacks on his

Naval history he hurled pamphlets of defense; and into the novels he poured once more—but now with deliberate purpose and plan—his views on the failure of American democracy and his hopes for its regeneration. In *Afloat and Ashore* (1844) he recreated in Miles Wallingford his own idealized youth, and in the Littlepage trilogy, *Satanstoe* (1845), *The Chainbearer* (1845), and *The Redskins* (1846), he traced the decline of the New York landed aristocracy which to him personified a lost ideal of democratic distinction in living. Age did not abate his zeal; *The Crater* (1847) is far more convincing as Utopian allegory than is the earlier attempt in this form *The Monikins* (1835). As proof of his unfailing creative faculty, this tale of a volcanic Pacific isle has enough romantic gusto to sustain its heavy economic theorizing. The humanistic ideal first presented in Leatherstocking had carried him through. He was the first but not the last American to prove his freedom of thought, act, and speech by criticizing all that he held most desirable in life. Man's failure to attain the perfection within his reach provides the tragic view of life in a free society. This truth Cooper was the first but not the last of our writers to realize.

Irving and Bryant had helped to create an art for America, but Cooper took the first strong step toward an American art. Starting where others had started, with an effort to learn the craft of fiction by imitating English novels that he had enjoyed, he took the normal course of trying to work American scenes, events, and people into his chosen forms. But he was too genuine—too spirited—to be content with any such limitations on his message. The United States, he felt, possessed institutions and distinctive opinions of its own, and no literature which failed to give them full expression could be called valid. He thus cut into the heart of his problem; and, by his third novel, *The Pioneers*, he was throwing out the last of his doubts and giving himself over wholly to the urgencies of his creative instinct. He had lived on the frontier, and he knew the city; his father had been the personification of American man, the settler who had transformed the wilderness into civilization; his friends were newspapermen, lawyers, seamen, doctors, woodsmen, almost every kind of man of action; he had himself sailed before the mast, explored the forest, played the country squire, and courted and won a belle of the city. Passionately committed to the American adventure, he was as critical of the defects in what he loved as he was vigorous in his praise. He was determined to put the whole of America, roots and all, into his books.

In Cooper the organic artist in America was born. He was the first writer of power to realize that a new literature must be created from the inside out, from the feeling to the form. Abandoning tradition and alien controls, he sought the sources of light and power in the life he knew at firsthand. Never wholly successful in disciplining his violent materials into manageable forms, he remained to the end an amateur in his art, but he made clear the job that must be done before America could have a literature of its own.

CHAPTER III

THE AFFIRMATION
Emerson, Thoreau

IT was finally Ralph Waldo Emerson, and not Irving, Bryant, or Cooper, who reconciled the abstractions of the romantic imagination with the realities of American life at mid-century. With him the center of literary activity moved from New York to Boston and, more particularly, to the quiet Massachusetts town twenty miles to the west, well named Concord. With him also romanticism in America became a matured system of thought and feeling, deeply rooted in the native soil but drawing strength from other literatures, other philosophies, other times.

The Knickerbocker writers did not at first like such New England dreamers as Emerson. Nathaniel Parker Willis, the migratory dandy of two continents who reported his gossip to the New York *Mirror* as "Pencillings by the Way," wrote after hearing Emerson lecture on "England," in 1850, that he had expected "a new addition to the prevailing Boston beverage of Channing-and-water," but discovered instead "a suggestive, direction-giving, soul-fathoming mind." His conversion was symptomatic, for by then America was learning to appreciate its major scholar-poet.

The "Channing-and-water" to which Willis referred was

the Unitarian faith of the elder William Ellery Channing, now secularized by the group of enthusiasts who had gathered around Emerson in the 1830's and 1840's and who were popularly known as Transcendentalists. Unitarianism carried the revolt against New England orthodoxy to the limits of theology, but the next step was still to be taken, that of pushing it beyond those limits into the airy spaces of pure moral abstraction. The inspiration for that final step came not from within the creed itself but from the waves of German and English literary romanticism that were beating against the Eastern coast. The blending of the restrained idealism of Puritan New England with the headier German variety then so popular in England brought about, in America, the climax of the romantic movement, with some aid from Plato and the Oriental mystics. Philosophically the result was not simple and clear; but dynamically it produced what was needed for imaginative literature.

The first step in the revolt was Channing's declaration of independence in his essay on "The Moral Argument Against Calvinism" (1820). The argument itself is simple; it merely points out that the doctrines of man's depravity and of God's arbitrary grace are inconsistent with a faith in "God's goodness and equity," which even Calvinists profess. But Channing goes on to reason that therefore "the ultimate reliance of a human being is and must be on his own mind. . . . Conscience, the sense of right, the power of perceiving moral distinctions . . . is the highest faculty given us by God." So much like Jonathan Edwards in personality and in religious devotion, this nineteenth century preacher of a revived faith reasserted the heresy which Edwards had fought against so valiantly a hundred years before, the doctrine of the freedom of the will. In so doing, he laid the foundations for Emerson's central doctrines of self-reliance, the moral sense, and the exact correspondence between natural and moral law. So intense a faith in the individual as the measure of all brought religious liberalism, political democracy, and literary romanticism together at last to produce works of art from the substance of American experience.

– 2 –

Ralph Waldo Emerson (1803–1882), like so many great men, is often remembered as he seemed in his age rather than as he was in his youth. The sage of Concord, surrounded by his followers, secure in his own peace of soul, a maker of systems, a guide of men, is a myth of the popular imagination. The young Emerson was the very spirit of revolt itself, impatient with tradition and respectability, challenging the convictions of his elders, and searching his own heart with a restlessness born of impatient curiosity. Throughout his long life the calm which he achieved and so successfully maintained was the fruit of constant struggle, the balance of opposing forces, the courage to question again tomorrow all that was settled yesterday. His philosophy is a way of living, not a system of thought. His writing is the record of his own "man thinking."

He came by his open mind quite naturally. Many of his forebears were clergymen, including Peter Bulkeley, the founder of Concord, and his father William Emerson, minister of the First (Unitarian) Church of Boston; but they were always independent in their thinking. "It is my humor to despise pedigree," he wrote in his *Journal* on reaching manhood. "The kind Aunt whose cares instructed my youth (and whom may God reward) told me oft the virtues of her and mine ancestors. They have been clergymen for many generations, and the piety of all and the eloquence of many is yet praised in the Churches. But the dead sleep in their moonless night; my business is with the living."

The "kind Aunt" was Mary Moody Emerson, a fiery little person, radical even in her orthodoxy, who was a frequent visitor at the Emerson home after the father's death. She supplied the sounding board for the childish questions of Ralph and his brothers, orphaned and impoverished at so early an age. The Church had provided for the widow for a time, and relatives helped, but the boys could spend little time in play. Family chores and school work occupied their days. The older brother William was the first to go to Harvard; Ralph followed from the Boston Latin School; his younger brothers Edward and Charles came in their turns, each working his way and helping the others, persistent in their common goal of knowledge and self-improvement. Emerson's tight-knit family loyalty in these years was doubtless the source of much of his later spiritual strength. William kept a school, his brothers taught, and all read and studied earnestly to satisfy the hunger of their active and growing minds.

Ralph was self-selected to carry on the family tradition and prepare for the ministry. "In Divinity I hope to thrive," he confesses in his *Journal* of 1824. "The office of a clergyman is twofold: public preaching and private influence. Entire success in the first is the lot of few, but this I am encouraged to expect. . . . Every wise man aims at an entire conquest of himself. . . . What is called a warm heart, I have not. . . . Physician, heal thyself; . . . My trust is that my profession shall be my regeneration of mind, manners, inward and outward estate." The somewhat sophomoric confidence of this amazingly accurate self-analysis is tempered by a deep humility, born of honesty. He became a successful preacher, both in the pulpit and out. For the time, it was his life.

The sermons of the young Emerson reveal a struggle to reconcile even the mild orthodoxy of the Unitarians with his passionate desire for complete personal integrity. His later cry, "Trust thyself: every heart vibrates to that iron string," expressed a temperamental rather than an intellectual conviction. In college he had debated in the Pythologian Club, read the Scottish rationalists, studied Socrates, and practiced writing and oratory. Textbooks and professors were, with a few exceptions, little more than obstacles to knowledge, for they did not assign "the most extraordinary book ever written," Montaigne's essays, nor did they ask him to read Bacon or Ben Jonson. His skepticism outran his orthodoxy in those days, but it left him without a much needed faith. When he later tried to preach the acceptance of miracles and sacraments, his voice was strained, unconvinced and unconvincing. All the melancholy doubt of a Byron or a Goethe was his, held within the firm frame of his New England conscience.

The tensions were too great, and the crisis came in 1832 on top of much personal sorrow and loss. He had successfully battled the tuberculosis which ultimately took three of his brothers, he had completed his studies at the Harvard Divinity School, he had succeeded to the charge of the Reverend Henry Ware at the Second (Unitarian) Church in Boston, and he had married Ellen Tucker. In 1830 his life had seemed full and promising; but in February of the next year his wife died and by the end of the next he had resigned his pastorate, preached his farewell sermon, and sailed for Europe. He was alone, discouraged, embittered. "I am my own comedy and tragedy," he admitted.

The immediate reason for his resignation was his unwillingness to administer the sacrament of the Last Supper. To the doctrine behind the ritual he had no objections; the issue was that of conformity. This was the first and the most dramatic of his assertions of the self-reliance which was to become his most urgent message. In the quiet of the White Mountains, he made his decision: he would never conform unless his mind and spirit were in harmony with his act.

When Emerson returned from Europe after a year of seeing ruins, scenes, art, and great men (especially Carlyle, whom he sought out in his Scottish retreat), he was ready to reconstruct his life: a new heart to his thinking, a new profession, and soon a new marriage and a new home.

In the Botanical Gardens in Paris, the young traveler had paused to observe the "occult relation between the very scorpions and man. . . . I say continually 'I will be a naturalist.' " A month after his return, he read a public lecture in Boston on "The Uses of Natural History." With it began the reconstruction of his "First Philosophy" and of his new profession. Accepting the romantic view that each natural form is "an expression of some property inherent in man the observer," he laid down the dualistic law of correspondence as the first plank in his new platform. The rest of his life would be devoted to expanding and expounding the doctrine that the inner, or moral, or divinely inspired law of life as perceived by the intuition is paralleled, point for point, by the outer law of nature with its multiform revelations as perceived by the senses.

All of Emerson's philosophy begins and ends with this simple proposition. To clear his path and to make known his way, he immediately set to work on three decisive documents: his carefully prepared statement of the new and living faith, the prose-poem *Nature* (1836); his courageous blast at formalism and tradition in learning and literature, "The American Scholar" address (1837); and his frontal attack on the same kind of enemies of freedom in religion, "The Divinity School Address" (1838). With the appearance of the first series of *Essays* (1841), based on the many lectures he had meanwhile delivered on science, literature, biography, and human conduct, his place in American literature was assured.

– 3 –

When Emerson returned to Concord in 1834, he was returning to familiar ground. The Old Manse above the sleepy river was, in a sense, the family home. His grandfather had lived there, and there as a boy he had himself spent many happy summer days visiting Ezra Ripley, then minister of the Concord Church. "They who made England, Italy, or Greece venerable in the imagination, did so by sticking fast where they were, like an axis of the earth," he wrote later. The next best thing was to return from whence one came. "The soul is no traveller."

Nature was written in his own study in the Coolidge house on the Lexington Road, which he had just purchased for his new bride, Lydia ("Lidian") Jackson, of Plymouth. For thirty-five years and more (until it burned—and again after it was rebuilt) this was the home of his growing family and the center of the intellectual and spiritual movement for which he was so largely responsible. Never have the roots of life been more deliberately and firmly planted.

A deceptively slim book, *Nature* reflects the new-found but militant security. It was the only book that Emerson ever wrote, as such, and it was scarcely more than a pamphlet. Yet it was his testament, for it contained in embryo all he was ever to say or feel or think again. From it grew the later essays, lectures, and poems like branches from a single trunk.

Its form is that of any of the later essays, though much longer. Schooled in the rhetoric of the pulpit, Emerson's prose is heard, not seen on the printed page. There is always the initial establishment of rapport with an unseen audience, usually in a paragraph recalling a familiar human experience or declaring a homemade text. Then follows a paragraph or two of bold generalization to galvanize the attention. Finally the persuasive ascent is undertaken in a spiral form of dictum, argument, and illustration, from the level of the relative to that of the absolute.

In *Nature* the text is a question: "Why should we not also enjoy an original relation to the universe . . . a poetry and philosophy of insight and not of tradition, and a religion by revelation?" The bold generalization follows: "All science has one aim, namely, to find a theory of nature. . . . To a sound judgment, the most abstract truth is the most practical." From the level of the sensory experience—the uses of Nature—the slow ascent begins. Commodity, beauty, language, discipline— these are the services that Nature may render to Man. Poetry, philosophy, science, religion, and ethics are Man's means of dealing with the dualism of the divine and the natural worlds that he thus discovers inside himself. In the full wisdom of Nature alone may his spirit hope to resolve this dualism into the act of worship. The Understanding (using the word in the romantic sense that he had learned from Coleridge to describe the lower level of logical apprehension) is not adequate to this task; only the Reason ("an instantaneous instreaming causing power") can distinguish the "axis of vision" from the "axis of things" and see always "the miraculous in the common." The heights have been scaled: "Every spirit builds itself a house, and beyond its house a world, and beyond its world a heaven." The prose poem is completed; the new doctrine that can accept the findings of science and apply them to the service of God has been pronounced.

Because this testament is based on a point of view, an "angle of vision," rather than a logical premise, the resulting philosophy remains fluent. Although Emerson speaks of truth, he is more concerned with the means of seeking it than he is with its own ultimate nature. His furthest point of certainty is "the moral sentiment" rather than a final verity. His best essays deal with ethical rather than metaphysical questions: self-reliance, experience, the role of the poet, politics, love, friendship, the uses of history, the law of compensation, circles. When he attempts definition of the absolute, as in "The Over-Soul," he ends by revealing a way of discovering God rather than by offering a clear notion of the nature of Deity.

It was this very quality that made him the spokesman for an age in which old dogmas were fading away, new laws were in the making. He could maintain certainty in the midst of flux, for his was an open universe; he an explorer rather than an oracle. People turned to him for guidance, but he resisted the role of the Messiah, refused to join clubs or sects, discouraged any attempt at system in his own thinking or at organization among his followers. Older idealists like Bronson Alcott and younger ones like Henry David Thoreau were equally drawn to him, even to the point of settling in or near his home. Practical Utopians like George Ripley who established the cooperative community of Brook Farm and women of vigorous intellect and reforming zeal like Elizabeth Peabody and Margaret Fuller found in him a friend who could help them in their projects without himself becoming involved. The Transcendental Club, an informal group of men and women of Boston and Concord who were strongly influenced by the new German idealism and who delighted in abstract discussion, met frequently at his home. Lesser writers like Jones Very, the younger W. E. Channing, and Christopher Pearse Cranch echoed his views and were willing, where he was not, to be known as "transcendentalists." And it was his vision and persistence that made possible the *Dial* (1840–1844), organ of the movement and most distinguished literary quarterly of the mid-century.

Essays, First and Second Series (1841, 1844), are Emerson's most widely known books. Each of these essays is a finely wrought work of art into which he threw his most mature and careful effort, yet each book as a whole is little more than a miscellany. The design of the individual essays does not extend to the volumes in which they are collected. Emerson meant them to be read one at a time and in any order. His method was to enter in his voluminous *Journals*, begun in 1820 and continued throughout his life, his first thoughts on life and books. These entries, which often have an incisive freshness that might later be lost, then became the "savings bank" to be drawn on for the lectures which, after 1833, constituted his main interest. The essays were a device for polishing these ideas, never designed to be delivered as lectures, except for occasional addresses like that on "The American Scholar," but inevitably retaining much of the tone of spoken discourse and the awareness of an immediate audience.

Representative Men (1850), based on lectures delivered in England during an intensive lecture tour in 1847; *English Traits* (1856), a by-product of his lecture series after his return; and *The Conduct of Life* (1860), lectures mainly in the West, complete the list of Emerson's major prose works. The first was the closest to a straight printing of the lectures as delivered, the second the nearest to a complete rewriting. In the last, the philosopher again attempted, as he had in his first book, *Nature*, to sum up the essence of his thinking. More settled in its inconsistencies than in its system, the matured Emersonian view of life presented a suspended judgment, a calm of soul obtained by the balance between forces, an admission of both fate and free will, of both divine and human sanctions. The strict philosophical mind has difficulty in accepting so relative a position; the literary mind requires it. Only when the spirit is steadily open to experience can literary expression reveal the length and breadth, the heights and depths of human thought and emotion. This Emerson succeeded in doing through a long life. His later and his posthumous collections show less creative power as his own powers failed, but they are illuminated by the same "lustres"—a favorite word with him—as are the early ones. Emerson, recorder of the American mind, is also its poet and its prophet. He was his own most "representative man."

– 4 –

As a poet, too, Emerson was a rebel. The limpid strain of contemplative music that flowed through Bryant and Longfellow found no echo of its melodic voices in the rough terse periods of his thoughtful and symbolic verse. In his own early poem "Uriel," he describes his treason to the conventions:

> "The young deities discussed
> Laws of form, and metre just,
> Orb, quintessence, and sunbeams,
> What subsisteth and what seems."

"The balance beam of Fate was bent" by such fearless questioning of the "stern old war-gods." "But now and then, truth-speaking things" were born of the young gods' courageous reopening of life's secrets.

A decade later, in the poem "Merlin," he reasserted his position—now with more confidence—that the poet who tunes his lyre to Nature's music will rediscover for himself essential truth:

> "The kingly bard
> Must smite the chords rudely and hard. . . .
> He shall not climb
> For his rhyme . . .
> But mount to paradise
> By the stairway of surprise."

Poetry to Emerson was not, as it was to Bryant, merely a suggestive art through which the poet could teach direct lessons of wisdom; it was a function of his own being as an individual seeking truth. The poet is the student, the receiver of wisdom; not the teacher. Poetry is moral, but it is not didactic.

Except that he was a reader of Coleridge, and that he absorbed from him the organic principle of the German idealists, Emerson paid little attention to his British contemporaries. The inspiration for his poetry and for his poetic theory came directly from Plato and from the seventeenth century British so-called "metaphysical" poets, George Herbert, John Donne, and their fellows. Form for him was inherent in substance because the laws of art must be equivalent at every point with the laws of Nature. The poets who sang in that great age of scientific inquiry following the disturbing discoveries of Galileo and Newton were forced to open their minds to the evidences of Nature even where they seemed to be in conflict with the supposed rules of an arbitrary God. The nineteenth century was facing a similar intellectual crisis. Once again the spirit of scientific inquiry was destroying old dogmas and re-asking the old questions. It was the very confusion of thinking in his age that attracted Emerson, as that of an earlier age had attracted Donne, to an attitude of skepticism. Only by it could he hope, as poet, to receive even faint glimmers of direct revelation.

Emerson's favorite image of the Æolian harp, the lyre that plays when its strings are caught by the breeze, aptly describes his view of the primary role of the poet. "Poetry was all written before time was," he tells us in his essay on "The Poet," "and whenever we are so finely organized that we can penetrate into that region where the air is music, we hear those primal warblings and attempt to write them down." The poet has his special function in the order of nature; he is "the sayer, the namer, and represents beauty." He is important to his age because "the experience of each new age requires a new confession, and the world seems always waiting for its poet."

In stating so clearly his case for an organic view of art, Emerson was describing not only his own method but the instinctive approach of most really great American writers. Only when the artist takes upon himself the responsibility for rediscovering a central vision can he hope to deal with a new experience. The earlier American writers had hoped to borrow their forms and methods from Old World authors, but Emerson told them: "it is not metres but a metre-making argument that makes a poem. . . . the thought and the form are equal in the order of time, but in the order of genesis the thought is prior to the form." Only by a totally fresh evaluation of his own experience, he might have added, could the American artist hope to find the form which is inherent in each truth he discovers. Melville and Whitman too were listening to this counsel.

Emerson's constant use of the symbol of the harp might lead one to suppose that he thought of poetry as an auditory art and that he would try to equate it with music. Perhaps because, as he tells us himself, his ear was poor, he turns rather to the image as picture to discover his language. Next to organicism, his most important contribution to American poetry was his use of the symbol. For him Nature was itself a symbol of the spirit, and particular natural facts were symbols of particular spiritual facts; finally, words were symbols of natural facts.

The word as symbol was for Emerson no accidental device, no convenient analogy; it was an integral part of the thought, the vehicle of truth. The poet who discovers the right symbol has revealed his share of truth. His is an intellectual and pictorial music, not heard but seen. His own poems at their best are rugged in meter, but their argument is conveyed in a sustained symbol: the sphinx, the parade of days, the snowstorm, Merlin the all-wise. This modern "metaphysical" poetry was Emerson's invention for America. One of the oldest of the methods of art, it required a reaffirmation before it could be used on the new experience freely by Thoreau, Emily Dickinson, T. S. Eliot. Emerson seldom wrote a perfect poem because of his failure to abandon the arbitrary laws of meter and rhyme that he rejected in theory and that he could not himself master, but in their singleness of vision and in their symbolism his best poems are designed on a grander scale than anything before Whitman. Without the discharge from convention that he had authorized, Whitman's release might not have occurred. No wonder Emerson wrote to the younger man, upon receiving one of the first copies of *Leaves of Grass*, "I greet you at the beginning of a great career."

– 5 –

The affirmation of Henry David Thoreau (1817–1862) was not so much one of words as of deeds. Emerson defined and expounded the special kind of idealism that New England rocks and winds had bred; Thoreau lived it first and then recorded his experience in his *Journal*. No two men ever were less alike personally nor more alike in what they thought man should do with his life in this world. If their relationship had been a harmonious, as it was a logical, outcome of their thinking, one could call it that of master and disciple. But to do so would be to violate the heart of Thoreau's sense of independence. First of all, he was beholden to no man; he was, in his ideal view, man alone and sufficient.

It is best, therefore, to think of him in his hut on Walden Pond even though he spent only a little more than two of his forty-five years there. Most men live lives of quiet desperation, he felt; he at least would live as deliberately as Nature and spend his hours in fishing and drinking in the stream of time. If he were to be a poet, he should act as one and make his life a poem. The building of the hut and the following of the seasons there was an experiment rather than an adopted way of life. If the doctrine of self-reliance were sound, how far

could one carry it? The best way to find out was to try. Just
do it and see where one got by mere elimination of as many
non-essentials as possible. Live by dead reckoning. Simplify.

He built on a small tract of woodland belonging to his
friend Emerson, only a mile from Concord. He could walk
over from his family's home—full of people and paying guests
—and work on his cabin, returning in the evening to a substantial and warm meal. The Thoreau family—mother, father,
brother, and sister—were closely knit in affection, but even
the most loving of people can intrude. He began to build in
March, 1845, and moved into the finished cabin on July 4th.
Still he could choose his times to be alone or with people. The
village was not far. "I learned this, at least, by my experiment;
that if one advances confidently in the direction of his dreams,
and endeavors to live the life which he has imagined, he will
meet with a success unexpected in common hours." At the end
he returned to the village because he had worn a path from the
cabin door to the pond; perhaps his mind was also beginning
to travel a beaten path. "I left the woods for as good a reason
as I went there. Perhaps it seemed to me that I had several more
lives to live, and could not spare any more time for that one."

He was wrong, of course, if he thought that he had learned
a lesson which he could apply to these other lives to make them
better. The Walden years were the highest point, the most intense moment of living. There he was most himself, genuinely
the poet in word and act. From the experience came, in one
way or another, his two real books, *A Week on the Concord
and Merrimack Rivers* (1849) and *Walden* (1854). His other
books were miscellaneous essays collected from the magazines,
or passages from his voluminous journals. In these two is the
essence of Thoreau as writer.

Thoreau was a native of Concord although not of the original migrant British stock. His father's family was English-speaking French of the Channel Islands, his mother's American Scottish Tory. This is the sort of mixture that the true American is made of, now as then. But to his fellow villagers, there was something strange and almost alien about this awkward and shy but vigorous boy with a slight "burr" to his talk. His temperament was retiring—so much so that he made relatively few friends in his years at Harvard—and his actions, apparently indolent, were actually energetic. He read much and walked more. From the earliest years he sought the still uncleared woodlands about the village rather than the society of his fellows. He may have learned silence by reaction to his mother, reputed the greatest talker in Concord, or directly from his taciturn father.

When it came time to choose a profession, he turned from those that were conventionally open to him as a Harvard graduate—ministry, law, medicine, business—and tried school-teaching as had Emerson. The "Concord Academy" that he and his beloved brother John opened was much criticized and immensely popular. John Dewey should have been there, for this was pragmatic education, learning by doing, exploring nature rather than books. Then he tried lecturing, and that, if anything, became his career. Never very effective on the platform, he followed the Emersonian pattern of entering observations in his *Journal*, preparing a lecture from them, and then refining the lecture into an essay. The direct conversational tone of even his most formal writing is perhaps a result of this presence of an audience in imagination if not in fact.

He began his *Journal* in 1837, and all his writing originates there. Almost his first words were: "To be alone I find it necessary to escape the present,—I avoid myself." But he sought out his brother for the idling trip on the sluggish Concord which was to provide the frame for his "books of days." The early pages of his *Journal* are subjective—romantic introspection—but with a hard core that prevents them from being sentimental. They emphasize the necessity for being alone, more in the mood of the fireside than of the moor. He is already setting his house—his soul—in order with ironic and deliberate self-deception. He knows Brahma and Buddha as well as the Christian God; he talks of reading but mentions few books by name. Gradually there are more specific comments about the details of nature, and the walks become more important. It was about then that he went to Walden Pond. He had assisted Emerson and Margaret Fuller with the *Dial* and had contributed many poems, essays, and reviews. He knew that he was a writer, but he did not know then, nor did he ever know, how to make a conventional book, although his work had an inner form; and he would not write what people were willing to pay to read. They might take what he had to offer or not, as they liked.

After the Walden experiment, he lived at the Emerson home while its master was in Europe lecturing. Lidian was kind to him, and his affections were awakened. Except for his unrequited early love for Ellen Sewall, this devoted friendship was the only break in his emotional singleness. Like many of the transcendental group, he idealized the relationship of the sexes and attempted to intensify it by putting it on the Platonic level. Such friendships were very common in this group of perfectionists—Emerson's letters are full of them—but Thoreau lived at the Emerson house no more.

When a gift of Oriental books arrived from an English

friend, he shared his treasure with Emerson, and with him took up the cause of John Brown when the slavery issue became too acute even for him. In this crisis, for the first time, both men turned thought into action of the more obvious kind and crusaded for the fanatic hero of Harpers Ferry. But Thoreau was no longer the poet, the man of moods and ideas. Still, as one biographer has called him, the "bachelor of nature," he was now more an amateur botanist and geologist, a collector of specimens, than a dreamer and wit.

It is his wit that really differentiates Thoreau from the other transcendentalists: "Museums are the catacombs of nature"—"I have learned that the swiftest traveller is he that goes afoot"—"A man is rich in proportion to the number of things he can let alone"—"Any man more right than his neighbors constitutes a majority of one already"—"There is need for a Society for the Diffusion of Ignorance." The reverse aphorism which carries a sting as it provokes a smile is Thoreau's trade-mark. Ben Franklin nods to him across the years with a sympathetic twinkle in his eye.

There is also a wisdom as well as a wit in the rugged and spiny prose that sets this man of Nature apart from many of the Concord poets and philosophers. The tang of the Maine woods and of the sea is in his sentences, as well as the peace of his New England town, and he can build, out of the common experience of streams and trees and fields of corn, figures of speech that reveal eternal truths. He can make a battle of ants and a conversation with a woodchuck seem like events in history. His words flow swiftly because his thought is clear and his emotions steady. The skepticism of all dogma and the faith in life that he shared with Emerson take in him a form more appealing to some readers because they are less theoretical, more closely tied to action. He can say: "Read not the Times. Read Eternities," and make it seem like the most practical advice anyone could give. Uncompromising in his war against materialism, opportunism, and hypocrisy, which he early discovered as the most dangerous of pitfalls in a free society, he could see the sandy bottom of the stream of time without failing in his job of fishing for eternities. Because he could rejoice in and use well the freedom that was given him, he seems not only the harshest critic but the greatest lover of his land.

Thoreau's most influential essay is that on "Civil Disobedience," prompted probably by his night in Concord jail when on principle he had refused to pay his poll tax a few years before. Gandhi read this well reasoned argument for passive resistance and became an ardent admirer of the American prophet of individualism who had gained so much inspiration from the Orient. Others in other times and places have found him an immediate and practical guide through the thickets of circumstance to the open fields of thought and feeling which are always just beyond. In Thoreau the affirmative argument had reached the stage of demonstration; the spirit of independence had become a way of life.

CHAPTER IV

THE ARTIST IN AMERICA
Poe, Hawthorne

THE organic theory of literary art, upon which Emerson and Thoreau so fully agreed, was the only possible one for a nation that had so much new experience to shape into expression as did the young Republic. "There are two classes of men called poets," Thoreau had written. "The one cultivates life, the other art,—one seeks food for nutriment, the other for flavor." In their cultivation of life these two men were uncompromising and tireless; in their cultivation of art they were deliberately sparing. They were artists of the word and sentence; in the larger forms they contributed only the necessary flexibility of mind and spirit for the creation of new symbols and rhythms. Originality and sincerity were their guides.

The idea, of which Thoreau spoke so lightly, that art can be in itself creation requires the kind of deliberate craftsman that does not appear very often in a new culture. It requires that the artist must finally pause in his living and take a position outside himself and his own thoughts and feelings if he is to extract meaning from experience. In the perspective thus gained, it is possible for him to recast the materials of life into forms of his own devising. Usually, in the evolution of a cul-

ture, this stage is reached only when society has become sufficiently stable to relieve the artist of concern for the pressing
problems and immediate economic needs of existence. It began to be reached in the United States between 1830 and 1855,
only to be disrupted by the westward expansion and the Civil
War of mid-century; but before the equilibrium broke down,
two writers succeeded in establishing firm ground for their
art in well considered literary theory and well constructed
literary forms. The originality and artistic genius of Edgar
Allan Poe and Nathaniel Hawthorne laid the foundations for
a native American literary tradition of conscious art, as Emerson and Thoreau had defined and expressed the primary
sources of native American literary inspiration.

– 2 –

So firmly fixed in the public mind is the portrait of the
typical romantic poet singing immortal words as he sinks pre-
maturely into the twin despairs of love and death that, once a
poet is identified with the romantic image, his own personality and artistry are difficult for criticism to recapture. Such
was the fate of Edgar Allan Poe (1809–1849). The known
facts of his life seem to provide the necessary outline for such
a portrait, but many of them were planted in his own day by
contemporaries like Rufus Griswold who had been stung by
Poe's just but acid criticism or who were jealous of his bril-
liance. The myth of blighted genius which early grew up
about him was fostered also by his own self-pity and his consequent eagerness to arouse the pity of others for his failures
and his regrets. It has been further augmented by the psychological interpretations of later biographers who often look to
the poet for a reflection of their own frustrations and fail to

appreciate the poetry through which he escapes to the harmony of an imagined ideal. Poe was the first American writer to succeed in creating a total life in art as a foil to the conflicts and frustrations of the human predicament. In so doing, he seemed alien to his time and his country, a strange dark bird like his own raven, appearing suddenly and as suddenly disappearing into the night.

Over against this picture should be set that of the finest critical mind of his generation, with a poetic sensitivity keyed to impressions of sight and sound, an intense introspective searching of soul, and a belief in the mathematical logic of the universe. Poe's art was the romantic art of contraries and of compensations. In his way he was as much the spokesman for America as were Cooper and Irving in theirs, but he gave voice to eternal human hungers for the unrealizable and the unrealized. His was the eagerness of the pioneer, astray in the wilderness, for the beauty and the richness of Old World culture, rather than the aspiration of the pioneer whose goals lie in a sunset that can be pushed further and further back toward the new and undiscovered country to the West. The intensity of his dreams and the firmness of his conviction of the validity of art as a way of life are as native to America as is Leatherstocking, for, like the portrait of Cooper's trapper of the north woods, they are the products of the special conditions of life on the Western continent at the period of its awakening cultural consciousness. Poe as introspective and deliberate artist may be thought alien to America only in that he moved further than did Cooper from the circumstances that conditioned his writing into the realm of the imagination where all artists are kin. American artists from Brockden Brown and Poe to Henry James and Eliot have suffered this fate. They have been thought of as expatriates while acclaim has come to them from abroad, and they have been denied a place in the literary history of the nation that first shaped their art because they idealized or criticized its civilization. Poe did not become the less American because he turned from the world of commerce to that of the imagination in an attempt to express his inner life rather than the life about him. His revolt was not merely an imitation of that of Byron or of Coleridge or of Goethe. It was his personal and private experience —although by contraries—with the America of his own day. His literary tradition was that counter to realism, and he was but the first of a series of such major writers in the literature of the United States.

Poe spent formative periods of his life in several of the northern coastal towns: Boston, where he was born; Philadelphia, where he did some of his best writing; and New York, where he gained his last fleeting successes; but at heart he was always a citizen of Richmond, Virginia, where he spent most of his boyhood years. The Southern chivalric ideal is at the center of his view of life and art. The myth of the Cavalier may not have much basis in economic facts of Southern history, but by about 1830, when Poe began to write, it was already established as the literary image of a society committed to the defense of an aristocratic order. Poe made it his own. His tradition is that of Sidney and the Elizabethan court poets and not that of the Puritan England of Milton, the London of Dr. Johnson, or the Cumberland hills of Wordsworth. His feeling for music, his idealization of women, his attempts to make the supernatural credible can all be traced to the lyric poetry, the ornate prose, and the romantic tragedy of the age of Shakespeare.

As artist, he was born to his role. His mother, Elizabeth Arnold, was a popular actress on the American stage who had played successfully a "dancing nymph," a rustic maid, and a series of more substantial parts up to that of Cordelia in *King Lear*. An early miniature of her shows the wide eyes and sensitive mouth of her even more gifted son, who probably inherited from his father, David Poe, the sharp mind and brooding spirit of his Irish ancestry. Edgar, at the age of two, had already lost both parents and was given a home by the Scottish merchant of Richmond, John Allan, and his childless wife. Surely the contrast between the Bohemianism of Poe's inheritance and the strict prudence of his early environment was sufficient to cause an inner violence that must erupt ultimately in some form. His life-long effort to find beauty and harmony in art must have some inverse connection with this division in his emotional background. His childhood was externally happy, internally moody and at times dark. Living the normal life of a boy of good social standing, he played, studied, fell in love, and prepared for college. At the same time he was writing poems of longing for unattainable beauty and for death:

> "From childhood's hour I have not been
> As others were—"

and reading them to his "Helen," the sympathetic mother of his school friend Bob Stanard. With the world-weariness of the adolescent, he cried:

> "Is *all* that we see or seem
> But a dream within a dream?"

Perhaps some of this sense of unreality came from the contrast of the winter darkness and ivied ruins which he remembered from a residence in London and Scotland when he was six years old, with the Virginia sunlight and freshness about him. More likely, it was self-induced, the inward turning of romantic youth, as much a product of reading as of living. It is hard to reconstruct that reading, but there is evidence that he read and studied much. The *Weltschmerz* of Goethe and Childe Harold, the haunted imagination of Coleridge, and the castles and tarns of Scott vie with the Greek sense of order and the neoclassical ideal of rational moderation which he may have learned from his year at Jefferson's University of Virginia. Although he was completely free of the religious inheritance of the New England transcendentalists, he claimed the same tradition of idealism from the Greeks through the Renaissance, and he was temperamentally more free than they to attempt a balance between emotion and reason in his art.

The quarrel with his guardian over gambling debts and the subsequent break with his whole early life reveal inner emotional tensions rather than the dissipation to which they are often attributed. His brief Army experience in South Carolina and his later dismissal from West Point are not so important as is the appearance in Boston of his first book, *Tamerlane and Other Poems*, in 1827. Two years later a revision, with new poems added, appeared in Baltimore, where he had joined his uncertain fortunes with those of his aunt Mrs. Clemm, mother of Virginia, his future child-wife, then a child indeed.

With a third edition of his poems (called "second") in 1831, Poe was ready to declare his poetic creed. His preface, the "Letter to Mr. B——," is a violent protest against rational control of the imagination as it was argued by Wordsworth and Coleridge. "A poem, in my opinion," he concludes, "is opposed to a work of science by having, for its *immediate* object, pleasure, not truth; to romance, by having, for its object, an *indefinite* instead of a definite pleasure, . . . to which end music is an *essential,* since the comprehension of sweet sound is our most indefinite conception." In his later and matured definition ("Poetry is the rhythmic creation of beauty"), he held firmly to the positive aspects of this proposition, although he recanted on his rejection of science or reason. Of the three divisions of the mind which he so often reiterated, Pure Intellect, Taste, and the Moral Sense, he took always as his own special province that of Taste, which he placed in the middle as mediator. In doing so he was not at first fully aware of the discipline of art itself which demands that its own structure of laws be understood before beauty can be fully realized. Later the effort to achieve mastery of this structure of aesthetic law became his consuming passion, "Unity" rather than "Beauty" his primary goal.

It was "Helen," standing statue-like in the window-niche, who brought him home

> "To the glory that was Greece
> And the grandeur that was Rome."

The classic restraint of this poem marks the turning point of his career in art. Before it, the long poems "Tamerlane" and "Al Aaraaf" wandered in the realm of pure sensuous beauty; after it, "The Raven" and "Annabel Lee" could be constructed with what, for some, seems an all too deliberate architecture.

Beauty, restraint, unity of effect—these are the three stages in Poe's mastery of his medium. The small body of his poetry, the best of which was not collected until the volume of 1845 and some not published until after his death, has had an influence far beyond even its own intrinsic worth because it is so perfect an embodiment of his theory of art.

The angel Israfel "whose heart-strings are a lute" and who, according to the Koran, was to sound the trumpet for the Resurrection, is Poe's symbol for the poet, as Merlin was to be Emerson's. Through him the earth-bound versifier could associate poetry with music, the real with the ideal:

> "If I could dwell
> Where Israfel
>   Hath dwelt, and he where I,
> He might not sing so wildly well
>   A mortal melody
> While a bolder note than this might swell
> From my lyre within the sky."

But there was no confusion of identity. Poe was not Israfel, nor was the world of the ideal to be attained as a day-by-day experience. In the mathematical order and harmony of music, the poet might find the necessary controls for his imagination. Chaotic fancy, lost in the labyrinth of the senses, could become a shaping power through aesthetic control of the emotions when projected to the level of the ideal. Neither Intellect nor the Moral Sense need be called upon to govern; in art itself the visual image and the harmonic pattern could be trusted to provide a universe of meaning and relation into which the disordered and worldly spirit of the poet might escape.

As his own life became more and more disrupted by the violent consequences of his divided personality, the wings of Poe's angel Israfel became stronger and the course of his flight more certain. Poems like "Ulalume," "Annabel Lee," and "For Annie" have a firmness of texture as symbol and rhythm which is belied by the emotional chaos that they express. Poe had found a way into the dark recesses of the human soul and he had created a form in which its torments could find direct symbolic expression. His poetry is insight revealed in music and picture, in rhythm and image. The further task for him, as well as for Hawthorne and later students of human motivation, was to give that insight a more analytical expression in fiction. Poe's own poems and criticism show how, in the romantic-organic philosophy, the imagination may, at the higher levels, create its own rules of order. Once he had conquered his own diffuse sentimentality, he tended to err in the direction of an almost mechanical formalism (as in "The Raven" and "The Bells"), but he never again made the mistakes for which he attacked his contemporaries Drake, Halleck, and Longfellow. His conception of the functions of the poetic imagination and the rules for its control had to be understood and applied by a whole generation of French poets before American poetry could continue from the point at which he left it.

— 3 —

The period of Poe's brief maturity was spent in Baltimore, Philadelphia, and New York, as the fortunes of his profession of editor and author took him. His marriage in 1836 to his ailing young cousin Virginia, then only thirteen, did little to alter his fixed vision of perfect beauty in the mirage of unattainable woman, although she more and more came to stand for this ideal. With her death in 1847, the image was complete. Bereavement, long an essential of his romantic ideal, was now an intense personal fact; but it had already been fully expressed in his poems ("The Raven") and in his prose tales ("Ligeia"). Experience followed only as confirmation.

Poe's turn to prose was immediately prompted by his need to earn a living. Befriended by the Baltimore novelist John Pendleton Kennedy, he became editor of the *Southern Literary Messenger* after winning a prize for his tale "MS. Found in a Bottle." His success was immediate in both fields, and only the volatility of his temperament prevented him from settling down to a relatively prosperous and secure way of life. Other editorial posts followed, notably that of *Graham's Magazine* (1841–1842), and his own *Tales of the Grotesque and Arabesque* were collected in 1840. In the final decade of his life, he was recognized and respected as a writer, as an editor he brought together the best literary talent of his day, and as a critic he was feared because his judgments disregarded sensibilities in order to demand an integrity which the current journalism was not willing to require.

Poe's fiction follows his theory as closely as does his later poetry. Less concerned now with beauty for its own sake, he realized that emotional impact on the reader is the primary purpose of a prose tale and he tried to discover the internal laws which produce the most impelling effect. An avid reader of *Blackwood's* and other contemporary magazines, he decided to exploit the Gothic methods with which Brown and

Freneau had already experimented. On the assumption that the most basic emotion is fear, he turned to the supernatural for his material. Here he had the aid of the pseudosciences of the time: mesmerism, phrenology, and other efforts to explore what we today would call the subconscious. In the area between waking and sleeping, between life and death, he found the senses most alert, the emotions least inhibited. Insanity, telepathy, and other abnormal or unusual states of the mind became instruments of his art. The phenomenal analytical power of Auguste Dupin—that forerunner of Sherlock Holmes—, the ability of the author's dead love Ligeia to seize and momentarily inhabit the dying body of the Lady Rowena, the failing mind of the distraught Roderick Usher at the moment when he, his family, and his very house are on the verge of collapse—such are the central figures of these blood-curdling tales. The outside world with its people becomes a mere system of symbols for the constructs of his deliberately overwrought mind.

The monitor in the artist's consciousness is never swept away by the horror of the tale. Poe, the creator, is in control. His early tales, like "A Descent into the Maelstrom," take their form chiefly from the sequence of events, but in the later tales the artist is as precise and deliberate in laying brick upon brick as is his merciless teller of the tale in walling up the unfortunate Fortunato in "The Cask of Amontillado." Plot, says Poe, is "that in which no part can be displaced without ruin to the whole." Again artistry is achieved, as in the poetry, by a studied unity and totality of effect.

Poe himself classified his tales as "grotesque," "arabesque," and "ratiocinative," to indicate variations in his intentions. The "arabesque" are those in which horror or other emotion in violent suspense gives the tale its power; in the "grotesque" tales, like "The Masque of the Red Death," the effect is achieved by a grim and ironic humor; in the "ratiocinative," of which "The Murders in the Rue Morgue" and "The Gold Bug" are the best known, the effect comes from the use of rational analysis in reconstructing a series of events in the best manner of association psychology. All three methods were developed rather than invented by Poe, but his careful study and systematic use of them made him the master of a new form, the short story of psychological effect.

In the last three years of his life, when Virginia was slowly dying and he had lost through his own restlessness his ability to hold a job and support her, his outer life became a more frantic seeking for pleasure, his inner life an effort to transfer his discovery of aesthetic unity to the laws of being. *Eureka, a Prose Poem* (1848), is testimony to his final effort to discover, in the mathematical plan of the Newtonian universe, the harmonious counterpart of the human soul that he had previously sought, and found, in art. It is ironic that, having denied and scoffed at the dualism of Emerson, he should at last have discovered a similar dualism of nature and art in his own metaphysics. But it was too late to rescue the poet Poe, now with emotions worn thin and nerves ready to snap, from the dissolution that his body had already reached, even though Poe the artist lived on.

– 4 –

Poe was one of the first critics to greet his rival in the prose tale, Nathaniel Hawthorne (1804–1864), as an artist rather than as a moralist. His review of *Twice-Told Tales* in 1842, when the second series appeared, contains perhaps the best early definition of the short-story form and ranks Hawthorne as the best practitioner of the art. The prose tale in contrast to poetry, he points out, seeks Truth rather than Beauty as its end, but it must have a unity of effect based on uniform style or tone and limited duration. To these requirements Hawthorne conforms, and his tales "belong to the highest region of Art—an Art subservient to genius of a very lofty order." His unified tone is one of repose, he consistently seeks Truth, he observes a necessary brevity, and above all, he has "invention, creation, imagination, originality—a trait which, in the literature of fiction, is possibly worth all the rest."

Critical opinion since then has supported Poe's verdict but not without wasting much time on the problems of moralism and sentimentality. Hawthorne's material was the ethical view of life of his Calvinistic New England ancestors, and his tales are almost always allegories with morals attached, but the author's own attitude toward his material is usually that of the artist: detached, critical, skeptical. The central theme of most of his stories is not sin as a theological problem, but rather the psychological effect of the conviction of sin on the lives of the early colonists. Like Poe, he was an explorer of the dark recesses of the human soul, and he used his art to reveal rather than to resolve the dilemma of human destiny.

Hawthorne's early life was a long apprenticeship for a comparatively brief period of literary activity. He was thirty-three before the first of his collections of short stories appeared and forty-six before he wrote a successful novel. Yet he never once doubted that he must become an author. When his sea-captain father died in 1808, and the boy was shut in upon himself in the old house in Salem by his mother's devotion to a memory, he read Spenser and Milton and prepared with a tutor for Bowdoin College. His shyness was deeply rooted and was always present, whether he was living the life of a recluse or was joining quite naturally with his fellows. Biographers have had difficulty in reconciling his long period of withdrawal and apparent misanthropy with the accounts of his genial relations with his college friends Franklin Pierce, Henry Longfellow, and Horatio Bridge, and later with his wife and children. There is no inconsistency; the shy and introspective personality may very well be unusually gentle and outgoing when he is genuinely at ease. Hawthorne pitied rather than hated mankind; he was burdened rather than revolted by man's heritage of sin.

The twelve-year period of relative withdrawal from society, when he lived in Salem after his graduation from Bowdoin, was a period of deliberate preparation for his art. He read voluminously and wrote the experimental *Seven Tales of My Native Land*, all of which he presumably destroyed. His first published tale, *Fanshawe* (1828), might well have been destroyed also, except for its partial self-portrait of the scholar-recluse grappling with the problem of living his own life and at the same time adjusting to society. In Fanshawe the worlds of thought and of reality were separate and irreconcilable; they were so for Hawthorne also, then and always. His personal story is one of a constant effort to adjust to living while preserving his own spiritual integrity; his tales are various treatments of this major theme. Like Poe, he made his best adjustment by the creation of art rather than, like Thoreau, by the arbitrary shaping of an independent course of life.

Success came when he learned how to get perspective on his problem by pushing it back into his own racial and national past. Living in the town where the witch trials had taken place, and involved in them through his direct ancestor Judge William Hathorne, he found it easy to become completely immersed in Salem history and in the lives of the Puritan colonists. Their problem was his problem, his problem theirs. The fact that with them sin was an awful reality while with him it was a psychological obsession only made them the perfect instruments to receive his skeptical speculations. His introspection could be exhibited in a fictional frame. He turned naturally to the extreme form of symbolism, the moral allegory, as the most nearly perfect medium available to his desperate needs for confession and for secrecy. Here he could say what he wanted to say and yet hide behind his symbols.

Gradually he was drawn out into the world by his old friend Horatio Bridge who arranged for the publication of the first volume of *Twice-Told Tales* in 1837 (second series, 1842) and by Sophia Peabody whom he married in 1842. Meanwhile he had sought a means of earning a living with the least possible concession to Mammon. An experimental residence at the Utopian colony of Brook Farm was wholly unsuccessful, probably because his motives were practical rather than Utopian. A post in the Boston Custom House was uncomfortable but adequate to his immediate needs. Only in the romantic interlude at the Old Manse in Concord, where he took his fragile bride, does he seem to have been completely happy. In 1846 he published his third volume of tales, *Mosses from an Old Manse*, and returned to the slavery of the Custom House once more, this time at Salem. He was not writing the kind of story that at any time—and much less at that time—would supply the means of livelihood.

Poe, with a sure critical sense, likened these misty tales

to the essays of Lamb and Irving. They have the familiar essay touch of a writer who is absorbed by his own speculations and is willing to drift as they take him. "So! I have climbed high," he explains in "Sights from a Steeple," "and my reward is small. Here I stand, with wearied knees, earth, indeed, at a dizzy depth below, but heaven far, far beyond me still." Even so he would prefer the "multitude of chimneys," with their secrets of humanity spoken in smoky whispers, to the loneliness of clouds. At this remove he can observe both a thunderstorm gathering on the horizon and a funeral taking place in the street beneath him. Neither a part of human destiny nor completely removed from it, he draws his lesson of life. "Man must not disclaim his brotherhood, even with the guiltiest."

There is both an aesthetic and a moral significance in this neutral position which Hawthorne took, neither in nor outside human life. As artist it gave him the perspective necessary for treating reality with the freedom of fiction, and as moralist it provided him with his message: the bond of sin—committed or thought—binds man to earth and so to a common fate with his fellows. The true Calvinist seeks conviction of sin as a preparation for a promised salvation; Hawthorne, the humanitarian heretic, sees it as an admission to the brotherhood of man and cares little for what may happen in an afterlife. His essays are speculations on this problem; from a steeple, in the "singular moment" of starting from a midnight slumber, at the "gate of dreams," on an imagined broad Western prairie—always at one remove from life either in time or in space.

His tales are the projections of these speculations into the observed lives of men and women—familiar people removed by the imagination to the colonial past: Young Goodman Brown who meets his lover-wife at a midnight rendezvous of evil spirits in the depths of the woods; the minister who, by wearing a black veil, hides a supposed sin but reveals his sinfulness and therefore his common humanity; Ethan Brand who has committed the sin of sins and whose heart is finally discovered to be of marble; the scientist who provides an antidote for the poison which turns out to have been the very life of his beloved.

The people of these tales never become much more than phantoms—vague symbols moving through a pattern of meaning which is an impersonal reading of life. The scenes, too, are sketched with the brush of an impressionist, in broad, vague, and blending strokes. The mood is tense, though tranquil, because the author feels so acutely the human tragedy that he delineates. Man (or woman) is his hero, endowed with the hope of perfection seen dimly through his Christian faith, but forever thrown back on himself to discover a dark salvation in the mystery of sin. Behind all Christian tragedy is the theme of the Fall, whether of man or of the angels, and the consequent struggle for salvation. Hawthorne shares this tradition with the Hebrew prophets, with Milton, and with Melville. In the shorter tales his art remains on the level of allegory, with its meaning almost extinguishing the reality of his people and places; in his longer romances he approaches the freedom of tragic vision. The Christian myth of Heaven and Hell, which to Jonathan Edwards was an urgent reality, was for Hawthorne the artist a system of acknowledged symbols through which to describe the predicament of nineteenth century man.

– 5 –

There was only one more collection of short tales, *The Snow-Image and Other Twice-Told Tales* (1852), not counting the collections in the "Tanglewood" series for boys and girls. The range of Hawthorne's art in this genre is not great, and he tends to repeat his characters, his themes, his scenes. The unity that Poe demanded, Hawthorne achieved in a dozen or more tales, but variety is lacking. It was his publisher-friend James T. Fields who came to his rescue in 1850 with the suggestion that he would gain more readers by a longer story. In *The Scarlet Letter* Hawthorne discovered not only a greater range, but an even greater depth. The characters of Hester Prynne and her lover, the Reverend Arthur Dimmesdale, are the first to step out from the frame of his speculations and become people in their own right. The theme is the now familiar one of a sin committed before the story opens and of the unfolding of the consequences of that act in the lives of a group of people. Here the sin is adultery, but Hawthorne does not share the absolute morality of the Puritan community which demands perpetual penance in the wearing of the scarlet letter "A." On the level of the higher and almost pagan morality which he seems instinctively to favor, Hester by her public and constant confession gains a kind of purity and strength which is not otherwise found in this God-fearing people. Dimmesdale, on the other hand, in keeping his part in the sin a secret while he appears to the world as a spiritual leader, suffers a moral degeneration that leads to his breakdown and death. Strangely enough, the third member of the triangle, the wronged husband Roger Chillingworth, is made the real villain of the piece in that he commits Hawthorne's sin of sins, the violation of the human heart, by exerting his almost hypnotic control over the young minister and deliberately causing his ruin. The codified morality of the Puritan community becomes in this strange tale the social complex against which the natural morality of earthly love revolts. The tragedy lies in the failure of that protest, even though the principals, the two who have committed the social crime, are ennobled by their ordeal. As Christian tragedy, the pattern of the action is set by the theme of the Fall, but salvation comes through acknowledgment of Satan rather than of God. Hester is, of course, condemned to eternal torment by this dispensation; but the tale is also a Greek tragedy because she is the woman of earth who has defied man-made law and has risen to heroic stature through the tragic flaw that must at last destroy as well as ennoble her. Hawthorne wrote better than he knew, and better than he could write again.

The ambiguity of his own position was completely revealed in this short and perfect work of art. He had fully accepted the terms of his material and had allowed his characters to state their own cases, exercising only an aesthetic control over their actions. His moral disinterestedness was much more nearly perfect than he imagined. In spite of himself, he had become in ethics the total skeptic who could view calmly the paradox of human will working its own destruction. He had joined society and his inherited faith in condemning Hester at the same time that he revealed why not only he but all men must love her.

Never again was he so detached from the life of which he wrote, and never again was he master of so concentrated an artistry. In the Preface to his next novel, *The House of the Seven Gables* (1851), he makes explicit the method that up to now was instinctive. He is writing, he tells us, a Romance, in distinction to a Novel which must "aim at a very minute fidelity, not merely to the possible, but to the probable and ordinary course of man's experience." A Romance, as a work of art, must also subject itself rigidly to laws, and sins unpardonably in so far as it may swerve aside from the truth of the human heart, but within these limits it has fairly a right to present that truth under circumstances to a great extent of the author's own choosing or creation.

Hawthorne takes full advantage of his writer's freedom in the loving care with which he reconstructs the past of his native Salem and in his choice of a House rather than a person for his central character. The House is a family as well as a physical fact, as it was in Poe's tale of the House of Usher, and the theme is a curse which carries down through the generations. The wrong that the Colonial Governor Pyncheon did to the revengeful Matthew Maule is visited upon the nineteenth century Judge Pyncheon and his pathetic cousins Hepzibah and Clifford. In leaving the house, Holgrave, the descendant of Maule, finally absolves the now crumbling mansion of its curse, but its life is past. A more sustained piece of writing than the last, this novel—or Romance—does not quite reach the same depths of understanding because it relies more on setting and theme, less on characterization. It tends to become diffuse where *The Scarlet Letter* was concentrated, panoramic where the earlier work was focused with cruel concentration; but its tragic intensity is no less.

The next two novels play further variations on the theme of conscience. Hawthorne's Brook Farm associates serve as models in *The Blithedale Romance* (1852) for a group of people who feed upon one another's hearts as they attempt to construct a social Utopia, but the two strong characters Zenobia and Hollingsworth fail to gain either Hawthorne's or the reader's allegiance, and the tragic outcome of the plot is therefore unconvincing. The delicately spiritual Priscilla and the scholar-recluse Coverdale are by now too much in control of the writer's own view of life, and the tendency to rely on melodramatic circumstances to carry the theme of hypnotic violation of personality weakens what might have been a unique masterpiece of psychological analysis. There is probably no novel of the era in which the role of the subconscious is so fully apprehended, so little understood.

Hawthorne's last completed novel, *The Marble Faun* (1860), is a product of his years of residence in Liverpool as American consul and of his travels in Italy. The scene is modern Rome, but the characters and theme are transferred from Puritan New England. The writer's hope to make his novel popular as a sort of guidebook was realized by the imbedding of long descriptive passages in the narrative with the result of a further extenuation. The theme of sin, retribution, and salvation, at least in this world, through confession, provides a frame for an elaborate plot in which fantasy and melodramatic incidents play their full parts. The faun-like ears of Donatello who loses his innocence but gains humanity by the knowledge of evil are unconvincing, and the plot of murder and confession is never realized on the symbolic level; yet there is a sustained delight in this novel as in all the others. However dark his imagination, Hawthorne's life in the world of make-believe was always intense, and he is able to convey that enjoyment to his reader. There is a witchery about his longer works which sustains even this last great story, in spite of a gradual relaxing of the controls which had made his first romance his greatest. It is the power of the artist who knows at firsthand the passions and problems of which he writes, but is able to present them without himself becoming entangled in their web. The agency of his perspective was allegory which, because it is used primarily for aesthetic rather than moral purposes, serves to supply a symbolic level of meaning to the imagined events. In spite of his deep concern for morality as the major force in human affairs, Hawthorne, like Poe, achieved in his best work an aesthetic detachment that made it possible for him to give to American life, at the moment of its first cultural renaissance, a critical presentation in literary art.

CHAPTER V

ROMANTIC CRISIS
Melville, Whitman

IF in Emerson and Thoreau the soul of the infant Republic had found its first affirmation and in Poe and Hawthorne its agony and its tragic voice, the times were ready by 1850 for a literary masterwork which would cry out with a timeless world cry of both faith and despair. Only of such stuff is great literature made, and of such were *Moby-Dick* (1851) and *Leaves of Grass* (1855).

The authors of these two works were born in the same year and died within a year of each other after living lives which virtually spanned the century. At no time were they further than a few hundred miles from each other except for brief journeys, and both looked to New York City and its environs as home. Both were profoundly influenced by the wit and patriotic fervor of the Knickerbocker writers and by the expansive idealism and imaginative range of the New Englanders, and yet there is no record of their having known each other personally or of either having made significant comments on the other's ideas or writings. Melville's important creative work was virtually complete by 1855 when Whitman issued the first experimental edition of *Leaves of Grass*. Two rebel giants, each created and inhabited for his span of years the sovereign kingdom of his own imagination. Writing with epic sweep and tragic vision, these two spoke to the ages; they had no need to nod to each other. They had in common the misunderstanding, verging on scorn, of their contemporaries, and they finally shared the acclaim of posterity.

In the popular mind their moods and messages seem to be in violent contrast. Melville's voice is the voice of irony and despair, his ultimate faith is in the certainty of evil, if faith can be said to have at all transcended his cosmic doubt. He seems the Devil's advocate in contrast to Whitman's voice crying out for confidence in life, in the future, and in the common goodness of humanity. Melville seems philosophically to link with Poe and Hawthorne; Whitman, with Emerson and Thoreau. But the contrast is illusory. It was Whitman who uttered the cry of joy in death which concludes his great ode "Out of the Cradle Endlessly Rocking," and it was Melville whose hero Billy Budd blessed Captain Vere for crucifying his innocence. *Leaves of Grass*, except for the blatantly assertive "Song of Myself," is a deeply sad tribute to man's weakness in the midst of cosmic splendor. *Moby-Dick*, like all great tragedy, purges the emotions of their violence and gives its lone survivor the steady eye of experience with which to look out upon the world.

The difference between *Moby-Dick* and *Leaves of Grass* is in the kind of epic poetry that each represents. There is the tragic or Promethean epic in which the poet defies his gods and gives humanity a voice of protest against fate, and there is the heroic or racial epic in which the poet speaks the common aspirations and faith of his people. American literature produced both kinds almost at the one moment.

– 2 –

Herman Melville (1819–1891) was a product of the up-state Dutch-British stock that Irving satirized in his Knicker-bocker's History and that Cooper and Paulding studied in their novels with loving care. Born and raised in the city of New York, he was as much a Middle States American as it was then possible to be. Six years of youth spent in the head-waters capital of Albany confirmed his deep-rooted provin-cialism, and a tightly knit family life inculcated the certainties of a Calvinistic creed and an economic security. If Maria Gansevoort had been a little more flexible in her social and re-ligious convictions or if Allan Melville had been a little less so in his world travels and manipulations of the family fi-nances, the rebel Herman Melville might never have devel-oped. Out of violent though probably suppressed emotional conflict at home came the will to kick against the stars. At the age of nineteen, according to his own somewhat fictionalized account, he was ready to ship for Liverpool, "as a substitute for pistol and ball," on the first copper-bottomed and fully rigged merchantman that he happened upon. This he did, and the outcast Ishmael was born in the heart of a shy and well mannered youth.

These most formative years of Melville's life are cast in the familiar pattern of romantic escape from hardships more imaginary than real. Actually, his departure was planned and understood by the widowed mother and the envious but help-ful older and younger brothers who went down to New York ahead and made the arrangements. The fictionalized young Redburn of the novel of that name left home in lonely des-peration of spirit and set out into the unknown in a mood of suicidal gloom. Actually, in these autobiographical novels the truth that Melville was following was, like Hawthorne's, that of the human heart only. His recent biographers have done much to correct the earlier ones who accepted them as actual records of what happened to their author. A comparison of the real and fictional accounts of this single incident opens the door to an understanding of the workings of a great imagination. No doubt the apparently quiet and happy boy who waved goodbye to his two brothers and elder friend as the *St. Lawrence* left her slip on her way to Liverpool with a cargo of cotton was, deep inside himself, the desperate and lonely exile from humanity that he later pictured. Melville was throughout his life a dual personality; he could live on two levels of consciousness and be fully and keenly alive on both at the same moment. The experience is a common one, of being caught up by an emotional situation and at the same time being critically aware of what is happening, but seldom is it made so articulate as in Melville's autobiographical romances. The suicidal lonely youth and the happy and favored brother who was off to glorious adventures were both there waving from the rail. And they collaborated later to make the novel *Redburn* a narrative of what happened and an extraordinarily accurate revelation of the inner conflict of adolescence. Even in this, one of Melville's lesser works, the artist could step into the breach and make the voyage of Redburn a symbol of the first meeting of youthful dreams with the hard facts of experience. The same process, far more intricate and involved, created *Mardi*, *Moby-Dick*, and *Pierre*, where passion and understanding reached their maximum intensity while the artist Melville retained control and direction of both.

The inner and outer biographies must proceed together, for that is how they were lived. With a guidebook to Liverpool that might have been used by his father many years before (the earlier biographers assumed that it had been), the apprentice-sailor dreamed of the sights he was to see while enduring the hardships of shipboard life and the insensitivity of his fellows. The poverty and squalor of the Liverpool dock area shocked him profoundly, for America confessed as yet to no real slums in her cities, but he probably saw little of England other than its one chief harbor and the surrounding countryside during his six-weeks stay. Much more—the hurried trip to London and the episode of the corrupt Jackson on the return passage, as well as many lesser details in the novel —are apparently but products of his imagination; and they are the best parts of the story.

On his return, he found his family in even worse financial circumstances than when he had set out, and he was soon off again, this time to the South Seas on the whaler *Acushnet* from New Bedford. On July 9, 1842, "Richard T. Greene and Herman Melville deserted at Nukehiva," according to the crew list sworn to by the captain. Greene was the "Toby" who plunged inland on the wild Marquesan island with his adventurous companion, hoping that when the natives appeared from the tropical underbrush they would be the less cannibalistic of the two tribes who were reputed to inhabit the island in a state of constant warfare with each other. But the idyllic residence with the natives which Melville describes in his first published novel *Typee* (1846) follows only the outline of the facts. History tells of no maiden Fayaway of the canoe and the inland pool and no watchful Kory-Kory to attend the fearful but contented captive. The escapes of Toby and then of the author are attested, as is the decrepit whaler *Julia* under another name, the new companion Doctor Long Ghost (of all Melville's people, the most lovingly and ironically drawn), and the adventures in and near Tahiti, as told in the sequel *Omoo* (1847). There the chronological parallel between fiction and fact is broken. The wandering sailor, after another whaling cruise in the waters off Japan, finally enlisted in the Navy in order to ship on the man-of-war *United States* and return from Honolulu to Boston, where he was discharged on October 14, 1844.

His marriage on August 4, 1847, to the daughter of Chief Justice Lemuel Shaw transformed the world wanderer into the respectable family man and citizen. From then on, except for a few brief trips, Herman Melville could be found in New York City or at his rural home Arrowhead near Pittsfield, Massachusetts. His brief friendship with Hawthorne, who was in nearby Lenox in 1850–1851, and a trip to the Holy Land alone in 1856 are the major events of his later years in so far as his writing is concerned. The psychologist is concerned with the inner violence often caused by a life of apparent conformity; the reader is interested only in the writings that supply his imagination with the probings and insights of an aroused but suppressed genius. From 1846 to 1852 Melville wrote and published furiously; from 1853 to 1857 he continued to write, but much of his imaginative abandon had given way to critical uncertainties; from 1858 to the end of his life, a period of over thirty years, he lapsed into comparative silence and his novels were almost forgotten. Melville had been a writer of promise, but . . . The early praise was swallowed by oblivion.

The revival of interest in *Moby-Dick* in the 1920's is one

of the most dramatic reversals in all literary history. From a by-line in the textbooks Melville became overnight one of the half-dozen major American literary figures of the nineteenth century. *Moby-Dick* spoke directly to the youth who had fought in the First World War, and once it had been redis-covered the other novels followed: first the stories of adven-ture at sea, *Redburn* (1849) and *White-Jacket* (1850), then the two symbolic romances *Mardi* (1849) and *Pierre* (1852), and finally philosophical allegories like *The Confidence-Man* (1857) and the posthumous *Billy Budd* (1924), as well as the short stories and poems. Melville, it would seem, had written as much and as well as the best of them.

– 3 –

Melville's art builds up to and away from the tragic epic *Moby-Dick*. It would present a confused and meaningless pat-tern without that central peak; with that focus it is an aes-thetic and interrelated whole.

So concentrated is the vision of this great book that it could be called merely a battle between the mad captain Ahab of the whaler *Pequod* and the mightiest of whales, the "white" monster Moby-Dick. In a previous encounter Ahab had been defeated, and bears the symbol of his defeat in a false leg made of whalebone. Swearing revenge, he sets out, actually toward a second encounter in which he will allow only total victory or total destruction. His obsession draws all his crew into the orbit of his passion, some willingly, some passively, some re-luctantly, and the voyage is undertaken. It concludes only in a victory which is also destruction.

The story, as told by Ishmael embarking on his first voy-age, falls into three parts: a long and circumstantial introduction in which the matter-of-fact youth is forewarned by various events and signs that this is no ordinary voyage, but ships in spite of all; the major portion of the book in which Moby-Dick is pursued through months of wandering over the face of the water that are filled with the incidents and the technical processes of whaling; and finally three whirlwind concluding chapters in which the adversaries are engaged in mortal conflict and resolution. Ishmael, the outcast, alone survives the wreck, to tell of it.

Other characters are grouped around these three: Ishmael, Ahab, the Whale. The three mates are New England men: the pious Starbuck, the blunt and humorous Stubb, the casual Flask. The three harpooners are all primitives: the Indian Tashtego, the Negro Dagoo, and the Polynesian Queequeg. Closer to Ahab are the mysterious Parsee Fedallah and the imbecile Negro cabin boy Pip. Starbuck casts over the story the light of conventional Christianity, Queequeg that of primitive pagan morality, but neither can overcome Ahab's will; nor can the warnings of passing ships that have heard of, seen, encountered, or fled from the object of his search with fearful results. The pursuit is relentless.

Melville began work on his book about a "whaling voyage" in the winter of 1850. By May he thought himself "half way in the work." Then that summer he met Hawthorne and reread Shakespeare. Apparently the whole concept changed while the writing was in progress, for a year later it still was not finished. Finally it was published in England in October of 1851 and at home before the end of that year. He had determined to do the "wicked book" that he needed to do and not merely another semiautobiographical romance. The narrative was supposedly completed first; then a course of reading and pondering filled in the other two levels in the rewriting. Saturated in the lore and facts of the art of whaling, he packed his novel so that it breathed sea air and reeked of boiling whale blubber; deeply moved by the problem of free man confronting his own destiny, he made his captain one of the company of Titans who defy both God and Nature. Fact became symbol and incident acquired universal meaning in this second composition. During that year Melville was writing, not the "whaling voyage," but a "strange wild work, and awfully symmetrical and reciprocal," which he described later as seizing his own tormented character Pierre in the novel of that name.

The change was not as sudden as these facts would make it seem. In his first novel *Typee*, Melville had made clear his belief that natural man in many ways is superior to his civilized fellows, and in *White-Jacket*, he had symbolized "the world in a man of war." His skepticism and his symbolism can both be traced back to his earlier works; but the real preparation for *Moby-Dick* was the loose-jointed, humorous, serious, satiric, poetic allegory *Mardi*. The voyage of Taji through the islands of an infinite archipelago in quest of the maiden Yillah is a rather obvious symbolic study of man's fruitless search for a vague ideal of beauty or self-completion, and the various islands provide a handy device for reviewing all the ways in which man has tried to reconcile his insatiable desires to the laws of God and Nature. At the end, Taji is still searching, as was his creator. *Moby-Dick* had to be a romance of moral inquiry and it had to be the allegory that Melville feared it might become.

Once he had determined to allow Ahab to ask the ultimate questions, he could give his imagination and his artistry full freedom to mold a gigantic work. The nature of good and evil, the power of the will to defy fate, the validity of those insights which contradict the apparent laws of experience, the eternal conflict of God and Nature in which man is caught—these are the issues that are raised by Ahab's defiance. In the person of Ahab, whom he conceived in total tragic abandon, he could ask questions that had no answers; in Ishmael he could stand by and allow reason to speculate on the events. Because he supplied no one formula of interpretation, he left his readers the same freedom he gained for himself—the ability to move back and forth between fact and meaning on the bridge of symbolism. He had mastered the art that Hawthorne's experiments had taught him because he had the fluidity of spirit to allow his book finally to write itself.

Quite rightly, the recent study of Melville has concentrated on his later and more purely intellectual work, for never again did he allow himself the emotional abandon required for his masterpiece. In the next novel, *Pierre*, he went "deep, deep, and still deep and deeper" as he strove to "find out the heart of a man." For a third time, he experimented with a literary method that might help him resolve the "ambiguities" of his own heart, but this time he chose one of total subjectivity. Because Pierre cannot escape from his author, he cannot finally ask his questions clearly. The most searching of all Melville's novels threatens alternately to become pure philosophy and pure melodrama. In *The Confidence-Man*, the short tales like "Benito Cereno" and "Bartleby, the Scrivener," and the poems—particularly the long and philosophical *Clarel* —he weaves rational webs of increasing subtlety and complexity, but is held by his growing skepticism from ever stating his case clearly. Finally, in *Billy Budd,* which did not appear in his lifetime, he returned to his central problem of man's moral dilemma, in the character of the boy-sailor caught fairly between the laws of man and the laws of God. No longer is there the nice parallel upon which Emerson rested his case. Like Johnson's *Rasselas,* Melville's speculations led only to a conclusion in which nothing is concluded, but, as in all great art, the reader may form his own answer in the clear and simple presentation of the problem that Melville here at last achieves; but what his own answer is or was, no one can know.

– 4 –

"Certain it is," wrote Melville, "that this great power of blackness in him derives its force from its appeal to that Calvinistic sense of Innate Depravity and Original Sin, from whose visitations, in some shape or other, no deeply thinking mind is always and wholly free." He was speaking of Hawthorne in the "shock of recognition" that came to him upon first reading the *Mosses from an Old Manse,* and as he wrote he thought also of the dark characters of Shakespeare through whose mouths are insinuated "the things which we feel to be so terrifically true, that it were all but madness for any good man, in his own proper character, to utter, or even hint them."

Another "shock of recognition" occurred not long after. Emerson received in the mail a volume by an unknown poet and sat down to write: "I am not blind to the worth of the wonderful gift of *Leaves of Grass.* . . . I find incomparable things said incomparably well. . . . I find the courage of treatment that so delights us and which large perception only can inspire. . . . I greet you at the beginning of a great career." The apostle of light acknowledged a new light of genius instantly when it appeared, as Melville had been quick to greet the blackness of Hawthorne. There are two roads to truth, through sorrow and suffering or through illumination, but both take the courage of conviction. Hawthorne inspired Melville to greater depths of occult wisdom than he could have probed alone; Emerson freed Whitman for mystical insights that were beyond his own ken.

"A great career, which yet must have had a long foreground somewhere, for such a start," Emerson added. He did not then know the part which he had himself played in shaping this articulate prophet of the American democratic man. First too fulsomely acknowledged and then too self-consciously denied, the debt to the elder seer was as obvious to Whitman as to his readers. It was almost as though Walt had stepped out of the pages of Emerson's essay on "The Poet," so exactly did his conceptions of the role of the poet and of the nature of poetry in general tally with the theory there laid down. There were other influences, of course, because the organic theory of poetry and the idea of the national bard were not the sole property of the Concord sage. Germany had her Goethe, England her Wordsworth, and Norway her Wergeland before Whitman appeared for America. Romantic egotism, beginning in the introspective intensity of the individual, readily becomes racial, national, or even cosmic as the times require. When this happens, the bard is created, and Whitman, because of the favoring circumstances of a democratic ideal and an open society, became perhaps the greatest of modern bards.

The moment of mystical revelation, when the consecrated poet is suddenly born of the ordinary man, is perhaps too uncanny to allow a tracing back of the "long foreground" of the event. Apparently such a moment came to the Long Island printer and editor some time between 1845 and 1855. "The story," says his biographer Henry S. Canby, "comes to the surface in 1847 . . . and it can be written concretely from then on." Before that, there is little indication of the special gifts of the author of *Leaves of Grass* in the simple facts of Whitman's life. Born of essentially the same stock as Melville, Dutch on his mother's side and New England British on his father's, he inclined to make much of his mixed blood as a cause of his genius. The place of his birth could have a special significance too, because Long Island was a kind of miniature continent that had received radical and restless offshoots of the Connecticut and New York colonies from the earliest days. The inland plains and fringing seacoasts gave a variety of scene which otherwise could be experienced only by the pioneer who traveled long distances. "There was a child went forth," Walt wrote many years later, "and the first object he look'd upon, that object he became."

His people made no claim to aristocracy as did Melville's. They were simple country folk on both sides, with little or no education, a large family that showed no special genius except in the one son. His father, a carpenter, had learned to read and had subscribed to radical journals, but his mother was nearly illiterate most of her life. The only religious strain of any real influence in the family picture was the Quaker, on his mother's side, which gave a simple idiom for the love which she and her son exchanged. When the family moved to Brooklyn in 1823, the poet in Walt looked out upon the objects of the harbor and of the busy little city as he had looked out upon those of the country, and these objects too he became. He was by birth and education "of the people" more truly than was any previous American author of note, and he learned in his own youth the conflict of country and city life which was to help shape the American literature of the future. The thousand miniature pictures with which Walt's poetry is studded were impressed on his memory in these early years, from the farm sounds and smells of early morning near the sea to the sights and sounds of busy city streets—he knew them all before he had reached manhood.

Most of Whitman's early jobs were in printing shops and newspaper offices which, as with Franklin, Mark Twain, and many another American author, largely took the place of schools. He had his own small paper, the *Long Islander*, in Huntington at the age of twenty, and he was teaching school and editing newspapers from then on at least to the time of his great change in the fifties. From the start he was a Democrat, a follower of Jackson, and he was active in politics. There is an oratorical overtone in much of the later poetry, as well as a tone of editorializing, that stems from these early experiences. When he decided to speak naturally, he did not speak, like Emerson, the words and phrases of the pulpit, nor, like Melville, the sonorous rhythms of Shakespeare and Milton. His natural language was the jargon of the daily press and the political stump speech, a novel but truly American and democratic base on which to build a new poetry.

Signs that a change in Whitman's life and thought was taking place began to appear by 1848. No one knew of the notebook he had been keeping for several years, in which was written:

"I am the poet of the body
  And I am the poet of the soul. . . .
  I am the poet of Equality."

To the world he was the respectable editor of the Brooklyn
Eagle, a haunter of the opera and theater and of art shows, a
political writer of party conviction, a healthy and well adjusted American, crossing the river by the Fulton Ferry almost
daily, mingling in the crowds on Broadway, and returning to
report it all in his paper.

The *Eagle* was the best paper in Brooklyn, and Walt used
its pages to celebrate the new spirit of expansion that followed
the Mexican War and the acquisition of large territories to the
south and west. Then suddenly he resigned under fire. About
the next seven years there is much mystery. We know that he
took a job on the New Orleans *Crescent,* that he left home
with his brother Jeff on February 11, 1848, and that he was
back in Brooklyn by the middle of June. Four months have
been stretched by legend to several years, and packed with
romance. An affair with a member of the demimonde, un-
acknowledged children, a mystical experience of poetic insight, travels through all parts of the West, anything that Walt
or his disciples and biographers wished to have in the "long
foreground" was created and assigned to this romantic interlude.

Whatever the facts, the experience was regenerative, and
the Whitman who returned was no longer a mere newspaper
editor; he was the poet and prophet of *Leaves of Grass,* self-
created but already speaking out boldly in his own free idiom
of life and voice. "The American poets are to enclose old and
new for America is the race of races. Of them a bard is to be

commensurate with a people," he was to write a few years later. Reading furiously, writing only occasionally as a free lance, trying bookselling and printing and carpentering, he seemed restless and aimless. Then, in 1855, he borrowed the press of his friends, the brothers Rome, and set up his own book. By July the first edition of *Leaves of Grass* with its posed portrait of the "rough" in slouch hat and shirt open at the neck, and with its generous wide pages and bold type, made its appearance. It was a new kind of book; it was the end of the romantic movement and the beginning of a new era in American literary history.

– 5 –

What Walt Whitman tried to do in this book was quite simply to lay aside any commitments to tradition or conformity he might have as a poet and to find out and express only what was inherently poetic about life in mid-nineteenth century America. His way was the organic way of art carried to its logical conclusion. Starting with an uncritical acceptance of life in its totality, he worked inward to his consciousness through his senses and his insights, and outward to the democratic masses of American people—and to mankind at large—through friendliness and love.

Even before he went to New Orleans, the basic plan of the book was in his mind, and he worked over its experimental ideas and forms for almost a decade before he offered his results to the public. His statement of his central driving idea in the Preface to the edition of 1855, when he first felt himself ready to speak, is essentially the same as that in the Preface to *November Boughs* in 1888, when he felt that he had said all that he was capable of saying and he could look backward over his accomplishment. This was "a feeling or ambition to articulate and faithfully express in literary or poetic form, and uncompromisingly, my own physical, emotional, moral, intellectual, and aesthetic Personality, in the midst of, and tallying, the momentous spirit and facts of its immediate days, and of current America. . . . Modern science and democracy seem'd to be throwing out their challenge to poetry to put them in its statements in contradistinction to the songs and myths of the past."

This is both more and less than the book actually accomplished. It is more because Whitman's actual experience with life in America was limited. He had not traveled much nor did he know the extremes of the upper and lower levels of American society. What he announced were ideals rather than facts, but his limitation was also his strength. In expressing what he called his own Personality, he was genuinely representative, in the sense that Emerson used the word for men who could reach to the principle behind the evidence. He provided the bridge between American facts and ideals and the universal hopes and failures of mankind. The book as it finally developed was a much more human document than that which Whitman at first designed because it grew in humility and wisdom as its author lived. Constant revision and rearrangement from edition to edition as new poems were added did not swerve it from its single purpose.

The long poem, or collection of closely related short poems, which occupied most of the first edition and which later was called "Song of Myself," really contains the gist of all that Whitman ever had to say, but he is so aware in it of the novelty and challenge in what he is saying that his apparent arrogance tends to interfere with an open acceptance of his message. His first words, "I celebrate myself, and sing myself," are quickly tempered by "And what I assume you shall assume," but their brash egoism has already left the shock that Whitman intended. It is necessary to accept the poet with the poem, for to Whitman life and art are integral. Through his senses, through his uninhibited imagination, through his violent joy in life and urge to creation, the multiform experiences of American life are poured. Even in those opening lines he is thinking of the self as a powerful and sensitive instrument for receiving and expressing, rather than as Walt Whitman of Brooklyn. He moves from himself to you and to others, to all humanity en masse about him, to the brave violence of his nation, to love and death, to the pantheistic God in every object, to the future and to eternity. Then:

> "I depart as air, I shake my white locks
>   at the runaway sun. . . .
> I stop somewhere waiting for you."

Given his abstract idea of Personality—so close to Emerson's concept of a self-reliance that results from unity with the Over-Soul—Whitman's thought moves outward in concentric circles from a concentration on the abstract value of his own self. Through all the intervening layers of friend, lover, the "en masse," nation, humanity, this idea of self moves from its fully realized inner core to the extreme outward limits of cosmic unity. The mystical experience rather than the logical mind must and can alone make this journey. The most limited and personal of poems becomes the largest and most nearly universal.

This "Song of Myself" was much altered with the years

and with later editions of *Leaves of Grass* as Whitman lost some of his youthful extravagance, but it never lost its original meaning of all in each. The final edition of the collected poems, which the poet prepared in his old age, was, he tells us, "the result of seven or eight stages or struggles extending through nearly thirty years," and the reader can recognize at least four: assertion, humility, humanity, cosmic fulfillment.

The second edition of *Leaves of Grass* (1856) carried forward the challenge of the first, but some time between 1855 and 1860, if we judge only from the evidence of the poems, Whitman experienced intimately the sorrows of love, bereavement, and death which had been largely theoretical to him earlier. There is a mood of depression and resignation in the new poems of the edition of 1860–1861 that is totally lacking in the earlier volumes. All brashness is gone in the somber brooding of "Out of the Cradle Endlessly Rocking" over the loss of a beloved mate and the final and joyful acceptance of death. To many, this is the poet Whitman at his greatest because he now seems at last to receive in deep humility the universal truths he had demanded so vigorously before. And the new symphonic forms here used seem to attain the natural music which Whitman's theory of composition had promised.

The next edition of the *Leaves* (1867) added the poems from *Drum-Taps* to mark a third stage in his poetic progress. When Whitman learned that his beloved brother George was wounded and in an Army hospital, he went to care for him, and then for the others who were stricken by the war. With the coming of sorrow, love for his fellows became more and more an impersonal bond with humanity, a principle of life closely associated with death. In these new war poems, and in their sequel, "When Lilacs Last in the Dooryard Bloom'd," the insistent personality of the poet becomes the universal principle that had been earlier proclaimed:

"Comrades mine and I in the midst . . .
Lilac and star and bird twined with the chant of my soul,
There in the fragrant pines and the cedars dusk and dim."

In the death of Lincoln, the poet had found the symbol for the suffering and death he had seen in so many forgotten soldiers; and in giving his love to the dead leader he gave it to mankind.

Now as Whitman approached the meridian, he began to see life as a whole. The *Leaves* of 1867 is the most vigorous, rich—and confused—of them all. Here for the first time, the Inscription "Oneself I sing" is placed first, the other poems drastically revised, and a few new poems in addition to those from *Drum-Taps* included. The book of life was beginning to take its final form. The theme of "Modern Man" is established deliberately and an attempt is made to develop it systematically through arrangement of existing poems; but the work is still unfinished because it was the poet's own life and he, as man, had still a quarter of a century to live. His uncertainty is evident in his feeling that perhaps the poems he was next to write would start a second book, and in his efforts to make clear his political and social philosophy in his only major prose work, *Democratic Vistas* (1871). He was at the peak of his creative powers, but doubts assailed his triumph.

These doubts made *Democratic Vistas* one of the truest and most moving of all statements of the theory of democracy, as it had been known and lived in the United States. Whitman accepted the basic faith of Jefferson that all men are good and that the best society is the one of the least government because it permits the greatest progress toward human perfection. In turgid prose he pleads that these States "sole among nation-alities" assume the task of putting into practice the "theory of development and perfection by voluntary standards and self-reliance." American democracy, which should be a grand ex-periment in the growth of individuals, had fallen upon evil days through the schism of war and the corruption of govern-ment. Here, for the first time, the poet admits the discrepancy between the ideal and the actual; but only to enforce the ideal. With a democratic literature to guide it, and with the advances in knowledge of modern science, the experiment can yet suc-ceed.

With his next poems Whitman launched boldly into the outermost rim of cosmic consciousness. The building of the first transcontinental railroad, the laying of the Atlantic cable, and the digging of the Suez Canal inspired him to sing his first poem of one world. The sea image, always present in Whit-man's deeper poems, here takes full command:

> "O we can wait no longer
> We too take ship O soul,
> Joyous we too launch out on trackless seas"

which circle the globe, but which also, like the seas upon which Melville's imagination sailed, carry the soul on a "passage to more than India."

> "O farther, farther, farther sail!"

The mystic experience of eternal time and space has carried the poet beyond the limits of mortality.

In 1873 Whitman left his government job in Washington and settled permanently across the river from Philadelphia in Camden, New Jersey, in order to be near his mother and his brother George. His strong constitution pulled him through the paralytic stroke of that year and gave him another twenty years, but his creative impulses were dulled. His many later poems contain the ideas but lose much of the power of the earlier ones. The loss was partially compensated by the recognition which was now coming to him, mainly through the British followers who had been attracted to him by William Rossetti's London edition of 1868. Like so many American writers, Whitman was appreciated first in Europe, more slowly at home. Surrounding himself with a small but devoted group which included Traubel, Burroughs, Bucke, and the British visitor Carpenter, he felt his influence at last taking hold. Slowly the plan of his life's book was clarified and *Leaves of Grass* took its "authorized" form. In 1881–1882, he gave the poems their final revisions, order, and titles, establishing the form he wished his book to take, but by now much of the gusto and extravagance of the earlier editions was gone. The reader may choose whether he wishes to follow Whitman through the stages in his growth or to accept the verdict of an old man on the lasting values in his work. In either case, he will discover the bard of American democracy.

CHAPTER VI

END OF AN ERA

WHEN Whitman admitted in 1871 that American facts did not agree with the ideal of the democratic man, he was but expressing an old dilemma in a new guise. Cooper had said the same thing in his day, and Sinclair Lewis was to repeat it in his. This discrepancy between fact and ideal is the creative force of an open society, for it supplies the dynamics of change. Only when the ideal of the free individual becomes too exactly identified with a particular phase of economic and political development does the structure of democratic society stiffen, buckle, and crack. For this reason the United States has successfully weathered crises under which almost any other form of society would have been destroyed.

Such a time of crisis in the history of the United States was the period 1855–1870. Three fundamental issues reached the breaking point in those years: the conflict between the agrarian ideal of Jefferson and the industrial ideal of Hamilton, the conflict between the plantation gentility of the South and the commercial gentility of the North, and the conflict between a culturally mature East and a raw and expanding West.

Although political historians would probably emphasize the conflict between the North and South as basic, and economic historians that between agrarianism and industrialism, the literary and cultural historian finds the third—that between East and West—by far the most immediately important. In this split is to be found the decline of one cultural cycle and the rise of a second. The battle between "idealists" and "realists" which provided the major issues of American literary history from 1870 on, is readily identified with the East-West geographical division, with the line of demarcation following the Allegheny Mountain range of the Eastern coast. As the civilization of the seaboard Republic expanded into the mid-continental river valleys and onward to the Pacific coast, it took with it the spirit of the old explorers and settlers, leaving the Eastern coastline to play the role which Western Europe had played in an earlier day: the seat of the culture left behind. At the same time, those Easterners who did not migrate turned with even more fervor to the culture of Europe and sought to strengthen their ties with tradition. Clinging to forms and habits inherited from colonial times, Eastern writers, whether Northern or Southern, thus developed a genteel conservatism which was reflected in literary propriety and sentimentality. The romantic movement as a dynamic force in American literature was over; only its ghost walked.

There is perhaps no better proof that the period of decline in the first major American literary movement had been reached than the death or silence of its leading writers. Bryant turned almost wholly to journalism after 1840, Cooper and Irving died in the fifties, Poe died in 1849, Thoreau in 1862, and Hawthorne in 1864. Emerson's last important book, *The Conduct of Life*, appeared in 1860, Melville's last important prose (with the exception of the posthumous *Billy Budd*) in 1857. Of these major figures, only Whitman survived the war in full creative power, and he was to identify himself with the future more than with the past by becoming one of the chief spokesmen for the continental nation and by serving as object of attack for the dominant Eastern writers and critics of the latter years of the century.

The writers in the East who did survive the war and who continued evenly on their literary ways were far less tempestuous than these individualists. Although continuing to use the romantic themes and forms now become familiar, their attitudes toward life and literature were conventional and reactionary. No more serious error has ever been made by literary historians than the identification of the genteel sentimentality of the Cambridge poets, for example, with the romantic movement in American letters, and of the Western realism of Mark Twain and William Dean Howells with some form of reaction or classicism. Realism was from the start a basic aspect of the romantic movement in French, German, Scandinavian, and British literatures. Romanticism per se is an attitude toward life and literature, a spirit of adventure and experiment, and not merely a given set of themes or interests. In its building of stable social and literary forms, the Eastern group of writers, which included Longfellow, Lowell, Whittier, and Holmes, played the role of reaction against the West's new wave of naturalism and a second major romantic impulse.

The rise of realism and the ultimate dominance of the West after 1870—not as West but as Continental Nation—is the theme of the second half of this book. The decline of the East—not as East but as colonial empire become Republic—can only be summarized as a concluding chapter to the story of America's first literary fulfillment. The American romantic movement rose, triumphed, and declined as the literary expression of the Atlantic seaboard Republic. A Continental Nation was at the same time in the making, and its literature was as yet unformed.

– 2 –

The defeat of the Southern cause in the Civil War was not nearly as serious a blow to literary as it was to economic and political history. By 1860 the South had already developed a culture of its own and was producing a literature to give it expression. The myth of the Southern cavalier had formed a literary tradition which had been expressed variously in the tracts of Thomas Jefferson, John Taylor of Caroline, and William Wirt, in the novels of William Gilmore Simms, John Pendleton Kennedy, and John Esten Cooke, in the poetry of Poe, Simms, Thomas Holley Chivers, and Henry Timrod, and in the orations of John C. Calhoun. First advanced as a way of life, it laid its foundations in an agrarian-slave economy that soon revealed inconsistencies with the humanitarian aims of democratic man. The chivalric ideals which it borrowed from a feudal past became more and more glamorous as they were pushed out of life and into literature. By 1860 the myth of the South was clearly defined in romantic poetry and fiction as an ideal of beauty and harmony.

The roots of the myth were dug into the very soil of the early settlements when the adherents of the Stuart kings sought refuge in Virginia. The wars of the Cavaliers and Roundheads that tore England apart in the seventeenth century were transferred to the new continent. Cavalier ideals throve in the flat tideland plantations of Virginia and the Carolinas, where vast properties were held for generations by single families like that of William Byrd. An agrarian economy fostered a wide distribution of the literate population, delayed the growth of cities, libraries, and colleges, and prevented any real break with British cultural and literary influences until the time of the Revolution, when they were forced to follow the political break. Even then the process was slow, and it was not until about 1835 that the Southern states began to show the literary nationalism that had been apparent two decades earlier in their Northern neighbors.

Richmond, Charleston, and Baltimore were the centers of this literary movement. Richmond was later to be the capital of the Confederacy, Charleston its principal port, and Baltimore its northernmost outpost, but in 1835 they were three provincial towns, each developing its own cultural life and its own literary set. It was in Richmond that Poe began his career by editing the *Southern Literary Messenger*, published the first of his macabre tales "Berenice," and crossed swords in his criticism with the Knickerbocker writers of the North. Charleston was the home of Hugh Legaré's *Southern Review* and of the novelist-poet William Gilmore Simms; Baltimore, of John Pendleton Kennedy, the friend and patron of Poe and author in his own right.

William Gilmore Simms (1806–1870) was the most versatile and representative of these Southern writers. The son of a poor storekeeper, he was an ardent admirer of the chivalric ideal, and did more than anyone else of his day to crystallize it as the Southern myth. A follower of Cooper in his choice of material and in his literary method, he went beyond his master in the variety of his romances and in his faithful delineation of life. *The Yemassee* (1835) is a story of Indian warfare in Carolina, *The Partisan*, in the same year, is the first of a series of romances of the Revolution, while his two Border romances, *Beauchampe* (1842) and *Charlemont* (1856) deal with the

Kentucky tragedy that also attracted Poe, Chivers and, in a later day, Robert Penn Warren. Slighted by his own society and struggling often with poverty, Simms produced a long shelf of romantic novels that idealized the Southern aristocracy at the same time that they gave a faithful picture of low-life characters and of primitive living on the Border. His criticism, addresses, poems (chiefly in the Byronic mode), biographies, and essays rank him as the most prolific and consistent Southern writer of his day. His literary career came to an end with the outbreak of the war even though he lived on for another decade.

In John Pendleton Kennedy (1795–1870), the Southern ideal found an even more accurate personification. A Baltimore lawyer by profession, his wealth made it possible for him early to become a patron of the arts. Beginning his own writing in the pattern of Irving's career, he produced in 1832 a series of pleasant chapters on Virginia life called *Swallow Barn* and, in 1835, a novel of the Revolution, *Horse-Shoe Robinson*, in which a rough but honest blacksmith, in the manner of Cooper's Natty Bumppo, squires an aristocratic young lady through the perils of Border warfare to a happy union with her patriot lover. This pattern of romance reached its most extreme Southern expression in *The Virginia Comedians* (1854) of John Esten Cooke, a Revolutionary romance that pulls all the stops of excitement and intrigue. This formula lapsed, of course, when the Southern Confederacy failed, but it was revived toward the end of the century in the romances of Thomas Nelson Page, James Lane Allen, and Mary Johnston. The fact that the life it represented had by then become a lost ideal added to its romantic glamour.

In poetry the Southern romantic movement stemmed

rather from Byron, Coleridge, and the so-called "graveyard" school than from the simple nature poetry of Wordsworth and the neo-Hellenic tradition of Keats and Shelley. The poetry of Chivers was so like that of Poe in its dark mood and its musical phrasing that unanswered charges of plagiarism flew back and forth for many years. Younger poets like Timrod and Paul Hamilton Hayne, who were members with Simms of the Russell bookstore group in Charleston during the fifties, carried on the same moody and melodious tradition, linking Poe in both matter and manner with the most original of all Southern poets, Sidney Lanier, who did his best work in the period of Reconstruction.

But it was in oratory, and specifically in the speeches of John C. Calhoun, that the spirit of the South was most unequivocally expressed. The famous "Fourth of March" (1850) speech, which attacked Clay's compromise and which was in turn answered by the "Seventh of March" speech of New England's Daniel Webster, was far more than a defense of slavery and states' rights. In it Calhoun spoke for a gracious and self-conscious South that was about to become a separate nation. Its distinctive culture had reached maturity.

The plantation economy of the South collapsed because of an inner flaw. It embodied most fully the agrarian ideals of Jefferson because it could not exist without them; it was wholly agrarian. As long as slavery could provide the cheap labor necessary for its continuance, the Southern pattern of chivalric living could persist and spread. It had penetrated the Mississippi Valley and had reached North as far as Missouri before it was put on the defensive and began its recession; but this did not take place until it had given full expression to its ideals and its code. The myth that resulted could not be eliminated by any war; it has persisted as one of the most valuable strains in American literary tradition.

– 3 –

The Northern agrarian myth of the yeoman farmer spread into the West at a time when it was being defeated in the East by a rising industrial capitalism. The broken dams, abandoned roads, and overgrown mill foundations of New England today bear mute testimony to an industrialism that began in colonial times and had, by 1835, created an essentially urban civilization along the coast. Boston, New York, Philadelphia, and Baltimore owed their importance rather to the fact that they were river ports than to the support of their rural hinterlands. When the Civil War decided that the Northern way of life should control the national future, the Northern pioneer and farmer moved out across the plains, with the roar of industry close behind him. The conquest of the West by the Yankee farmer was the most decisive factor in its development. The conquest of the Yankee farmer in his turn by the machine was in progress at the very moment when he was gaining respite by moving West.

Economically speaking, the outcome of the Civil War encouraged an industrial economy for the nation, developed cities after the Northern pattern, and dealt the death blow to the agrarianism of the South, but the patrician culture of New England was as much a product of the dying past as was that of the plantation. In literature the romantic ideals of the socially privileged found their full expression in the writings of Longfellow, Holmes, and Lowell even more than in those of Simms and Kennedy. The literary movement founded by Bryant, Irving, and Cooper in the twenties leveled off into the confident music of the Cambridge poets after the violence of its few really great writers had subsided. As New York became the commercial capital of the nation, and its literary culture became dissipated in the rough-and-tumble journalism of the rising daily press, and as the capital city of Washington was taken over more and more by the equalitarian followers of the Jackson tradition, the old patrician culture of the North retreated to the elm-shaded streets of the Boston suburb where it could stand its ground within the safe limits of Harvard Yard. While the Concord group was dreaming its transcendental dreams, the Cambridge Brahmins were more practically entrenching themselves in the achieved dignity of a matured culture. When Lowell succeeded Longfellow in the Smith chair at Harvard in 1855, and when two years later the *Atlantic Monthly* was added to the journalistic empire long ruled by the *North American Review*, the literary dictatorship of New England gentility was assured for many years in spite of war and westward expansion.

The spirit of intellectual and social aristocracy which found expression in the Brahmin poets was a part of a larger movement which included oratory, history, and humanistic scholarship in general. Study and travel in Europe were as much emphasized by the Cambridge "aristarch" as they had been by the seventeenth century Virginia gentleman. When Edward Everett and George Ticknor went together to the University of Göttingen in 1815–1819, they set a pattern of training for the democratic scholar-gentleman that persisted for a hundred years. The one became Professor of Greek, the other of Modern Languages, at Harvard, but the lives of both were devoted as much to the popularization as to the acquiring of learning. American culture at mid-century was shaped by a natural or self-appointed aristocracy which idealized and lectured to, but did not mingle with, the common man.

The common man was eager enough to be lectured to and instructed. Not only were the colleges thriving and expanding, but every town of any size from Maine to Georgia and westward into the Ohio Valley had its local lyceum. The Lyceum Movement, founded by Josiah Holbrook in 1826, in ten years made lectures on natural history, popular sermons on morality, readings of contemporary literature, exhibitions of the wonders of science, together with less intellectual forms of entertainment, the regular offering of three thousand centers throughout the United States. A more and more aristocratic, idealized, and Europeanized scholarship, with the aid of a great wave of democratic zeal for knowledge, produced Emerson the moral lecturer, Agassiz the scientific demonstrator, Prescott the historian, Parker the religious orator, and Barnum the promoter of circuses.

Pulpit and forum alike were caught up in the vogue of popular oratory. Daniel Webster thundered at a crowd of five thousand on a Vermont mountaintop during the Whig convention of 1840, while Phillips Brooks, Henry Ward Beecher, and Theodore Parker filled the New England meeting houses with spellbound listeners.

The vogue of popular history was closely related to this passion for the spoken word. In their search for a national past, the New England intellectual aristocracy led the common man to his own archives and with him discovered the discoverers. When Washington Irving turned his attention to Columbus and the expansion of Spanish power in the New World, he found that William Hickling Prescott had already staked out a claim and was nearing completion of the first of his

exciting narratives of Latin America. Prescott in his turn guided
the younger John Lothrop Motley to the Dutch empire, while
the most gifted of them all, Francis Parkman (1823–1893), undertook to tell the intricate story of British and French conquest and rivalry on the North American continent. Struggling
against a frail constitution, Parkman's passion for the Northern
wilderness and unexplored plains took him to Wyoming at the
age of twenty-three; but the effort completely broke his nervous stability and he was forced to dictate rather than to write
The California and Oregon Trail (1849), the first of a long
series of vivid narratives which were more than history because they had the imagination of the best of fiction and the
dramatic tension of a vast conflict between men and nature. In
the end it was apparent that Parkman had been all his life
deeply concerned with the clash between ordered democracy,
as represented by the British, and military dictatorship, as represented by La Salle, Frontenac, and the French attempts at
Western empire. Unable to make up his mind as to his own
preference, the Brahmin historian wrote his own emotional
conflict into the drama of his narratives and, without violating
historical fact but selecting and shaping it for justifiable emphasis, created a prose epic of westward expansion.

– 4 –

It was this general thirst for learning that finally broke
down the antiquated classical curriculum of the colleges and
opened the way for the study of American history and the
modern languages and literatures. George Ticknor had inaugurated the movement in taking the Smith Professorship of
Modern Languages at Harvard in 1819, a chair later held in
succession by Longfellow and Lowell. It was Longfellow,

however, who most successfully caught up the spirit of the times and identified it with his own personality. The Brahmin scholar who wrote equally well of his own country's simple colonial ways and the dim romantic cathedrals and castles of Southern Europe, and who could be both learned and democratic at once, was the accepted master of the American literary world for a generation.

Essentially a singer in a minor key, Henry Wadsworth Longfellow (1807-1882) was the most widely read and loved of American poets of his day—or of all English-speaking poets of any day. He was also the bard of the American people, not because he spoke the truth about life in his own or any other time as did Whitman, but because he made articulate and memorable the simple dreams of average humanity. When at the age of sixty he received an honorary degree at Oxford, it was remarked that his white hair and beard seemed drawn on over a young face. In that figure is portrayed the paradox of the learned and revered poet-bard who had remained through life at heart a child. His final dramatic poem *Christus* (1872), in three parts, which was to sum up the whole view of life of a major poet, was less popular but had no greater complexity than the beloved lyrics of his first collection *Voices of the Night* (1839).

Longfellow came of an old New England family. He spent his boyhood in the seacoast town of Portland, Maine, and he studied at private schools and at Bowdoin College. Want was never near, books were never far away, for this sheltered youth. In politics a Federalist, in religion a Unitarian, and in literature a romantic, he shared the inheritance that had shaped Bryant's career, and the calm simplicity of the personal voices of the two poets is much the same. Unlike Bryant, the younger man early went to Europe and immersed himself in the storm and stress which he was to share in milder form with Goethe and Byron. Homesickness, unrequited or bereaved love, and self-pity provided the background for that most famous of all hymns of faith and courage, "The Psalm of Life":

> "Life is real! Life is earnest!
> And the grave is not its goal."

What at first seems perhaps only an overwrought statement of the obvious is actually the cry of a heart, by its own confession, "rallying from depression," and asserting a doctrine of active self-regeneration rather than one of passive acceptance of defeat.

Alone during his first student-residence of three years, Longfellow took his wife with him on his second trip to Germany in 1835, but there she died in childbirth. Returning, once more alone, to teach at Harvard, the young scholar-poet brought with him memories of happy and melancholy days spent in the cafés and galleries of Europe, now already to the American a far-away treasure house of romance. As Irving had created an imaginary England, Longfellow in the travel sketches of *Outre-Mer* (1833–1834) and in the semiautobiographical romance *Hyperion* (1839) wrote his own dream world into the realities of a Europe now emerging from its great age of reasserted nationalities and reclaimed cultures. The cathedrals, the art galleries, and the new and vital romantic literatures of the Scandinavian countries, of Germany, France, Italy, and Spain, took their places in his mind beside the now legendary colonial past of the New World and the writings of contemporaries like Hawthorne and Emerson. The village blacksmith of Cambridge and Hans Sachs the cobbler-poet of the quaint old town of Nuremberg are one, and a skeleton in rusty armor dug up on the shore at Fall River becomes a Viking warrior who can tell a rousing tale of seafaring and fighting, of love and death. Longfellow's art of giving the young civilization a cultural past by blending the romantic unrealities of two worlds into one formed for Americans a habit of mind that lasted for more than a century. The vigorous assertions of cultural autonomy that had given life to the work of Cooper and were soon to produce the poetry of Whitman were softened in Longfellow to a twilight glow in which differences could merge and conflicts die. His reverence for Europe and his idealization of the American past were the foundations of that tradition of gentility against which the realists battled for three generations.

Longfellow's major work includes three narrative poems, *Evangeline* (1847), *The Song of Hiawatha* (1855), and *The Courtship of Miles Standish* (1858), in which, together with numerous shorter poems, he puts into galloping meters the history and legend of colonial times. It does not matter that he takes such liberties as he wishes with the facts and draws on his sources heavily where they can be of service to him in order to create stories of conventional love and sacrifice, sorrow and joy. The tales that he has told have themselves become parts of the American legend, more real than the history on which they are based. Like Cooper's Indians, his colonials provide the rest of the world with their ideas of what Americans were really like, for his poems were translated and read and memorized in every country of the globe. Whether in Dante's *Divine Comedy*, which is likened to a cathedral, or in the cottage of Priscilla and John Alden at Plymouth, Massachusetts,

"The tumult of the time disconsolate
To inarticulate murmurs dies away,
While the eternal ages watch and wait."

Longfellow conveyed his serenity to his active and impatient
countrymen and gave them an easy escape into what seemed
eternal verities. He is the poet of things half remembered and
of things wished for rather than of things as they are or were
or will be. His art was at its best in the chiseled simplicity of the
sonnet and the easy grace of the familiar ballad rather than in
the more ambitious narratives of his middle years.

The pattern of Longfellow's life was repeated in many of
his contemporaries and friends, among them the distinguished
Boston physician and wit, Oliver Wendell Holmes (1809–
1894). Born in Cambridge of New England stock, schooled
at Andover and Harvard, with almost two years of study and
travel in Europe, he was the very ideal of the American literary
gentleman when he issued his first volume of poems in 1836. In
Holmes the security of social position and accepted literary
standards and forms produced verses which were pithy rather
than sentimental, adding to Longfellow's gifts the one which
had been most lacking, a sense of humor. His celebration of the
frigate "Old Ironsides" caught the public imagination and prevented the scrapping of the battle-scarred veteran. Thereafter
his poems spoke directly to the times, and usually to the occasion, with sharp relevance and mild irony. The most famous
of them, "The Deacon's Masterpiece," told, in a simple narrative of the "wonderful one-horse shay," a moral tale of how
that which is perfect in all its parts will of course wear out all
at once and collapse. The reference to the fall of the Calvinist
religious system was there for those who could read between

the lines, but it did not spoil the immense joke that the un-suspecting deacon played upon himself. In his essayist role as the "Autocrat of the Breakfast Table," Holmes carried the same common-sense logic into other departments of human life, and in his novels he applied what was then known of medicine and psychology, perhaps for the first time, to the clinical study of human motivation in fiction. More a coffee-house wit than a melancholy romantic, Holmes did his part to tie waning American romanticism more tightly into the British and European tradition, as had Longfellow, by making his compatriots aware of themselves and of their history.

The youngest member of the group, James Russell Lowell (1819–1891) was also the most versatile. Sharing Longfellow's sentiment and Holmes's wit, he became the idol not only of Cambridge but of all America by simply being what it seemed most desirable for him to be, a natural aristocrat and a success-ful literary man. The ideal which he finally set before a Har-vard audience as the aim of university education was a por-trait of himself as "not a conventional gentleman, but a man of culture, a man of intellectual resource, a man of public spirit, a man of refinement, with that good taste which is the con-science of the mind, and that conscience which is the good taste of the soul." A native of Cambridge, he spent his whole life in the comfortable family home, Elmwood, among his books, looking out from his study windows with a deep concern for human sorrows and joys, traveling far to absorb the cosmopoli-tan cultures of Europe, and lecturing and writing earnestly in the causes of humanity, democracy, and nationality at home.

Before his marriage in 1843 to the charming and ardent Abolitionist Maria White, Lowell's love of life was expressed in simple and romantic lyrics and in that exuberance which had rusticated him from Harvard in his senior year. It took the cause of slavery to focus his thinking, and for a few years he spoke with a vigor that was matched only by the poet Whittier and the journalist William Lloyd Garrison. The year 1848 brought all of his talents into full expression with three ambitious and different poems: "The Vision of Sir Launfal," a modern version of an Arthurian romance; "A Fable for Critics," in which he wittily summed up the virtues and the weaknesses of his literary friends in the manner but without the acidity of Pope; and the first of the "Biglow Papers," dialect verses in which he commented, with homespun wisdom, on the issues of the day, particularly the doctrine of manifest destiny and the Mexican War. In his versatility lay his weakness, for any one of these poems could have provided the foundation for major work if he had followed through the creative lines that it suggested. Only the "Biglow Papers" had a sequel.

Instead he traveled in Europe, where his wife died, and returned to the professorship of French and Spanish which Longfellow was then relinquishing at Harvard and to the editorship of the new *Atlantic Monthly*. From then on, he was lecturer and critic rather than poet, speaking with the voice of authority to younger men like William Dean Howells, bringing to his students a love of the British and European classics, and urging on his country an ideal form of democracy in the cultivation of moral excellence.

As literary critic, Lowell was preeminent in his time. His catholic tastes, his wide scholarship, and his earnest quest for values helped him to formulate a creed by which he could measure artistic excellence, past and present. He combined sensitiveness to impressions, historical understanding, and ethical judgment in the belief that, because literature is the ideal representation of life, it should give pleasure by uplifting the spirit of man. His breadth of view made him responsive to Aeschylus, Dante, Chaucer, and Shakespeare, but the confusion of morals with manners is apparent in his clever but insensitive comments on such of his contemporaries as Thoreau, Whitman, and Emerson. The ideal in life was still, at the end, best viewed from the study window.

− 5 −

The Civil War broke out into open conflict on the issue of slavery. For the short period when emotions overruled all things else, the Abolitionist cause swept less immediate issues aside and reasserted with renewed humanitarian zeal the ancient American doctrine of the rights of man. When John Brown lectured in Concord for the second time in 1859, even Emerson and Thoreau dropped philosophy and became partisans; Lowell, Whittier, and Harriet Beecher Stowe had long since made their views militantly heard. It was a time when literature must turn from its larger concerns to the crisis of the moment.

The earlier antislavery societies were led by such idealists as Emerson's friend Bronson Alcott and the devoted William Lloyd Garrison who founded the *Liberator* in 1831 and continued it for thirty-four years. A movement of the people, it was not taken up by the Brahmin leadership until they had been shocked by such violence as the murder of Elijah P. Lovejoy in defending from a mob his Alton, Illinois, Abolitionist press in 1837. Slowly the prominent scholars, poets, historians, and religious leaders of New England were drawn into the cause. By 1846 Lowell was protesting the Mexican War as fought in the interest of the slaveholder in his *Biglow Papers*, and by 1850 Calhoun had identified the Southern nationalist cause finally and irrevocably with the right to hold slaves.

The leading literary spokesman of the New England view was the humanitarian Quaker John Greenleaf Whittier (1807–1892). A farm boy who learned of poetry through a love of the Scottish Burns, he began his own poetic career by singing of the beauty of simple things. It would seem that, like Longfellow and Lowell, without their learning but with more intimate knowledge, he would write of the common man whose history was the large history of his nation. Friendship with Garrison, however, turned him to the cause of social justice, and he edged his pen with acid. From 1833 to 1859, his best energy went into the Abolitionist movement, in founding his own Liberty party, and in editing newspapers in the cause. After the war Whittier continued to write of the New England scene, but now in the mood of hymning a just and friendly God and a friendly and happy people.

The vogue of Whittier's poetry was great because it used the language of the masses, and it spoke of matters of intense concern to the common man. Just how influential it was in crystallizing, as Tom Paine's *Common Sense* had in an earlier day, the complicated issues of a war into a simple cause that men could fight for, can probably never be estimated. It is somewhat easier to assess the power of a tract in fiction, *Uncle Tom's Cabin* (1852). President Lincoln was not far wrong in greeting Harriet Beecher Stowe with the words, "So you're the little woman who made the book that made the great war." The story of the high-minded Negro slave Uncle Tom "just growed" like its own mischievous Topsy until it sold over 300,000 copies in its first year and countless thousands of pirated copies in the years following, both at home and abroad.

Its unauthorized dramatic versions further increased its popularity as it wrung the hearts of audiences from Broadway to San Francisco. Probably the most widely reprinted and reread novel ever written, it so stimulated world concern for its cause that a century later the status of the Negro seemed still, to most European commentators, the primary issue in American civilization.

Yet Democracy continued to survive its unsolved problems. As the patrician codes of both North and South dissolved into myths in the heat of war, the ever flexible principle of the rights of man adjusted itself to the new nation that was being carved from the West. Mark Twain's first collection of tales and sketches appeared in the same year (1867) that Longfellow completed his translation of Dante.

THE

SECOND FRONTIER

In 1769 Daniel Boone set out to carve the Wilderness Road into unexplored Kentucky; a century later, in 1869, an impressive group of government and railroad officials met at Promontory Point, Utah, to drive in the golden spike that completed the first transcontinental railroad. In the interval one civilization reached and passed its maturity; another was born. The Continental Nation of 1890, stretching from ocean to ocean and from Canada to Mexico, differed in ways other than size from the new Republic of 1790, hugging the level Atlantic seaboard. The world of Mark Twain recreated that of

Washington Irving in bolder colors on a far larger canvas.

Most of the changes in the character of American civilization either took place or became apparent between 1850 and
1890. First there was the painful healing of the wounds of war.
The North, weakened by the conflict and uncertain of its
own destiny, fumbled the stupendous task of reconstructing
an economically and spiritually depleted South. The West
alone, because it had experienced only the fringes of the conflict, could move into the future with confidence.

The absorption of the vast trans-Mississippi tract into the
Union which Lincoln had saved now proceeded in orderly
fashion. The last continuous acquisition of the continental
United States, the Gadsden Purchase on the Mexican border,
took place in 1853; the last continental territories, Arizona and
New Mexico, were admitted to statehood in 1912. Meanwhile
the population of the nation was increasing rapidly, as Franklin
and some of the other farsighted colonials had predicted that
it would. During the first half-century after independence, it
climbed steadily from four to seventeen million; it jumped to
sixty-three million in the second half-century; and by 1950 it
had passed the 150 million mark.

Much of this increase was the result of immigration which
came, during the period of greatest territorial expansion and
settlement, mainly from Ireland, Germany, and the Scandinavian countries. Toward the end of the century the influx
from Southern and Central Europe and from the Orient increased rapidly but it was slowed almost immediately by quota
legislation. Ethnologically, the Americans were still, as the
thirteen colonies had been, mainly Teutonic in racial origin,
but their strong British character had faded into a more cosmopolitan type.

By 1900 the language that they spoke was no longer

British. In idiom, pronunciation, and vocabulary it had acquired so many new characteristics that it became American
in a strict and definable sense. Other cultural characteristics,
like habits of living, fashions, and folkways, created similarly
new patterns from old materials. Out of the Westward migration and the orientation of the American people to a continent
had developed, at least in outline, a new civilization. By 1950
that outline had been filled in to the smallest detail.

– 2 –

Two economic processes combined to create this result:
the process of expansion and the process of industrialization.
The earlier economic historians of the United States followed
the lead of Frederick Jackson Turner in attributing the change
exclusively to the westward movement of the frontier. "This
perennial rebirth," he wrote in 1893, "this fluidity of American
life, this expansion westward with its new opportunities, its
continuous touch with the simplicity of primitive society, fur-
nish the forces dominating the American character."

Except that he claimed to be telling the whole story when
he was telling only a part of it, Turner's thesis was essentially
sound. At the boundary of the settled and unsettled land, the
meeting of the Old World with the New was being continually
repeated; the culture of the Continental Nation was made as
that of the first frontier had been made. American territorial
policy as formulated by the Northwest Ordinance of 1787 was
an extension and correction of British colonial policy. The
British yeoman farmer who had cleared the wilderness in preparation for planting the garden of the world and converting
the heathen to the blessings of trade was the conqueror of the
American West in spirit, though now he spoke an Irish brogue,
or a German or Norwegian dialect, the clipped drawl of the

Connecticut Valley, or the rich round syllables of the South. It was an agrarian frontier in which the individual was king.

The overland trails did not follow the routes of the earlier French and Spanish explorations; they pushed more directly westward, piercing the Allegheny range through the Hudson and Mohawk valleys of New York and thence into the Great Lakes area, by the Cumberland Road in Western Maryland and out into the Ohio River Valley, or along the southern slope and the Gulf Coast into the swampy Delta country and on into Texas.

By 1825 the Middle Border was pretty well settled and had its own small cities with their newspapers, libraries, and colleges. Ultimately the pioneers converged at Independence, Missouri, to take the Santa Fe Trail to the Southwest or the Oregon Trail to the Northwest in order to cross the Continental Divide. Here the expeditions of Frémont and of Lewis and Clark had made ready for the covered wagon. The Mexican War opened up vast new lands in 1845, and by 1849 the discovery of gold in California further accelerated the process; but rich lands still provided the main incentive. The San Joaquin Valley of California was the last garden of the West, first with its wheat and then with its fruit. There is an uninterrupted line of descent from Daniel Boone to the Joad family of John Steinbeck. By 1870 the fertile western slope had its own towns, and the typical American way of life was established in them, but even the Homestead Act of 1862 could not fill the broad expanse of prairie lying between.

The culture that resulted from these migrations was more complex than that of the early Republic. The Indians, by being gradually pushed West, had learned to resist, and finally, crowded into their barren reservations, had succeeded in maintaining their folkways until, in the twentieth century, the white man came to appreciate what he had by then almost totally destroyed: the tradition of American Indian culture. The scattered Spaniards and French who had been left behind by their receding colonial empires, whether in the Gulf port of New Orleans or in the missions and ranchos of the Southwest, had settled into a way of life that was absorbed rather than destroyed by later migrations. Furthermore, the new groups from Europe—the Germans in Wisconsin, the Swedes and Norse in Minnesota and Iowa, the Bohemians in Nebraska— learned how to retain their cultural autonomy while contributing their full share to the historical process of expansion. The pockets of settlement left behind by the western wave were almost as various in their cultures as the Europe from which their people had come.

One result was an American folk tradition that was native in the end because it borrowed from everyone. Partly racial, partly occupational in origin, the ballads and the tall tales of the West started as echoes of older memories. The English country dance, with its jig tunes and its singing games, took on a bolder and simpler character in the Western granges; Irish, Norse, and Welsh giants became heroes of the lumber rack and the riverboat; cowboys sang deep-sea chanties and country love songs to their herds as they rounded them up on the prairie.

Because there was too much to do and too little time to be sad, much of the tragic gloom of Old World folklore turned to rough humor in the New. Skepticism, mixed with belief, exaggerated the feats of the giant lumberman Paul Bunyan beyond credulity and turned them to laughter. The effort to outdo the other fellow in solemn-faced lying developed the tall tale, core of the new folk literature. Such Western writers as Artemus Ward, G. W. Harris, Mark Twain, and Bret Harte took the milder Down East humor of Josh Billings and colored it to match the Western scenery in size and variety. Europe laughed again at Mark Twain as it had at Washington Irving's Knickerbocker; Bret Harte squeezed out the sad sweet melancholy of life from the mining camp as Irving had from the simple countryside. Sentiment and humor were unabashed together on the frontier.

Local color, sentimental memories, the relief of laughter —a new American literature was growing once again from the roots of the new plantings. The traveling minstrel shows picked it up and mixed the lore of the Negro with that of the prairie to make a strong and sometimes unpalatable brew. Slowly it reached the stage of writing. By 1870 Bret Harte, Mark Twain, and W. D. Howells were publishing their observations in the form of tales and sketches in the *Overland Monthly* of California, the *Atlantic Monthly* of Boston, and *Harper's Monthly* of New York. They were welcomed because the realism, the sentiment, the novelty, and the laughter in what they wrote were traditionally American. Youthful and crude in their exuberance, they were renewing the childhood of a people and reasserting the pioneer spirit of independence that Jefferson and Whitman, Franklin and Emerson, had preached, each in his way.

– 3 –

When Irish immigrants laid across the foot of Walden Pond the tracks of the new railroad to Fitchburg, Thoreau watched with interest. This was the way to the West, but it opened far more than territory. In 1893 Chicago celebrated in a World's Fair the triumph of the railroad and, with it, the triumph of industrial capitalism in her Western empire. Even while the Civil War was still in progress, the infant Republican party had, by high tariffs, national banks, and railroad subsidies, thrown its lot in with the cause of industry; by 1890 the country had over 150,000 miles of tracks. The assignment of alternate sections along the right of way by the Government had given the railroads a whiphand over the farmers as the Far West opened. Cutthroat competition threw vast new economic power into the hands of the few. As the Vanderbilts, Jay Gould, James J. Hill, and E. H. Harriman built up their railroad empires, the financial fortunes of the country rose and fell with their plans and speculations. Periods of prosperity and panic alternated so regularly as to seem the results of an economic law of business cycles. The large operators absorbed the interests of the men and communities from which the starting capital had come, only to fall into failure themselves and lose their railroads to the bankers, especially the House of Morgan. Soon finance capital discovered its own method of control in the Trust, later to be developed into the Corporation. The rails were followed by Western Union, Standard Oil, Carnegie Steel, and hosts of lesser combines, all of them controlled more or less by the bankers. "Wall Street" became a symbol of the new power, while at the same time another power began to take shape in organized labor. The nation was shocked when, in the Haymarket Riot in Chicago on May 4, 1886, seven policemen and one rioter were killed by a bomb. Dramatically the cleavage of American society between the forces of capital and labor was displayed, and the long task of political readjustment to a new economic society was begun. The great city, the factory, the machine were to shape the twentieth century American. The industrialism of the East was to take over the future of the West.

The rise of industry on the Atlantic coast had begun in colonial times, and by the end of the eighteenth century it had become dominant from Massachusetts to Pennsylvania. Alexander Hamilton and John Adams had written on the virtues of manufactures, the issue upon which they and the party of Jefferson had divided. The Massachusetts Federalists had provided the principal opposition to the Louisiana Purchase in 1803, and it was they who had first threatened secession from the Union in 1814. The opposition of Lowell's Hosea Biglow to the Mexican War thirty years later was further protest against the expansion of an agrarian economy in the pattern of the South. The conflict between agrarianism and industrialism was written into the Constitution, and in large part it caused the Civil War. When the Industrial Revolution hit America in full blast after the war, it but intensified a situation already existing.

In the West the first phases of the conflict took the form of a clash betwen the Northern free farmer and the Southern slaveowner. In either case, the West was to provide the raw materials that the East needed. The coal, wheat, cattle, precious metals, and finally oil that were to be drawn from it to enrich the North and to give shape to the future United States required at first an agrarian context. Thus as political democracy retreated from the East, it was reborn in Andrew Jackson and Abraham Lincoln. It was Lincoln rather than Douglas who spoke the ideals of Jefferson, and yet it was largely through Lincoln's Republican party that the pioneer spirit of independence was finally transferred from the farmer to the entrepreneur.

Before the close of the century, industrialism had moved into the Great Lakes area as the last wave of the frontier movement, the Continental Nation was complete, and financial capitalism was at the wheel. The rationalization of the ideals and values of the farmer-pioneer to fit the unimpeded growth of big business provides the key to an understanding of the changes in American civilization between 1870 and 1910. At heart the pioneering Henry Ford was not too different from Daniel Boone or Captain John Smith; John D. Rockefeller exploited oil as Thomas Jefferson had tried to exploit land, although with less idealism. The philosophy of the free individual and the economic doctrine of laissez-faire were applicable to the so-called Robber Barons as well as to the Puritans, even though somewhere along the road certain basic values seemed to have become inverted. Assumptions which had been developed by an agrarian economy were forced to adjust in a few years to an industrial economy without sacrifice of ideals and habits—an obvious impossibility. There were inevitable distortion, sophistry, and disillusionment as the concept of the simple American pioneer became more and more romanticized and the facts of American industrial life became more and more complex and ugly. The rise of the railroad, the factory, and the city was the final stage of the frontier process. When the tractor and bulldozer moved onto the farm, whether in Vermont, Oklahoma, or the San Joaquin Valley, the wilderness was tamed. When the road to the White House started from the sidewalks of New York rather than from the log cabin, the process of the Industrial Revolution was completed in the United States.

The political and economic process itself is no part of this story, for literature deals with what man thinks and feels about his environment rather than with the environment itself. Henry Nash Smith has recently supplemented Turner's thesis of the frontier by revealing the persistency of the myths of the free individual and the garden of the world in the West despite economic changes. The existence of such myths is a fact of American civilization itself; because of them the effects of the Industrial Revolution in the United States have been different from those in any other part of the world. New doctrines such as conservation, cooperation, government regulation and industrial bargaining have been developed in their name to block the totalitarianism so common elsewhere. The tragic paradoxes of complex modern American life and the struggle of the free individual to maintain his integrity in the face of rapid economic and social change provided the dominant themes of the second American literary renaissance.

CHAPTER VII

LITERARY REDISCOVERY
Howells, Mark Twain

T HE story of American literature from 1865 to 1895 is that of a vast adjustment to a new set of conditions for living. Fortunately the United States was not alone in facing such changes. European nations were consolidating their gains after a period of revolution and shifting boundaries. Technological advances and the rise of industry were creating social change in England, France, and the newly unified Germany and Italy as rapidly as they were in America. The era of revolutions was over, and one of vigorous and competitive living had set in. The spirit of nationalism was everywhere providing motivation for building new empires abroad and making new social patterns at home.

Throughout the Western world, as in the United States, literature began to pay less attention to general ideas and more to the immediate facts of life. This movement took two forms: interest in "one's own back yard," and experimentation with more literal methods of writing. Regionalism and realism took the place of imagination and idealism. The novel superseded drama and poetry as the most popular and usable form of literary art. In England, Thackeray, Dickens, George Eliot, and Trollope turned to studying humble folk and their ways, leaving the heroics of history and the rise and fall of kings and martyrs to Tennyson and Browning; in France, Balzac developed faithfully and minutely his "Comédie humaine," providing a model for novelists in the new manner every-where; and in Russia Turgenev inaugurated a literary move-ment by his sketches of country life. America was fortunate now, as she had been in the timing of her first national growth with that of the romantic movement, in being offered by Eu-rope a point of view and a literary method which exactly suited the new set of conditions resulting from the Civil War and the opening of the West. Life in the here and now must be rediscovered and restudied.

There was plenty to rediscover in the America of 1865. Vast areas of the West were unknown, except by the vaguest sort of hearsay, to Eastern readers of magazines and novels; the South was going through distressing but important changes; even the North was experiencing a new sense of the past and of the value of regional differences as the Civil War cut it off from its former way of life. The materials for a regional and realistic literature were abundant in a nation of vast area and rapid change.

Gradually, in the backwash of the frontier wave of mi-gration, regional characteristics began to assert themselves. In 1871, when William Dean Howells of Jefferson, Ohio, took the key post of editor-in-chief of the Brahmin *Atlantic Monthly*, there suddenly and simultaneously appeared re-gional sketches and verses in Indiana, Missouri, California, Maine, and New Orleans. The man who was to define realism in American fiction was also the principal sponsor of the re-gional awareness that seemed to spring up in widely scattered areas—obviously the product of a common impulse, using local lore and characteristics in the first phase of a literary movement that was national on a continental scale.

Such characteristics were determined by a variety of causes, but mainly by the origins of the settlers, both past and present, and by local economic factors which created special occupational interests. The old "Northwest Territory" was now the "Middle Border," and was soon to become the agricultural and industrial heartland of the nation. Extending from the Alleghenies to the Continental Divide and from the Great Lakes to the confluence of the Ohio, Missouri, and Mississippi rivers, its level plains and deep waterways created very rapidly a people interested in doing and thinking similar things. Rich enough in resources to promise economic self-sufficiency in a few years, it cultivated the same confidence and materialism that had characterized the earlier Connecticut Yankee. The first settlers were in fact mainly Yankees who easily absorbed the German and Scandinavian farmers who followed them. A common faith in the self, in the land, and in an unterrifying and helpful divinity gave the Middle Border people a sense of being in the main stream of the American tradition, whatever their origins. Democratic, agrarian, and self-confident, the "Hoosier" of Indiana or the "Pike" of Missouri inherited all the traits of the earlier "Yankee."

This grass-roots American appeared, dialect and all, in Edward Eggleston's *Hoosier School-Master* and in John Hay's *Pike County Ballads* in 1871. The pious sentimentalism that Eggleston brought from his strongly religious background was mixed in equal proportions with a detailed and good-natured interest in the common things and in the quaint characteristics of local living. A simple love story provides a handy plot for a careful picture of humble folk and their ways. Eggleston, who was something of a scholar in his interests, made a special study of the local speech and helped to set the pattern for the use of sometimes unreadable dialect in all such tales. In similar fashion Hay used a swinging ballad meter to tell the tales of Jim Bludso, heroic captain of a burning Mississippi steamboat, and of other supposedly crude characters who have hearts of gold. Later, the Middle Border was to appear drab and unsatisfying in the harsh tales of E. W. Howe and Joseph Kirkland, but in the seventies and eighties it was full of promise and good will.

The same spirit was reflected in the tales and poems of the Far West, especially those of the lumber and mining camps. Bret Harte immortalized the gold fields of California with the sentimental but effective tales collected in *The Luck of Roaring Camp* (1870), and was summoned on a triumphal transcontinental crossing to Boston as a salaried contributor to the *Atlantic*. His promise and his art waned, however, when he deserted his own gold mine of characters and country. His was a single strike, not for him to repeat, even though Mark Twain wrote of the same untamed Far West in *Roughing It* with greater success and the Oregon poet "Joaquin" Miller sang its largeness:

"Room! room to turn round in, to breathe and be free
To grow to be giant, to sail as a sea . . .
My plains of America! Seas of wild lands! . . .
I turn to you, lean to you, lift you my hands."

The older parts of the continent likewise furnished colorful material for the new movement. New England seemed, after the war, to be given over to the women for purposes of fiction. After her success with *Uncle Tom's Cabin*, Harriet Beecher Stowe turned to simpler tales of country life in *The Pearl of Orr's Island* (1862), and Sarah Orne Jewett used the same Maine coast in her *Deephaven* sketches (1877). Jane Austen furnished much of the inspiration for these very American studies of quaint fisherfolk and rocky islands and bays, which were developed in *A Country Doctor* (1884) and *The Country of the Pointed Firs* (1896).

The South took a few years to regain her composure, but by the eighties her rich store of local color, earlier tapped by Augustus Baldwin Longstreet in *Georgia Scenes* (1835), was rediscovered in the Negro tales of Joel Chandler Harris, *Uncle Remus: His Songs and His Sayings* (1881), and by the New Orleans sketches of George W. Cable, *Old Creole Days* (1879). More mellow and restrained than the studies of the Middle and Far West, these tales of New England and the Old South used a similar mixture of realism in dealing with the present and romance in dealing with the past. Before the close of the century, there was hardly a section of the country that had not furnished its supply of quaint local characters and heroic bygone incidents to create a regional movement that was to shape American fiction until well into the next century.

– 2 –

On one point many of these regionalists were not clear: the distinction between fact and fiction, reality and romance. Writers like Eggleston and Jewett had a strong impulse to write only of life as they knew it at firsthand, but mixed with this interest was the readers' demand for the conventional love-story plot and characters and for the glamorous history of many of the regions. A further complication was the sense of social injustice that writers like Harris and Cable felt for such special groups as former slaves and Creoles. Glamour had an ugly side as well. Perhaps the reason that the regionalist movement failed (except in the case of Mark Twain) to produce a masterpiece before the middle nineties was its lack of a critical guide to work out some of these difficulties.

Such a guide appeared when William Dean Howells (1837–1920) took over *Harper's* "Editor's Study" in 1885 and formulated the rules of fiction to which he had long since devoted his creative efforts. "Truth and sanity" were the simple touchstones that he offered to young and old writers and readers with tireless insistence in his monthly columns for almost thirty-five years. "Let fiction cease to lie about life; let it portray men and women as they are, actuated by the motives and the passions in the measure we all know," he wrote in his essay on Mark Twain. Turning from the "false theory and the bad manners of the English school" of criticism to the sounder methods of Balzac and Turgenev, he found that "the art of fiction, as Jane Austen knew it, declined from her through Scott, and Bulwer, and Dickens, and Charlotte Brontë, and Thackeray, and even George Eliot, because the mania of romanticism had seized upon all Europe." Failing to remember that realism was one of the main issues in the revolt of Wordsworth and the other nature poets against the formalism of an earlier age, Howells identified "romanticism" with "romance" or "make-believe," and set up a false antithesis that has troubled literary historians ever since. Feeling that health lay only in that realism which is "nothing more and nothing less than a truthful treatment of material," he was actually repeating Hawthorne's distinction between the romance and the novel, and he was taking the opposite side of the argument (the side that Fielding took) from that of Hawthorne. He felt—and rightly—that the new generation of storytellers would have to start afresh with a frank look at the world about them.

The clarity and conviction of this critical position, rather than its historical accuracy, made it a rallying point for the new realism which was to become the dominant current in American fiction for the next half-century. Howells started where a new movement must start, with simple first principles; his failure to realize the full significance of his position explains why, in late life, he felt himself left completely behind by Dreiser and all who followed him, and why in his prime he was the dean and lawgiver of American letters. In developing his attack on romance, he stressed four main points: that the commonplace rather than the unusual offers the best material for fiction; that character is more important than plot; that the writer should reveal the good in life as more "real" than the evil; and that realism is the expression of democracy and therefore peculiarly suitable as an American method.

Like many literary critics who are also creative writers (for instance, E. A. Poe, Henry James and T. S. Eliot), Howells was making a critical theory out of his own best practice. His early work had been the travel essay and what he called the "psychological romance," the simple record of the actions of ordinary people that he knew well (including himself as the Basil March of many of his novels), and it was to this kind of writing that he returned in his later years. Best known for his social novels, he himself considered the unpretentious but psychologically acute *Indian Summer* (1886) his best.

Howells was a country boy who, in good American fashion, made his way in the world by industry and honesty, and he appreciated these traits in others. A boyhood in a small Ohio town prepared him for his later life in the literary centers of Boston and New York mainly because of the encouragement of a father who mixed religious mysticism and a love of poetry with poor business sense and a flair for journalism. Young Howells and his brothers were brought up with the stain of printer's ink on their fingers and an insatiable appetite for books. Howells, when he made his first literary pilgrimage to the East and interviewed Lowell in Cambridge, came as a poet and a newspaper correspondent, offering his verses to the editor of the *Atlantic* and sending home a report of the interview. His immediate welcome by Lowell and Fields encouraged him to look to a literary future in Boston, an ambition which was fully realized when he took from Fields in 1871 the editorial post which Fields had inherited from Lowell.

A campaign biography of Lincoln had meanwhile won him the consulship at Venice, and his four years there had produced his first prose work, *Venetian Life* (1866). These gentle commentaries on everyday life in a foreign land, first contributed to the Boston *Advertiser*, were the work of a novelist rather than of a journalist in that they were concerned more with people than with ideas and events. It was only a small step from them to his first real novel, *Their Wedding Journey* (1872), the thinly disguised honeymoon trip of the author and his bride, Elinor Mead of Vermont, to

Niagara Falls. A little more plot was introduced into the Italian tales which followed, but the only growth that can be observed in Howells's special gift of the slightly ironic domestic novel of manners is in his idea of "complicity." Gradually he learned that the conduct of any one human being influences the fate of many others far beyond his own control. This larger knowledge he learned later in life, chiefly from his reading of Tolstoi. It led him also into a study of Gronlund's *Cooperative Commonwealth* and an interest in Socialism, finally producing a group of stories in which the personal is temporarily overshadowed by the social concern.

Howells is known to modern readers mainly through four of these social novels, *A Modern Instance* (1882), *The Rise of Silas Lapham* (1885), *A Hazard of New Fortunes* (1889), and the Utopian *A Traveler from Altruria* (1894), because in these he seems to be speaking most directly to the future. The first, a study of incompatibility in marriage, the place of women in society, and the institution of divorce, pioneered a long series of such novels by Robert Herrick, Robert Grant, David Graham Phillips, and others in the early years of the next century, but it is still most memorable for its understanding of the character of Marcia Gaylord, whose marriage to the irresponsible newspaper reporter Bartley Hubbard goes on the rocks. Similarly, in the second of these novels one is inclined to forget the social theme of conflict between the *nouveau riche* and the entrenched but impoverished Boston society in the more human theme of the rise and fall of the paint manufacturer Silas Lapham of Vermont, his plain but worthy wife, and his lively daughters. Even in so complex and thorough an analysis of American urban life as *A Hazard of New Fortunes*, there is a temptation to become absorbed in the house hunting of the Marches when this alter ego of the author accepts Fulkerson's offer to edit a paper sponsored by the oil-rich but untutored and insensitive farmer Dryfoos. The problems of social inequality, new wealth, exploitation of labor, and strikes, which give the story its action, plot, and meaning, become of less interest than the author's—and the reader's—zest for details.

These were the doors to a more meaningful fiction which Howells opened by his advocacy of realism, and his rediscovery of the common man, but he was temperamentally unfitted to enter them himself. His own purest art was finally, as he realized, to be found in the quiet irony of an Indian summer courtship in Italy or in the silver-wedding journey of his old friends the Marches. His acute awareness of the subtleties of human character made him a superb critic of detail while others moved on to explore the social problems he had raised, to exploit with a bolder humor the paradoxes of American life which he had discovered, and to show that the common man in America was not to be wholly understood by a limited and faithful study of the commonplaces of his daily existence.

– 3 –

Principal among these others was Samuel Langhorne Clemens (1835–1910), better known as Mark Twain. The first major American author to be born west of the Mississippi, Mark Twain *was* what Walt Whitman talked about and what Howells described. Whether a child who never grew up, as one critic believes, or a genius whose very faults are his virtues, as another would argue, this son of the heartland came to symbolize the variety and range and power of the American spirit. The Mississippi was his bloodstream and his hands reached across two oceans. The incurable optimism and humor of the frontier was written into his earliest work, and the dark dismay of its failure into his latest. Responsive to every fact and mood of his time and place, Mark Twain was the artist of the folk, the teller of the tales that make a people. Unconscious of the larger meanings that his own best works convey, he gave to others the perspective that he could never quite define for himself. His art was natural, organic, wholly valid. Always it was the voice of a people; at its best it was epic.

The boy Samuel Clemens was native to the river town of Hannibal, Missouri, the steamboat stop above St. Louis, which through Mark Twain was to become the home town of all boys everywhere. Actually he was born a few miles to the west, in the crossroads town of Florida to which his parents had emigrated from Virginia by way of Kentucky. Erect and earnest, John Marshall Clemens never quite made a success of the law or the land in any of the communities along the way at which the family paused, and the lively Jane Lampton, his wife, brought up the children mainly by courage and conviction. Sam, the second son, was sickly in childhood, inheriting his mother's verve and imagination in a frame that was toughened only by the will to survive. Humor is often the result of an overacute sensibility balanced by a more than usual endurance. To see the incongruities of life and to tolerate them is to laugh. This was the paradox of Mark Twain as he recreated himself in Tom Sawyer and in Huck Finn. Tom was the Sam Clemens who sought the violence and excitement of life in a frontier town, Huck the sensitive dreamer who puzzled over man's inhumanities. The two were never reconciled in the boy of Hannibal nor in the man who lectured and was read around the world; but through them he did his best writing.

He could not do it right away because the largest ingredient in his art was memory. His earliest stories and sketches are about more immediate experience, his rediscovery of the American character and scene. Apprenticed to his brother Orion, he early got that basic training in realism which he shared with Howells and almost all the others in this new generation of American writers by reporting for a small-town newspaper. As a journeyman printer, he made his first trip East, visiting the principal cities and working on their newspapers. In a few years he wandered back to his native Mississippi Valley. This he next explored as a cub reporter on a river steamboat, learning the twists and shoals and changes of the sluggish monster as many schoolboys learn their Latin grammar. As if to complete his knowledge of the continent, now reaching from New York to New Orleans, he next set out by overland stage with his brother Orion as secretary to the Secretary of the Territory of Nevada. From there he went to California and on to Honolulu as miner, printer, but mainly as reporter. Finally, the *Alta California* sent him as correspondent with one of the *Quaker City*'s earliest Mediterranean cruises to Europe and Palestine. At the age of thirty-four, Sam Clemens had seen more of the world than many a diplomat or professional traveler.

His first sketches were the reports of a sensitive journalist. In the rough and tumble of the river town or the mining camp, life's contrasts were sharp, and the practical joke was the height of humor. *The Celebrated Jumping Frog of Calaveras County and Other Sketches* (1867) told of Angel's Camp and the California gold country of Bret Harte and

Artemus Ward. The tale of the frog loaded with buckshot had often been told, and the ruse of the petrified man required more daring than originality, but this was the folklore of the frontier. Already a successful lecturer because of his skill with the grand lie of the poker face and his Southern drawl, Mark Twain could put these same qualities into the printed word. It was the chord common to all America; his response to his audience was total, as was theirs to him, from the start.

The Innocents Abroad (1869) and *Roughing It* (1872) told of his travels East and West in the same mood. Written for the newspaper reader of the day, and little revised when collected, these sketches had the freshness of a happy response to life as it happened. The shrewdness that lay behind their apparent lack of guile gave them their charm. In a day of sentimental travels to the Old World and of eager curiosity about the New, the young reporter's mock innocence was the perfect base for obvious and good-natured satire on man's little hypocrisies. It was all in good fun when the "doctor" refused to be taken in by the Roman guide and preferred to tell him a few things about Christopher Columbus, or when Sam Clemens was himself taken in by the sharpers of the mining town of Virginia City, Nevada; and it was put into the record in a tone of naïve wonder that exposed shams and revealed essential truth. The reader felt his superior knowledge, and a good time was had by all.

Mark Twain's marriage in 1870 to the frail and protected Olivia Langdon of Elmira, New York, was the turning point in his life because it put an end to his wanderings and made him suddenly respectable—not because it changed his character in any important way. Its principal effect on his work was the corralling of the roving reporter and the release of the artist into his own world of memory. The ideals that led Mark Twain to his mate were his long before he met Olivia Langdon, as a picture in her brother's locket, and fell in love with her. The contrast between the rough, plug-chewing, smoking, swearing sinner and the gentle, whimsical suitor already was fully formed before Mark Twain humorously exaggerated it and won his suit with letters of recommendation from former cronies to the elderly citizen of Elmira who was the stern father of his charmer. It all happened right out of the books.

As a consequence Mark Twain's most productive years, 1873–1890, were spent in Hartford, Connecticut, as a respectable citizen and father of a family, and his first literary effort of those years was a collaboration with his neighbor Charles Dudley Warner, *The Gilded Age* (1873), in which he attempted to mix his West with Warner's East. The only survivor of this unhappy experiment was the irrepressible Colonel Beriah Sellers, undoubtedly one of the great characters of all fiction, the archetype of the impecunious, optimistic, get-rich-quick American. In the contrast between the humble realities and the grandiose schemes of his cousin James Lampton, Sam Clemens struck his richest vein. Here he discovered the focus of memory that was to bring to literary life his own boyhood.

Three books that are really parts of one masterwork, *The Adventures of Tom Sawyer* (1876), *Life on the Mississippi* (1883), and *The Adventures of Huckleberry Finn* (1885), grew out of this discovery. Taken separately, they vary greatly: the first is almost wholly narrative—a story written for boys, full of the horrors and joys of childhood, flowing apparently on the surface of experience; the second is a collection of sketches and impressions of the great river, taken partly from memory and partly from fresh observation; the third is the "sequel" which knits the whole group together, the story of a boy but no longer a story *only* for boys. It is a folk epic, for by now the mighty river has become a symbol of that with which man must forever contend but in which he can put his only faith. In the perspective of this third, all three books have an unsuspected depth and a further meaning.

At the start, it was to be all about Tom Sawyer and his gang. Tom was, of course, the Sam Clemens that wishful thinking of the respectable citizen of Hartford recalled from his lost youth, rather than the Sam who actually grew up in the Mississippi Valley town. Time had trained the artist to blot out or to emphasize various details with a sure hand. Ten years of childhood were telescoped into a single summer, and people and places were freed from the bonds of accuracy to a region where they could reveal a higher truth. Hannibal became St. Petersburg, and there are originals for all the characters. Huck Finn, Injin Joe, Becky Thatcher, Aunt Polly, even Muff Potter and the Widow Douglas. The hide-out on Jackson's Island and the dark recesses of the cave were later immortalized as tourists' shrines because they shared Tom's immortality. Mark Twain had written better than he knew. All the cruelties and fears of childhood could be expressed in the pirate-Robin-Hood Tom, side by side with its wonders and joys. Because his break with the past had been complete, Mark Twain had captured a kingdom into which the deeper passions of childhood that survive in every adult could escape and live again. In his last sad years his repeated efforts to write once more of Tom and Huck is sure proof of the meaning of this book in his own psychic life. It serves others in the same way; and no one need think his search for the eternal womb of life unnatural.

Next to being a pirate, the best thing was to be a pilot on a Mississippi steamboat. The river held all adventure, and the pilot was its master. When Howells asked Mark Twain for something to start off the 1875 volume of the *Atlantic*, Twain, full of these memories, sent in a series of sketches which were published as "Old Times on the Mississippi." Now there was no Tom Sawyer between him and his memories; he wrote of his own experiences as cub pilot in learning channels and shallows, he wrote of the history and the geography and the fickle personality of the river, and he wrote about the people who lived along its banks and in the rafts and barges and boats on its surface. Such a water-soaked book had perhaps never before been written—unless it be *Moby-Dick*. A sheer massing of details is sometimes the best, or only, way to recreate an image of grandeur, as Whitman and Melville knew. Out of Mark Twain's memories and his facts, the river spirit rose.

Eight years passed before his publisher suggested a trip down the full length of the river and enough new papers to make a book. The second half of *Life on the Mississippi* came of this trip. Of course it lacks the inspiration of the first half, but the experience reawakened more memories and encouraged Mark Twain to complete a third manuscript that had long been laid aside. Huck Finn might never have had a book of his own but for this.

The unevenness of Mark Twain's genius is nowhere more obvious than in his masterpiece. Taking refuge from both his drunken father and the Widow Douglas in his Jackson's Island hide-out, Huck was deserted by his author for many years. The runaway Negro Jim rescued him for literature as he in turn attempted to rescue Jim from slavery. Together they make a raft and float down the river in one of the noblest and perhaps the humblest of all Odysseys. Mark Twain had found his great theme in the remembered splendors and squalors of bygone Southern civilization, as William Faulkner was later to do also and more fully. The antics of the two river rogues, the "King" and the "Duke," offset the tragedy of the Grangerford-Shepherdson feud, and the fixed morality of man is balanced against the fluent morality of nature in Huck's ponderings on the justice of a law that demands the return of Jim to his owner. It does not matter that the escaping slave had only to cross to the Illinois side to gain his freedom, or that Miss Watson had died and set him free in her will anyway; ignorance and error are more real than truth because they are shared by Huck and Jim and they provide the tight frame of pathos and drama of their story. Mark Twain's inner life as a boy is discovered and made articulate in this story as the child mind has seldom been in literature.

When Tom Sawyer joins them, the story loses its depth and returns to the level of the earlier book. The last third is in the old mood, with some of its freshness gone, but Huck's deep revolt against being "sivilized" had taken shape from his meditations during fog-bound Mississippi nights and would always be there to comfort or to disturb his civilized author. It would also be there for the reader who was starting on a voyage through the strange and ruthless Nature of the machine age, different in all respects from the Nature of Emerson and Thoreau and Concord. The twisting, changing, heartless, sluggish Mississippi had told a different story.

– 4 –

The difference between Tom and Huck is the difference between the early and the late Mark Twain. The creator of Tom was a lover of life, filled with its mysteries, alarmed by its terrors, amused by its inconsistencies and contrasts; the creator of Huck was essentially a skeptic or agnostic who had turned against mankind because of its inhumanity to man. From 1884 to the end of his life, the inner Mark Twain was a different person from that of his public image. On the platform or at home, with his shock of white hair, his genial smile, his white suit, and his black cigar, he was the beloved humorist, ready with a quip to counter any catastrophe. In his heart he thought of himself as a disillusioned cynic whose personal life had ended in a succession of tragedies and who believed in nothing. Was the change sudden, and, if so, what had caused it? Or was it a natural and inevitable result of what the man was and what the times had become? The answer to these questions, upon which no two critics have agreed, holds the key to mysteries greater than those in the life of any one man.

One of the first signs of change came in a book written ostensibly for children, *The Prince and the Pauper* (1882), the story of a prince who exchanged places with a subject and learned at first hand of the poverty and tragedy in the average human life. With the scene set in Elizabethan England, the events were far enough away and long enough ago to allow devastating things to be said without a chuckle. The violence that underlies humor could be expressed without recourse to the cover of laughter. The fact that this is the book in which Mark Twain became absorbed when he laid

aside the half finished *Huck Finn* should tell much about what
was happening to him. Huck was too close to his innermost
self to be a comfortable companion. Prince Edward's story
could be told straight and nobody would—nobody actually
did—recognize its appalling meanings.

A Connecticut Yankee in King Arthur's Court (1889)
makes the case even clearer. It was a far more overt satire,
even though its author insisted that it was merely a "contrast."
The idea of transplanting a modern man to a past or future
time or to a remote or imagined country in order to comment
on the present is a common literary device, and extremely
popular at the time that Mark Twain was writing. Edward
Bellamy's *Looking Backward* appeared a year earlier, and
W. D. Howells's *A Traveler from Altruria* five years later.
Literally hundreds of lesser Utopias with satiric intent were
published both in England and in America during these years
of fundamental social, economic, and intellectual change. To
attribute Mark Twain's book only to the events of his private
life is to wear blinders.

A Connecticut Yankee is especially revealing because it
can be read with equal enjoyment on either of two levels, as
a lighthearted burlesque with Mark Twain's humor at its best
or as a devastating satire on American society, the mechanical
age, and human nature in general. It should be read as both
because here the early and the late Mark Twain were in
working harmony. The "Boss" is a person in a story, but he
also represents the successful American businessman, and his
removal to King Arthur's Court provides an easy contrast of
modern ways—the ways of democratic capitalism—with the
ways of feudalism. Against the squalor and tragedy of the lot
of the medieval peasant, the autocratic authority and corrup-

tion of the Church and Court, and, underlying all, the essential cruelty of human nature, are revealed in all their blackness. The debunking of the shams of chivalry and of romance that provided much of the humor in so early a book as *The Innocents Abroad* becomes here a direct attack which is humorous only to the insensitive. At the same time the antics of the knights are as absurd as those of the mock royalty on Huck's raft, and as worthy of ribald laughter. Nor does the Boss himself and all he stands for come off unscathed. At times he is as ridiculous and blind as any King Arthur, and his society is as corrupt and absurd as any feudalism. Although in the end the balance tips in favor of democratic capitalism, there is little enthusiasm left for human society when the Boss uses modern mechanistic knowledge in a wholesale slaughter of his knightly opponents. And it is Merlin's magic which puts him to sleep so that he may awake in the nineteenth century.

This book was written when Sam Clemens was at the height of his popularity as writer and lecturer. He had money to waste, and he had a happy home, a loving wife, and three beloved daughters. An investment in an unsuccessful type-setting machine and in a publishing business which failed were the beginnings of his personal troubles, to which his disillusionment has been so often attributed. While on a lecture tour around the world in an effort to pay off the debts for which he was only morally responsible, he learned of the death of his favorite daughter, and not long after he lost a second daughter and his invalid wife. His own failing health contributed to his gloom as he dictated to his secretary, Albert Bigelow Paine, excerpts for an autobiography which he believed would burn the very paper on which they were written and could not be safely read for fifty years.

There is no question that, about 1890, Mark Twain lost that hairline balance between fact and fiction which had been the secret of his greatest work. Perhaps the cause was merely advancing years, perhaps specific events in his life, perhaps the general trend of the times—most probably all three. The mind of a man past fifty-five may be just as keen as it always has been, but it is not as flexible. Attitudes and ideas become more fixed and more sharply contrasted. The sense of losing former powers is distressing, and the effort to recapture them is depressing if it fails. A few authors—Henry James, for example—may succeed in the effort and do their best work in later years, but Mark Twain did not succeed, perhaps because he ceased to grow in imagination, turning his efforts rather to the recapturing of his three best creations: Colonel Sellers, Tom Sawyer, and Huck Finn. Only one new character of importance appeared in these later books. Starting as Pudd'n-head Wilson in the novel of that name (1894) and ending as the young Satan of the posthumous *The Mysterious Stranger* (1916), a totally cynical commentator on human nature moved into the center of Mark Twain's imagination. His philosophical position is clearly enough stated in Pudd'nhead's diary, carefully elaborated in the essay "What Is Man?" and fully illustrated in "The Man That Corrupted Hadleyburg." Basically it is an acceptance of the new position suggested by the science of Darwin and his followers that had apparently deprived mankind once for all of his free will to act in a mechanically predetermined universe. But in addition to this cause for hopelessness, mankind, in Mark Twain's later view, is unable to assume a merely passive role because he is blighted by a moral sense, which is to drive him on to unspeakable cruelties because of his sense of guilt. And finally there is a good chance that the whole thing is a dream. This, as Mark Twain finally realizes in the character of Satan in *The Mysterious Stranger*, is man's only hope. In that realization—which turned bitterness into stoicism—he found an answer to his personal distress and loneliness and to the riddle of life in general. If it was only a dream, it did not matter.

It was, of course, all a dream, as literature must always be. Sam Clemens of Hannibal had once more dreamed the American Dream but he had reshaped it to his times. Because he was, in his best years, close to the life he pictured, loving its smallest detail in memory, he was able to change with a society that was undergoing one of the most rapid transformations that human society has ever experienced. His art, as long as it was immediately responsive to life, succeeded where a more rigorous and arbitrary art would have failed. Mark Twain was the folk genius of his time and place. In him the literary discovery of the Continental Nation moved from record into art.

CHAPTER VIII

ART AND THE INNER LIFE
Dickinson, James

THERE were many who followed Mark Twain into a vigorous acceptance of the expanding continent and the expanding world of the modern mind, but there were also many who reacted against all that the West called for and all that the Industrial Revolution and the new science demanded. By 1890 two roads of future development in American literature were clearly marked: the road that led to an open acceptance of nature and of things as they are, and the road that led inward to an exploration of the consciousness, to tradition, to restraint, and to concern for form. In an earlier day Poe and Hawthorne had in one way or another followed this second road, and in a later day it was to be followed by T. S. Eliot and Faulkner. This was the "back-trail" in a deeper sense than that in which Hamlin Garland used the term, yet it was somehow associated with the Eastward look and the search for tradition. Un-American as it often seemed, American literature could never have matured without it, could never have become more than a series of reports from the moving frontier. Introspective writers like Poe, Emily Dickinson, and Henry James were as much products of American culture as were Whitman and Mark Twain.

In method the two kinds of writers that appeared after 1870 were similar in that they both sought to reveal reality: the one of the outer world and the other of the inner world, the one of the unknown West, the other of the familiar East. Realism also opened the frontier of the mind and spirit as skepticism took the place of faith. Instead of the outer world, the West, the future, these fugitives from action explored the inner world of their own spiritual being, their cultural inheritance, and their past. Not content with such superficial rejection of American rawness for European gentility as one finds in the nostalgic idealism of Longfellow and Lowell, Emily Dickinson and Henry James discovered new depths of understanding through introspection and a faith in the integrity of art. In their respective retreats of garden and salon, these two artists carved out universal truths from their limited experiences.

– 2 –

For Emily Dickinson (1830–1886), retreat was into the absolute. The recluse of Amherst, Massachusetts, became one of the great poets of all time, and perhaps the greatest of all women poets, without stirring from her garden in the quiet New England town. Her universe was that of the soul; her special task was to make that universe articulate. This she did in gem-like verse that resembled nothing written before or since.

Was her poetry the expression of life lived or of life repressed? Does she tell of experience or wish? So successful was she in guarding her secrets that it is almost impossible now to reconstruct the life out of which her poetry was made, even if ever it was in any way specific. She writes of God, man, and nature with a knowledge that does not seem possible in one so sheltered. Never was there a person to whom so little happened who suffered and rejoiced with such intensity. She knew love and death as few have known them and survived, and yet who it was she loved and lost, her friends and biographers are unable or unwilling to agree upon.

There is a temptation to start with the stereotype of the New England nun, of which another writer of the day, Mary Wilkins Freeman, made a famous story. There was something about the way women lived in the late nineteenth century that encouraged repression. Glimpses of Sophia Hawthorne, Olivia Clemens, and many another idealized and sheltered wife tend to reveal an image of neuroticism that had provided its own system of values. Pale, dressed in white, devoted to their husbands and children, or consecrated to their God, they were waited upon, protected, repressed. The sex that was not permitted expression in literature was not even openly acknowledged in life.

The unmarried woman often died at an early age of the restrictions put upon her by society. Dress and habits allowed no free exercise that could promote health. Driven in upon herself, she lived intensely in the mirror of her own unrealized passions, and burned out her energies in silence. For her, Emily Dickinson provided a voice. Nature was her close and loving, although sometimes exacting, friend. Her religion had no church because she could converse directly with her God on personal terms. Whether she loved this man or that, or none at all except in her imagination, makes little difference to her poetry, for she knew love with a depth and violence that could come only from repression. Death, too, was always present, but whether it was someone dear to her who had just died or the sudden conviction of death itself is unimportant. Because most other avenues of expression were closed, her brief stanzas come to hold the distillation of all that it means to be human. They are her letters to the world, which she wrote but failed herself to mail.

No one who knew her well seemed to think of Emily Dickinson as morbid or withdrawn. Happy and outgoing, she loved and was loved by her family and her circle of intimate friends. Edward Dickinson, her father, was a man of considerable means and strong personality, a lawyer and treasurer of Amherst College; Emily Norcross, her mother, the exact opposite, was gentle and dependent, devoted to the care of her family until after her husband's death in 1874, when she became an invalid. Her younger daughter Lavinia, or "Vinnie," like Emily, never married, but did not share the beauty of Emily's spirit. Austin, the eldest, in the pattern of his father became a lawyer and leading citizen of Amherst, which he never left. He married Emily's early friend Susan Gilbert, a woman of aggressive wit and worldly charm, and lived next door to his parents' home on Main Street, where "Sister Sue" became for many years the confidante of the poet.

To her close-knit family Emily devoted herself completely after one year at Mount Holyoke Seminary. There had been nothing unusual about her childhood in its activities and friends, but her retirement from the world does seem to have had a deliberate intention to prompt it. She had attended district school and Amherst Academy, where she was known as a wit, and she loved her garden. To her friends she was outgoing and affectionate. She seldom left Amherst, although she had been to Boston on occasion, and once, at the age of twenty-three, to Philadelphia and Washington. Only in her unwillingness to "renounce the world" for a heavenly master did Emily seem different from her fellows; her independence made her hesitant to accept the joy of a nineteenth century Christian conversion. She felt herself too worldly! When she found that she could not share the unquestioning faith of her fellow students, she did not return to the seminary. Her own retirement from society came soon after, but it was to preserve rather than to renounce the self—there was more Yankee than Calvinist in her move. Perhaps she had been reading Emerson's recent essay on "Self-Reliance." Certainly the faith to which she retired had the skepticism of the Transcendentalist rather than the submission to God's will of the Calvinist.

Perhaps a failure in love, as gossip has it, was the immediate cause. There was a young lawyer in her father's office whom she called her "tutor" and who, before his early death, encouraged her in poetry and in religion, and there was the Philadelphia clergyman whom Emily saw only on a few occasions before he moved to the Pacific coast but who retained "an intimacy of many years" in the "box in which his letters grew." Both or either of these could have provided a focus for unrealized passions in the sheltered imagination. In any case the experience was there, and it was sufficient to produce, within a very few years, a sheaf of poems such as no woman had ever before composed.

It is too easy to assume that feminine modesty and the shyness born of her withdrawal had caused the delay in publication of most of these poems until after her death. The symbol of the pale Indian pipes, which her neighbor Mrs. Todd drew for the cover of the first volume of her poems, was never approved by its author; and the poems which Emily Dickinson wrote were not the outpourings of a hurt and inward-turning spirit. Art offers two ways to those who turn to it from life: a blinded wandering in the deep recesses of a sick-ened personality, or the depersonalized and hard forms of disciplined and complete expression. Emily Dickinson chose the latter. Hers was the poetry of craftsmanship rather than that of confession. Apparently she failed to publish because she could not find a way to reach the world on her own terms, and she would not accept compromise. From the first, she was writing as though to be read, but she was satisfied merely to enclose her poems in letters to her friends rather than in the covers of a book if in that way they could be accepted without alteration. Sister Sue, Mabel Todd, Samuel Bowles, Helen Hunt Jackson, and Josiah Holland were among those to whom she showed them for advice.

Once she came near to finding an editor who could help her, but even he tried to alter her supposed carelessness of craftsmanship. Thomas Wentworth Higginson, clergyman and editor, to whom she sent her poems, was acute enough to recognize their worth, but even he tried to smooth out the violent rhythms and the more obscure meanings when he later helped to prepare them for print.

The poet herself was courteous when such advice was given her, but she quietly ignored it. She knew better than any of her "tutors" what she wished to say and she was exact-ing in her ways of saying it. The general reading public that asked for meter that is smooth, rhythm that is easy, and words that are limited to only one obvious meaning interested her not at all. She was willing to wait.

Like John Donne and the English metaphysical poets whom she so resembled, Dickinson's understanding of the meaning of words was subtle and complex, her ear for music could assimilate discord as well as concord, and her images were drawn from life and from books with a sure but infinitely various authority. Only the most complex art could be made to include the depths and variety of those things for which she demanded expression. The resources of American poetry which the metaphysics of Emerson had already stretched with images as violent as those of Herbert and Donne, and that Poe had enriched with a darker and more complex music, were further opened and deepened by these deceptively simple stanzas. Emily Dickinson sought to reconcile the finite to the infinite without relinquishing the integrity of the human soul or the validity of physical nature. In the idiom of New England theology that she had renounced, she caught and forced into expression the skepticism and doubts of the age of science which was to come. Not printed until the 1890's, and hardly understood until the 1920's, poems which were written shortly after the Civil War reached with the firm note of authority a public that had experienced a World War. Her retreat had been into a realm which does not change, and her letters were to a world which had, like her, reached a point of irreducible paradox. Fully disciplined art alone could stand firm against threatened chaos.

– 3 –

Henry James (1843–1916) offered American fiction the same discipline that Emily Dickinson provided for American poetry. It was through the rejection of his times and his society that he became the spectator and analyst rather than the recorder. His alienation was both from the America of his birth and from the changing concepts and values of the mid-nineteenth century. Whereas Poe and Hawthorne had understood the dilemma of the artist as a forced choice between the world of the imagination and the world of fact and had chosen the former, Henry James made art a fact. Because the American as artist was the central dramatic figure of his best work, James succeeded in treating the dilemma realistically. The protagonist of his fiction was always a projection of at least a substantial part of the author's self, whether a writer or painter in many of the shorter tales, or a woman or man whose art was the conscious reshaping of the self to its own best potentialities, as in the longest and best of his novels. The artist in the story was always Henry James completely depersonalized and made the object of a clinical analysis and evaluation. This gift of projecting himself against a screen of perceptions made it possible for James to develop fiction into a complex and exacting art. The modern novel owes many of its basic principles of composition to his theory and practice.

Again a close-knit family life first shut out the world. The family was founded in 1789 by a North of Ireland immigrant who was not averse to making a fortune to pass on to his heirs, together with a strong Calvinistic sense of moral rectitude. William of Albany was the stuff out of which family empires are made. Providing the means of leisure to at least two of his succeeding generations, he endowed them with a conscience as well as with a bank account. Henry James, Senior, revolted violently against such parental and divine restrictions, but Fate was unkind to him. A childhood accident left him lacking a leg which had been burned and then amputated. He became a thinker rather than a doer, a religious mystic and a seeker of culture. With the means to indulge both himself and his family, he traveled freely in the abstract realms of the newer and freer religious sects then fashionable and in the actual world of European capitals and galleries. His was the rejec-

tion of the society to which his children were born. The novelist, Henry James, Junior, was brought up in a family in
which blood ties alone were to be counted upon. The securi-
ties of a settled religious system and of a community to which
he could belong were never his. The bonds between him, his
brothers and sister, his father and mother, were unusually
strong, but he was free of commitment to either God or country. There was still enough of the family fortune to justify
him in the choice of a life as a consumer rather than as a pro-
ducer. He could simply remain detached. He would, in his
own phrase, try to be one of those upon whom nothing is lost.

In an essay written in 1884 as an answer to a lecture by
the British critic Walter Besant, Henry James made clear his
distinction between a realism of fact and a realism of method.
He was not a philosopher like his brother William, but he was
quite certain that the only reality lies in the impressions made
by life on the spectator, and not in any facts of which the
spectator is unaware. Realism is therefore merely the obligation that the artist assumes to represent life as he sees it, which
may not be the same as life as it "really" is. By making the
conscious self of the artist, as discovered through his own sensibilities, the final measure of experience Henry James shifted
the grounds of realistic art from the outer to the inner world.
From this point on, he applied the techniques of the realist to
life as he knew it with even more exacting care than did Howells, but he was freed, as Howells and Mark Twain were not,
from the suspicion that he might not, in the first place, have
seen reality clearly. To James this problem did not occur.
What he saw was, in so far as his function as artist was concerned, the only reality to which he owed any allegiance.

The problem of how to be an artist was complicated by

that of how to be an American. Just as he made himself hypersensitive to life in order to reject it—or rather, to push it away from him into the perspective of art—he made himself overaware of what it meant to be an American by turning his back on the country of his birth and living a large part of his life in England and in the capitals of the Continent.

His father was partly responsible for this restlessness, because he kept the family on the move. Born in New York City, Henry with his three brothers and one sister was educated by private tutors in Geneva, Paris, and Bonn. Even when in the United States, they were as much at Newport as in New York. A deep and lasting relationship with his psychologist brother William developed first during these years, a mutual dependence from which both boys instinctively attempted to free themselves, never with full success. Yet they pushed each other on and were largely responsible for the intellectual success which each achieved. Both attended Harvard—Henry in law, William in science—and both settled first in Cambridge. Each went through some sort of "crisis" in early manhood, although William's was deeper than Henry's and his subsequent moral conviction stronger. An injury to his back, the result of an accident while watching a fire, gave Henry one further reason for removal from the play of boys of his age and cultivated in him the role of an observer. Solitary wanderyears in Europe while still in his twenties confirmed him as a bachelor of society, a welcome guest at any function where cultivated and intelligent people met, a member of no family or social group.

How much should be made biographically of his friendship with his cousin Mary Temple, particularly during one New Hampshire summer when he and two other young men were paying her court, is difficult to determine. Marriage does not seem to have been an immediate hope even then; but with her death Mary Temple became the most important inspiration and model for his fiction, the prototype of the young girl who asked all of life and was deprived of even a moderate share. The event struck home to him and became the focus of his life-long contemplations on justice, morality, and fate, but the girl herself does not seem too urgent an object of desire at the time. In the novels which she inspired there is always a young man standing apart and giving her only his intense curiosity, understanding, and sympathy. This young man is James. If he could establish his objectivity in love, he was pretty sure never to be at a loss for it.

At the age of thirty he was committed to the role of cosmopolitan, having virtually no home of his own, a wanderer mainly in Europe. After a stay in Paris where he saw much of the Russian Turgenev and the Frenchman Flaubert, he settled for a time in London, with frequent visits to the Continent. He was now the committed artist in fiction, ready to devote his life to the creation and improvement of his art.

The short stories and novels which he wrote in the decade 1871–1881 established his point of view and method and set up the three major themes of his career: the contrast of American sincerity and crudity with European deceit and culture, the conflicting realities of life and of art, and the substitution of psychological for ethical measurements of good and evil. Thereafter his books became more complex as art and more profound as commentary on the human predicament, but they never went beyond these primary issues for their material.

These were the years when James as an American sought

to solve the riddle of the American character, and as an artist to reconcile the life of art to the realities of love and life. In his first published novel, both themes are present in Roderick Hudson, a young artist whose studies in Rome are brought to an end by the fascinating Princess Casamassima, an American expatriate who has become wholly identified with the sophistication of European ways and values. Roderick reveals the insensitive egoism which for James was always the primary weakness of the American character, as well as an inability to resist an infatuation which draws the artist from his consecration to art and into the maelstrom of passion. The burden of the double issue is too much for even a character of fiction to bear, and in subsequent stories James focused his attention on one or the other of Roderick's dilemmas.

In *The American* (1877), *Daisy Miller* (1879), and *The Portrait of a Lady* (1881), and in a number of lesser works, the problem of the expatriate occupies his main attention. In no novel is the international issue more fully presented than in the tale of Christopher Newman, self-made wealthy American who has the temerity to assault the fortress of the ancient Parisian family of Bellegarde and attempt to carry off the princess, the beautiful but somewhat remote Madame de Cintré. His failure is a moral victory for the integrity of his national character (for in Newman, Henry James has most fully presented an individual as the prototype of his countrymen), but it is a somewhat hollow nobility which the rejected lover displays in refraining from using the family secret to destroy those who have become his enemies. The melodramatic plot holds the reader's interest and has preserved this story, whereas James's other and more subtle treatments of the same theme are less often read, but it distracts both him and his reader from the more important aspects of the clash of old and new cultures.

In his next try at the theme, James frankly calls his *Daisy Miller* a "study." The expatriate Daisy is "an inscrutable combination of audacity and innocence," a riddle of daring naïveté as insoluble to James as to her American and Italian suitors. She defies the conventions of European society and falls a tragic victim to her own innocence—not of masculine deceit but of malarial fever. Again the drama depends upon circumstantial rather than upon psychological complication for its complex, but James has taken a long step forward in his understanding of the American by allowing a young girl to stand for the national character. Daisy's struggle for full self-realization in defiance of conventions is much more subtly presented than is Newman's effort to add the amenities of a riper culture to a life of material gain. Daisy's values are more nearly James's own.

The much fuller and more leisurely analysis of Isabel Archer in *The Portrait of a Lady* carries the theme about as far as it will go on the level of cultural contrast. In Isabel herself and in the men whom she meets on her road to self-realization, James has presented almost every degree and kind of cultural difference—from the brashness of the American Caspar Goodwood to the subtlety and corruption of the Europeanized Gilbert Osmond, including the blunt British honesty of Lord Warburton and the dispassionate sensibility of Ralph Touchett who plays the role of the observer. The richness of psychological texture in this novel probably owes much to its author's memories of his cousin Minny Temple and of her tragic failure to discover the life in herself before death overtook her on the quest, but James has deftly transferred the mortal illness to the observer of the event and has saved Isabel from Minny's fate by assuming in the selfless Ralph her malady. Much could be made of these transfers from fact to fiction if one's aim were to analyze the author rather than his art; but, whatever meaning the tragic memories may have had for James, their meaning as fiction is profound and rewarding. Now the outcome does not seem to matter when Isabel unhappily and unconvincingly rejects her last avenue of escape and returns to her duties as wife and foster mother; the full cycle of lost innocence has been explored. A far more satisfactory representative of American freshness and candor than Christopher Newman or Daisy Miller, Isabel Archer herself seems to realize that experience has brought to her some of the rewards as well as most of the disappointments of the corrupt culture into which she has been betrayed. If this is life, she seems to say with James, let me be one of those upon whom no part of it is lost. Events and eventualities do not matter, only a fuller comprehension of the human lot.

In his fictional handling of a problem so close to his own experience, James here succeeded in gaining for himself that complete detachment of art from life which he had come to feel was so essential if art were to be wholly free. His own emotions never seem to become entangled in those of his characters even where the events of the story most nearly parallel those of his own experience. But the artists of his fiction find no such simple escape from the dilemma. The harassed heroes of his many stories on this theme seldom escape. In "The Lesson of the Master," the younger man learns to sacrifice his worldly love to the more exacting mistress of his art only to have his "master" ironically reverse the case and take the girl for himself; in "The Middle Years" a complicated involvement with a dying countess spoils the first and only chance of an elderly novelist to capture the artistic success which had eluded his youth; and in "The Aspern Papers" the effort to exhume the life of a dead poet from his letters raises the final question of whether or not the personality of the artist is distinct from the personality of the man and therefore becomes the rightful possession of his public. These are only a few of the short and longer stories by James which together touch upon almost every possible phase of the problem, but the nearest to his own answer is probably found in "The Real Thing," where the models of the painter so accurately express in their own persons the concept which the artist wishes to portray that they deprive him of his creative freedom. A professional model who could act rather than actually be the kind of person she was modeling, and who knew nothing of the meaning of her pose, was superior because she would not interfere with the "real" thing, which for James existed only in the mind of the painter until it was transferred to the canvas. Here, in almost explicit allegory, is the central principle of James's aesthetic philosophy.

– 4 –

Having found its range, intensity, and special quality in *The Portrait of a Lady*, the art of Henry James apparently faltered and for almost twenty years became diffuse and uncertain of its direction. The best product of these years was the short tale or novelette, of which James tried a variety, but he also wrote much criticism and made relatively unsuccessful excursions into drama, biography, and the travel essay. Then in 1902, at the age almost of sixty, he suddenly returned, as it were, to the scene of his triumph and produced three massive novels of the kind that he had built around Isabel Archer, *The Wings of the Dove* (1902), *The Ambassadors* (1903), and *The Golden Bowl* (1904). Rejected by all but the most ardent of his followers because of what seemed an unnecessary prolixity and complexity, these three carefully and intricately wrought tapestries of fictional art have finally claimed their place as masterpieces of a kind diametrically opposite to the free power of *Moby-Dick* and *Leaves of Grass*. In them he realized for himself, and for all novelists who were to come after, a specialized but completely developed art of fiction. Craftsmanship had triumphed.

The increased psychological depth and the complexity of style and structure in these last great works were, of course, the results of what had seemed to be pointless experiment. The illusion that he might have a career in the drama had been a reasonable assumption from the increasingly dramatic quality of his work, but James had failed miserably on the stage because he attempted to write not his own kind of drama but the artificial comedy that was then popular. Many of his novelettes have the quality of good theater, from the early *Washington Square* (1881) to *The Sense of the Past* (1917), and have made successful plays when dramatized by others, but the London theater of 1890–1895 was not ready for works of largely psychological interest. The attempt to write plays helped James to develop the very objectivity that he had been striving for in fiction, but it was not a happy experience for him to know so complete a failure with the public.

Much more rewarding were the series of short novels that he wrote between 1897 and 1901 in which he dealt with far more acute conflicts in human relationships than he had used in his earlier novels. *What Maisie Knew* (1897), *The*

Spoils of Poynton (1897), *The Turn of the Screw* (1898), *The Awkward Age* (1899), and *The Sacred Fount* (1901) might be thought of as a series of variations on the theme of evil, mostly as it appears in children and as it takes the form which had so obsessed Hawthorne—the violation of one human heart by the possessive will of another. Maisie comes to know "everything" at an early age by observing the misconduct of her estranged parents who share her custody in six-month periods. Thrown upon the confidences of governesses who are themselves involved in the illicit affairs of the elders, Maisie's education in evil serves to sharpen her wits and to commit her to a silence that is taken for stupidity. She might well have become the heroine of the later novel, Nanda Brookenham, who, having arrived at the "awkward age," is able to participate in the intrigues that go on about her. Avarice is the evil in *The Spoils of Poynton*, wherein the physical possession of a great house and its valuable collection of art objects and furniture becomes inextricably involved in the personal relationships of a mother and her son, a lover and his mistress. And in *The Sacred Fount* the vampire theme is only superficially hidden beneath the polite surface of English country-house society.

The nameless evil of *The Turn of the Screw*, about which there has been so much controversy, is therefore not too difficult to comprehend. It is nameless because, like evil in the tales of Poe and Hawthorne, it is malign only in its consequences. James's tale may be regarded as pure melodrama—a mystery or ghost story written for the sake of terror alone—but it is surely more than that. The hold which the dead Peter Quint and Miss Jessel have on the two living children is daemonic; whether it is interpreted as the result of a curse or of psychotic perversion will depend on the reader's habit of mind. And the question of whether the new governess who tells the story is agent or victim of the curse will depend on the reader's own whimsy. James is deliberately as ambiguous as the evil of which he writes. His aesthetic detachment has developed to the point at which he can present the most horrible of moral situations without auctorial comment.

It was in this mood that James returned to the central story of his life, the loves and death of Minny Temple. Now as Milly Theale of *The Wings of the Dove,* her intense spiritual vitality in a diseased body offers her cousin and probable suitor a moral problem of the utmost fascination for his scientific fictional analysis. The earlier Minny, Isabel Archer, was charged by life to expend her modest inheritance in discovering what she could of experience in a European adventure. Milly's wealth was fabulous and her charge was to satisfy her equally fabulous demands for a maximum of life's "vibrations" in an appallingly short time before her nameless malady took her off. With all its elements thus heightened, the treachery of her lover and her friend need not be so overt as that of Madame Merle and Gilbert Osmond, who had conspired against Isabel. Kate Croy and Merton Densher are not necessarily villains; they are provided with the excuse that they are making Milly happy in allowing her to believe in Densher's devotion to her during the few short days or months left to her. Milly's realm of which she is the fairy princess is real only to her, and surely the kindest act is to join in the game, especially as in that way the winning is only a matter of waiting for the natural death of the victim. The evil in Densher is perhaps only weakness of self-deception, but that in Kate is all the more intense for the one last suspicion that she too is merely being kind to her friend. Such things are relative; there is no final moral scale for such values. James himself uses the figures of windows and balconies from which one may dispassionately observe the princess and her friends. Milly is seen, not seeing, but she appears in so many and such oblique lights that the full intensity of her tragedy is forever printed on the mind. Subtly the central symbol of the story—starting as the Dove —becomes the Wings. It is not that Milly is a helpless and beautiful creature victimized by the events and people of her life; she has wings on which she can soar. The tragedy lies in the end of flight.

In many ways the weaving of the intricate pattern of Milly's life and death is the culmination of James's art—certainly if that art be measured in sensibility. But he himself thought *The Ambassadors* a finer work, and most of his critics seem to agree. Written on a less moving and essentially comic theme, it engages the sympathies of both writer and reader less intensely, but it leaves a more satisfying sense of completion. Here is a pattern of narrative in which there is no flaw. From the moment when Lambert Strether, who is to rescue Chad Newsom from the wiles of a French adventuress, meets his confidante Maria Gostrey at Chester and discusses with her the mission which has brought him to Europe, until that of his parting from her, his mission fulfilled in a way that he had not suspected, the story never swerves from its perfect roundness of architectural structure. This is the old theme again, the naïve American in conflict with the complex values of European society, but, in Strether, James has at last found an American who, like himself, is subtle enough to experience a complete spiritual enlightenment. Because the issue is so clearly a conflict of values in which the author is the wholly dispassionate observer, the comic spirit controls the action from start to finish. By recapturing the spirit of his own youth when he brought his bride on a honeymoon visit to Paris, Strether learns to value before it is too late the vibrancy of life that Madame de Vionnet has brought to the errant Chad Newsom. Instead of being the Ambassador from Woollett, Massachusetts, charged by Chad's mother to bring him safely home, he becomes the object of a second mission by the brashly American Pococks of whom there is no danger of conversion. Thus Strether, who until now has looked upon the central situation of Chad's affair as through many windows, moves into the center by acquiring someone through whose eyes he can himself be seen. As the concentric circles of the plot pattern are drawn inward to the vibrant core of meaning, other circles are provided on the outer edges which Strether had at first occupied. It is the image of the stone tossed into the pond, but now in reverse: the movement is steadily toward, rather than away from, the center.

"The business of my tale," said James in his later preface, "is just my demonstration of this process of vision." Nothing happens except that Strether learns by at least seeing that it is now too late for him to live. His detachment completes the perspective view of his creator. For once, and finally, James had written a tale which is all pattern and is not confused by the necessity of action.

Never again did he achieve so satisfactory an illustration of his theory of fiction. *The Golden Bowl*, his next major work, is provided with as neat an arrangement of human relationships as one could ask for, and the Bowl gives symbolic expression both to the roundness of that little world and to the flaw that destroys it; but the novel lacks the gay irony of its predecessor, and the mechanisms of its structure are more obvious. Only in some of his short stories, like "The Jolly Corner" or "The Beast in the Jungle," did James again reach the level of his purest art. As so often, his success in these tales resulted from a use of his own repressed experience—here the fear of meeting a second phase of his own personality some-how embodied in another—and from treating it with complete objectivity. The most self-centered and subjective of all American writers of fiction had—like the similarly introspec-tive poet of Amherst—succeeded in an art of total revelation through perfect workmanship. Henry James and Emily Dick-inson had demonstrated that the exploration of the individual consciousness could reveal the reality of the inner life as ef-fectively as Howells and Mark Twain had disclosed the reality of the world about them. The back-trail of rejection had led into the heart of the American experience.

CHAPTER IX

A PROBLEM IN DYNAMICS

Adams, Norris, Robinson

THE decade of the 1890's was one of sudden and swift cultural change. Whether or not there is validity in the superstition that the end of a century actually marks the end of an era in the affairs of men, the rule seems for once to apply. In this *fin de siècle* the forces which had shaped the Continental Nation found their first important literary expression, just as, a century earlier, the surge of nationalism that followed the Revolution had become a literary as well as a political and economic movement.

During the early years of this decade the last of the nineteenth century Titans died, Lowell and Melville in 1891, Whitman and Whittier in 1892, leaving no survivor of the romantic movement, for Bryant, Longfellow, and Emerson had died a decade earlier, and Cooper, Irving, Poe, Thoreau, and Hawthorne at mid-century. There was a genuine sense of literary void as the control which these masters had exercised over the ideas and forms of literature passed to the hands of seemingly lesser men or of leaders who could not discover a way to lead. Howells never quite got over the feeling that he was inadequately filling the role of Lowell, Mark Twain offended rather than amused the aging prophets when he tried to lighten the solemnity of the famous Whittier Day dinner by buffoonery, Henry James settled permanently and comfortably out of immediate reach in London, and the lesser poets and critics of New York and Boston—Aldrich, Stedman, Gilder, Stoddard —were willing to admit that theirs was the level plain after the descent from the mountains.

The literary movement which rose to combat this dying romanticism began to play a more vigorous role in the middle nineties than it had in earlier years. Finding its roots in the realism which had attempted to absorb and to portray the expansive forces in the new nation, it gained philosophical depth from the theories of the new evolutionary science, understanding of the human consciousness from the advances in the infant science of psychology, social significance from the makers of systems of society who followed the Industrial Revolution wherever it went, and encouragement from a more intimate knowledge of contemporary French, German, Russian, and other Continental European literatures.

The term "naturalism" is far too limited to describe the new intellectual and literary movements which American writers of the nineties began to share with these Europeans. It was the still fumbling attempt to discover adequate ways of giving expression to views of the universe and of human destiny which were everywhere supplanting the views of the Enlightenment. The Newtonian universe of limited forces and systematic organization, and the Lockean universe of the rational mind, were being hard pushed by concepts of a less logical and less self-determined Man. British and European thinkers like Darwin, Marx, and Freud were formulating theories of nature and human nature which would before long take the place in the general mind of those of Newton, Adam

Smith, Rousseau, and Locke. American literature had before this shared with the literatures of other nations a passionate return to Nature; Wordsworth, Goethe, and Emerson were all naturalists in this sense. In the nineties the call for a return to Nature was again sounded, but agreed ideas about Nature were changed. A machine, ruthless and inhuman, had displaced the mountains and ivy-covered ruins upon which a poet could impose his ideas of moral order. Man was being pushed out of the center of the biological world, and his will was being taken from him by such theories as that of natural selection, economic determinism, and subconscious rather than conscious motivation.

The ingrained optimism of the American character and the close link between basic democratic-agrarian theory and ideas of perfectibility and progress that had guided the growth of American society made the acceptance of these new ideas less easy to Americans than to Europeans. The concepts of the romantic era persisted almost to the end of the century and gave the trends toward social realism and psychological determinism a tough battle. Howells, Mark Twain, and other realists had, by 1890, succeeded in their demand for a fresh and unprejudiced examination of the facts of American life, and a more skeptical and scientific view of personality was appearing in the novels of James and the poems of Emily Dickinson. As literature undertook its normal task of giving expression to life, it was inevitably plunged into an era of experimentation and uncertainty. The literary movement of the nineties was an attempt on the part of a new group of American writers to describe life in general and life in America as it appeared to the dispassionate eye of the new science.

One important by-product of this movement was a close

bond between American and Continental European writers and a loosening of the bond with England. Most of the influential popularizers of the new science, like Spencer and Huxley, were British and were early heard and read by impressionable Americans like Mark Twain, Bellamy, Howells, and Garland, but British writers of fiction and poetry like Hardy were not influenced as deeply or as soon by the new ideas as were such Continental writers as Dostoevski, Zola, or Hauptmann. Whereas Longfellow and Lowell read the romantic and idealistic poets and dramatists of France and Spain, Howells, James, and Mark Twain early discovered Turgenev and Tolstoi, Balzac and Zola, Marx and Nietzsche. In his essay on the experimental novel (1880), Zola presented the most germinal single idea to be absorbed by American writers of the *fin de siècle:* the belief that the exact methods of experimental physical science can and should be applied by the writer to the analysis of society and the individual. The essay itself was probably not read by many, if any, Americans, but Zola's attempts to apply his theory to his own fiction were well known to Norris, Crane, Dreiser, and many others. Through this new naturalism American literature was to become an important part of world literature in the next few decades. By supplying a core of fundamental ideas about God, man, society, and nature, it served to focus the second renaissance in American literature as transcendentalism and the romantic philosophy had served the first.

– 2 –

The American response to the ferment of the era was vigorous and practical. To a people accustomed to translating thought into action quickly, the only need was for a working formula once the philosophical doctrine had been made generally known. In William James they were offered a philosopher who laid the foundations of modern psychology by applying a practical methodology to the quest for truth; in Edward Bellamy, a sociologist who devised a system for controlling capitalism through social morality; and in Henry Adams, a historian who sought to explain the American tradition quite scientifically as a phase of cosmic evolution. These were only a few of the many thinkers in all fields of knowledge who appeared between 1885 and 1895 to resolve the dilemma of modern man into a working formula of social behavior. Learned societies sprang up on all sides to bring together scholars in the various fields of history, literature, economics, and physics in the common hope of reducing all knowledge to ascertainable fact by the use of experimental techniques. It was the great day of science.

American philosophy had never been abstruse. The early Puritans had found ways of putting God's will to work on the job of clearing a wilderness and building cities, and the nineteenth century liberals and transcendentalists had stressed experience rather than metaphysics as the measure of truth. Benjamin Franklin rather than Jonathan Edwards set the pattern of the American mind with a philosophy that was later to be known as pragmatism, even though the term itself was not invented for a hundred and more years, and Emerson's Over-Soul became finally little more than a moral sentiment committed to good action. The philosophy of Pragmatism, as Henry's brother William James developed it, was a revolt against the rationalists. Frankly anti-intellectual, it urged a "looking away from first things, principles, 'categories,' supposed necessities; and of looking toward last things, fruits, consequences, facts." William James defined but did not invent it when he declared that "ideas (which themselves are but part of our experience) become true just in so far as they help us to get into satisfactory relationship with other parts of our experience." The open universe thus proposed gave a sense of release to the open mind; here was the ultimate statement of the right of the individual to push the frontiers of thought as far as they would go.

Pragmatism opened the door for the development of experimental psychology, and William James led the way. If experience is the only measure of truth, science can proceed to a laboratory analysis of human conduct without more ado. During his own mental "crisis" of 1870, James learned to accept the terms of empirical science as a substitute for the religious mysticism of his father and set to work to devote the remainder of his long life to the study of human motivation. In 1876 he set up the first American laboratory of psychology at Harvard, and in 1890 he published his definitive work *The Principles of Psychology*. In 1896 he delivered his lecture on "The Will to Believe" at Yale, and in 1902 he issued his lectures on *The Varieties of Religious Experience*. Although not himself a part of the so-called "Social Gospel" movement, James did more perhaps than any other American thinker to sanction the secularization of religion and the growth of organized social idealism which found concrete expression in such reforms as the Single Tax movement, fathered by Henry George, and the Nationalist movement that developed from Bellamy's social Utopia, *Looking Backward: 2000–1887* (1888). The major contribution of James's philosophy lay in its success in calling a moratorium in the clash between traditional religious dogmatism and the new science during a period of rapid intellectual and cultural change.

The American faith in social reform by evolution rather

than by revolution surged forward to meet the new problems. Always hospitable to Utopian dreamers like the British Robert Owen and the French François Fourier, American thinkers from Franklin to Emerson had thrown the weight of their sympathies to the thousands of experiments in living that had formed Utopian communities in the backwoods from the earliest colonial days. Most of these experiments did not find expression in books and were forgotten when the good will that founded them was exhausted, but toward the end of the century there came a change in the movement. With the closing of the frontier, Americans began to write rather than to live their social dreams, and a kind of fiction that can be traced back through Sir Thomas More's *Utopia* to Plato's *Republic* became epidemic. Of these books, *Looking Backward* is the best, both as a structure of social thinking and as an imaginative work.

Like James, Bellamy accepted the will to power, the materialism, and the pragmatic method of the new science without giving up the traditional American faith in human integrity and perfectibility. Patterned in method closely on the *Republic*, Bellamy's American urban Utopia of the year 2000 was an idealization of industrial capitalism, in which man's sense of social responsibility was seen to control and organize the primal urge toward an extension of being. The democratic form of state capitalism that he allowed his young Bostonian to discover by falling asleep and projecting himself more than a century into the future was realized in many essential respects by the later reforms of the New Deal. By 1950 the Government had come to resemble closely the Great Trust that Bellamy saw as the resolution of conflict in a competitive society, slums were fading into housing projects as he proposed, and many of his self-imposed controls on economic exploitation had become law.

It would carry this account too far afield to explore other applications of the empirical method to the problems of American living as science moved into scholarship, education, government, religion, and all other departments of American life. In literature it gave immense support to the methods and ideals of the realists at the same time that it presented the problem of human destiny in forms that classic theories of comedy and tragedy could not resolve. The times needed a literary man who could at least state the issues of the new order both in human and in cosmic terms.

The historian Henry Adams (1838–1918) inconspicuously offered himself in this role.

History in the hands of the major American historians had become largely a narrative art. Although they made use of documents, the Brahmin Prescott, Motley, Parkman, and Bancroft lacked the philosophical depth and scientific thoroughness of their German contemporaries. The essential difference between them and Adams was that they wished to tell a story in narrative perspective, he to solve a problem in civilization by analyzing it at one point in depth. His problem was to find out just what makes democracy work and to expose its flaws together with its virtues; his point of attack was the period of Jefferson and Madison which lay between that of his grandfather, John Quincy Adams, and that of his great-grandfather, the second President John Adams.

Adams's preparation for his work seemed accidental—and probably was in part—but it could scarcely have been more specific or thorough. As a younger son in the Adams dynasty, he was brought up on mountains of family papers. After graduation from Harvard, he was sent to Germany, where he pretends to have learned only the language, but later evidence in his work belies his modesty. As his father's secretary, he spent the Civil War period in the American Embassy in London and for the first time learned about government and diplomacy from the inside, although as a spectator. Short of stature and retiring of temperament, he early chose the career of journalism in lieu of politics or law, but on the highest possible level. Writing for the newspapers and the quarterlies was for him a way of moving men and nations, a kind of statesmanship once removed from action, a form of teaching in which mankind was the pupil. An avid reader, he knew his Gibbon and his Michelet, but he found them wanting in scientific method. Inspired by his friend, the geologist Clarence King, he studied Comte and Lyell, Darwin and Marx, to find out whether history could be a science as well as an art, and decided that it could be both although no one had yet demonstrated the way. If he could understand fully the laws behind the documents in the formative period of the Republic, he could demonstrate a new principle of historiography as well as expose the causes of a great historical event. To this end he devoted his life.

The careful reader of Adams is not misled by his claim to failure. He thought of his seven years of teaching at Harvard as an interruption, but he was a brilliant success at inspiring young men, and in doing so he humanized himself. His editing and writing for the *North American*, the *Nation*, and other journals was largely anonymous, but when his essays were collected by himself and others, they revealed a steady progress in method, style, and understanding. By the time he and his wife settled in Washington, D.C., in 1877 to be near the papers in the State Department, he was ready for his great task. Twelve years later, the nine-volume history of sixteen American years was completed and published.

Ostensibly a factual account of the administrations of Jefferson and Madison, it is actually an analysis, on the broadest possible scale, of the rise of a new form of human society to a position of power in the Western world and of the consequences of that shift of power. His speculations on the origins and consequence of democracy reach backward to the earliest colonial times and forward past his own day into the immediate future. Incidentally, in telling of America's absorption of the rights and dreams of large segments of the British and French colonial empires, he gives as good an account of the fall of Napoleonic power and of the reshaping of British imperial policy as can be found in any history. His book deserves a place beside De Tocqueville and Lord Bryce among the definitive analyses of the democratic system, but it is unique in that it is the only one to proceed from the inside of the problem outward. And he documents an idea which he was to repeat many times in the voice of a prophet: that the powers of the future would be Russia and the United States.

Meanwhile tragedy had struck home for him in the suicide of his wife. Speculations as to the reason are relevant only as they suggest the motives for a basic shift in Adams's hopes and plans. The blow fell as he was working on the last of four sections of his history, and he had to push himself to complete it. Suddenly he lost all the incentive toward a masterwork, deliberately obscured its plan and structure, offered it with sufficient apologies to prevent the public's interest, and took off for the South Seas with his artist friend John La Farge.

The historians were not fooled. They recommended him for honorary degrees and made him president of their national association, but no one accepted his challenge to write the history of the United States as proof or disproof of the scientific laws which he had illustrated by a case study rather than explicitly expounded. "The scientific interest in American history [was] centered in the national character, and in the workings of a society destined to become vast, in which individuals were important chiefly as types." Jefferson, the man of ideas and will, saw his policies apparently fail whereas Madison, by following the drift of events, came out at the end with a kind of victory. The people were in a mood of conquest and expansion because they had the need and the resources for a larger life. The national character had been shaped by a common experience, and Henry Adams, historian and student of society, had only to discover and reveal the laws of mind and matter which had somehow brought this about. In doing so, he joined the labors of the scientific historian to those of the artist. The *History* was, in spite of its author's successful attempt to obscure the fact, an organic work of art because it took its form and structure from the laws of nature scientifically discovered and revealed. It was rational, cold, and ruthless in its methods and conclusions. It remained largely unread—the first definitive work by an American in the new naturalism.

— 3 —

The change in Adams in 1885 was a release of his emotional energies and his imagination from the stern discipline to which he had subjected them in his role as self-appointed pioneer in scientific history. It was possible partly because the work was done—together with its satellites, the lives of Albert Gallatin and John Randolph and the lost life of Aaron Burr—but it was immediately brought about by the shock of his wife's death. Never again, except for one brief time on the island of Tahiti, did he attempt to write history. Just when he thought he had put history into his past, an intimacy with the once reigning family of the tiny distant island gave him in capsule form an illustration of the historical process that he had been trying to understand in his own family and nation. The wise old "Chiefess" (whom he persuaded to tell her memories of former greatness) was a kind of Henry Adams, the last of a once powerful family; and the involvement of this Pacific isle in the clash of empires was another illustration of the march of forces over which the individual could exercise no control. Published "ultimisso privately," in a few copies only, the book was his farewell to his first profession.

He now became the philosopher of history, the teacher of teachers. From events he turned to causes, from record to meditation. To the casual observer, he lost his sense of direction and became a mere connoisseur of arts and ideas, but behind the façade of failure was a new and deeper purpose. His own efforts to relate history to some organic process in the evolution of man's destiny had not been understood. The first task was to help the historians face their own problem: to discover and apply to science what had become little more than a narrative art. The change was one of medium rather than of basic purpose, but it required an increased freedom for the insights that underlie reason, a release of the naturalist, the mystic, the artist, who had been held in such stern control.

In his presidential address to the American Historical Association in 1894, he made his position clear: historians must renounce their past generalizations as inapplicable to the modern world; if they fail to create a working generalization of their own, they will be forced to accept that of the pessimists whom physical science was already spawning. While warning against the defeatism of contemporary thought, he was calling for what he could not himself produce, a formula by which man could retain his dominant place in the universe.

The human problems which concerned him most had already found expression in the anonymous novels, *Democracy* (1880) and *Esther* (1884), both of them about women whose intuitive curiosity led them to study the sources of human power, the one in the politics and society of democracy, the other in the realms of scientific and religious speculation and of art. When tragedy struck home to him the next year, his reaction was first stoical silence, then a slow beginning of the long preparation for the two great privately printed works, *Mont-Saint-Michel and Chartres* (1904) and *The Education of Henry Adams* (1907), and a lesser work, *A Letter to American Teachers of History* (1910), which was to serve as a binder for the other two. Written in a tone of the elder teacher who had retired from active life and who was now privileged to meditate idly on problems which for him no longer demanded solution, this single work in three parts stated the basic problem of modern man in terms so deep and broad that a new symbolism had to be constructed. Adams laid the foundations for modern literature even more than for modern history by asking questions with which literature alone was competent to deal. He succeeded where others who were more openly committed to literary art, like Hamlin Garland and Frank Norris, were to fail; he translated the new naturalism into meaningful forms of disciplined art.

A decade of rest and travel with congenial companions like the artist John La Farge, his old student Henry Cabot Lodge, and his three closest friends Elizabeth Cameron, Clarence King, and John Hay, was a necessary preliminary; another decade of secret and silent meditation and writing was an inevitable consequence. Before his death, the *Chartres* (1913) was revised and given to the public; immediately after (1918), Lodge issued the *Education* as a miscalled autobiography; and a year later his brother Brooks Adams collected his essays on the philosophy of history into a garbled volume to which he assigned the misleading title *The Degradation of the Democratic Dogma* (1919). A new generation of young men who, like Henry Adams, felt themselves to be balanced precariously between a dead past and an unborn future turned to him for wisdom and guidance. Through this "lost generation" he was finally heard.

The secret of Adams's final triumph as a man of letters lay in his ability to reconcile reality and myth by the use of symbols. He had reached the conclusion that "chaos was the law of nature; order the dream of man," but neither law nor dream could be rejected. Unwilling to accept the way of revealed religion, he could nevertheless admit that man had realized his dream of order most successfully in the system and ritual of an organized church. In their worship of the Virgin, the builders of the great cathedrals of Europe had achieved a unity of feeling and thought which the modern world had apparently lost.

Mont-Saint-Michel and Chartres is ostensibly a travel essay for young girls, the nieces with whom he had visited the cathedrals and the "nieces in wishes" who alone would have the intuition to understand him. In mood of airy humor, the "Uncle" takes his charges on a pilgrimage to places forever sacred, in which mankind had discovered all hope and belief. Approaching the century of purest faith, 1150–1250, and its shrine at Chartres, through St. Michael's earlier church on the Norman isle and the songs of the minstrels, Adams leads his reader to the symbol and the fact of the Virgin in whom an age had for once realized the unity which is the dream of all men of all times. No student of architecture could describe the pointed arches, the stained-glass windows, the statues standing silently in their niches, with greater care and comprehension than does this elderly tourist. When the travelers leave the sacred portal, they have been converted not to the faith that built the church, but to the church itself as a symbol of man's dream. The realization is of art rather than of religion. With a chuckle, the skeptic-mystic leads his charges to the library for a study of the scholastic philosophers who had given expression in words to this simple and steady cosmic view: Abélard, St. Francis, and the greatest architect of them all, Thomas Aquinas, who had reconciled Aristotle and the Christian faith. Here, he seems to say, is unity discovered and then lost; how can it be regained? Surely not in reason, for the Virgin was the perfection of irrationality; not in renunciation, for the Virgin was the mother of man, the intercessor for his sins; not in life in another world, but in this. Mary represented the force that could never be reasoned away or extinguished by the machine; she was man's protest against fate.

The *Education* was written for the young men who might perhaps learn a riper wisdom from the experience of this forgotten historian. If they were to discover the new law of history that would make it a science, they must understand their own time and extract from it a working generalization. All that the physicists themselves could offer was a machine, exhibited at the Chicago Fair in 1893, which could generate power forever, but which, if one were to believe Lord Kelvin, was merely extracting energy from matter in order to dissipate it. The Dynamo offered a kind of unity, but it was the unity of disintegration. Was this the law which the historian must learn to obey and to interpret?

There was a man, Henry Adams, who had been born in an older world of illusions but who had survived, fossil-like, into this frightening new one of relentless and inhuman force. Perhaps by retracing with him the steps in his "education," the young man of the twentieth century might profit by his mistakes and discover the central meaning of the new dispensation. In this way he might hope to avoid the pessimism and mechanism which seemed to be closing in.

The Uncle was not quite so gay on this second pilgrimage because in his heart he preferred the society of his nieces, but he undertook it with as light a spirit as he could muster. In making of himself a symbol, he could at least escape from the limits of a personal view and could thus identify himself with the future. His past could then be the past of everyone who, as an American and a democrat, and as a lay scientist and amateur philosopher, had with him lived through the most rapid changes that any civilization had yet experienced. The new law of unity might not be found, but the persistence of man's need for such a law could be demonstrated by his very unwillingness to become reconciled to failure.

The comic and ironic manner of these twin essays in destiny

is deceptive of their depth and wisdom, for the reading of life which they together present is that of tragedy rather than of comedy. All is presented and nothing resolved. When a work of art has taught man again the paradox of life on his earth and in his time without costing him his sense of the value in living, it has won a place among the epics and comedies and tragedies that comprise the literature of the world. Adams's masterwork did just this at the dawn of a new century and of a new era in man's experience. All that there remained for him to do was to write his *Letter* to his fellow historians; but none of them were listening. Only the young men heard.

– 4 –

Whether or not Adams's final works constitute a single literary masterpiece may remain a matter for discussion. The author himself considered them unfinished, and his editors and critics have done much to diffuse any single important meaning they may have had. But there can be little doubt that their structure of symbols stands at the beginning of the movement in thought and culture which gave force and form to the second American literary renaissance. Through his understanding and accepting of the description of the universe presented by mathematical physics and evolutionary biology, Adams laid his foundations firmly in the new naturalism which was stirring the literatures of Europe to fresh creative effort. His skepticism helped him to develop what Eliot was later to call the "objective correlative" to his experience and through it to achieve expression for the modern man in art at least a generation before American writers in any numbers succeeded in following him.

Meanwhile the new movement developed in a less rarefied

atmosphere, and its prophet was a simpler man than the hermit-scholar. In 1891 Hamlin Garland, of Wisconsin and Iowa, who had gone East as a young man, offered his *Main-Travelled Roads*, a collection of grim tales of the failure of the frontier hope. The story which lay behind these unadorned sketches of actual life was told later in *A Son of the Middle Border* (1917) and their literary intention described in *Crumbling Idols* (1894). In the faltering insights of this son of the prairie, American naturalism found its first unqualified statement and illustration in fiction. The doctrine of realism had descended from the sunny slopes of Howells and Harte and Eggleston, through the somber and factual plays of James A. Herne and Bronson Howard and such uncompromising novels as *The Story of a Country Town* (1883) by E. W. Howe, *Zury: The Meanest Man in Spring County* (1887) by Joseph Kirkland, and *The Damnation of Theron Ware* (1896) by Harold Frederic, to a level of realism which was a reading of life as well as a literary method. Pessimism was making its inroads without benefit of fresh insights or more flexible methods of expression. Creative genius was needed rather than honest mediocrity.

For a moment it looked as though the needed spark might be supplied by Frank Norris, Stephen Crane, or Jack London, three fiction writers of courage and power. All three were men of striking literary gifts who opened themselves to the influences of the new ideas about Nature, Man, and Art which were abroad. All wrote vigorous and provocative novels and short stories, but no one of them finally succeeded, as Dreiser did later, in accepting the limitations as well as the opportunities of the new naturalism and with its aid developing a consistent purpose and method in fiction.

Because of his buoyancy and energy, Frank Norris (1870–1902) is perhaps the most appealing of the three. In his essays collected as *The Responsibilities of the Novelist* (1903), he leads the way toward new powers, but at the same time he reveals his own confusion when he advocates a fiction which "proves something, draws conclusions from a whole congeries of forces, social tendencies, race impulses, devotes itself not to a study of men but of man." Three such forces were strongly at work in his imagination: an inheritance of the conventional ideals of simple and literal realism as Howells conceived it, a belief in the raw power of primitive nature probably derived from Nietzsche, and an ideal for a reformed social order in which a vague religious revelation would miraculously correct without destroying the system of American democracy. He was further torn by an impulse to follow new paths and by a desire to reach a popular audience through magazines that were wholly unsympathetic to most of the experiments he wished to try. His quandary is best illustrated by the lightly autobiographical romance *Blix* (1899) in which the dilettante hero is awakened to serious literary effort by the love of a woman of the new type—independent in mind and heart without losing a kind of Gibson-girl charm—and the realization that writing must honestly express the life that he knows. His own dilettantism had had its day in the society of art students in Paris and in the neo-Bohemian circles of San Francisco, but it was at Harvard under Lewis Gates that he read Zola and wrote his first outright "experimental" novel *McTeague*, not published until 1899. This story of a crude, animal-like dentist and of his violent impulses and ugly surroundings is told with the honesty and force of Zola's tales of the Paris slums. Nothing like it had ever been heard of before in American literature; but much that was like it would follow.

Norris's most impressive work was the prose epic *The Octopus* (1901), the first of a proposed trilogy which was to follow the Wheat, symbol of the life force, from its planting in the Western plains to its export to starving Europeans. Only two of the three parts were written, because their author died before undertaking the final novel which was to have been called *The Wolf*. The second, *The Pit* (1903), built on the theme of anarchic speculation on the Chicago grain market, lacks much of the gusto and sweep of the first. But in *The Octopus* Norris gave all he had. Adopting a symbolism which anticipated that of the Virgin and the Dynamo of Adams, he told the story of battles between the wheat growers of the San Joaquin Valley of California and the monopolistic Southern Pacific Railroad as a symbolic struggle between the primitive force of fertile Earth and the non-organic force of the machine. When he allows himself the luxury of a complete naturalistic fatalism, his treatment of this elemental conflict is superb, but his inner censor too often intervenes and his most impassioned passages tend to dissipate into vague religious mysticism. Even so, *The Octopus* opened the way to a new kind of primitive epic that later writers such as Wolfe and Steinbeck were to develop. The most ambitious of American novels up to its time (with the exception of *Moby-Dick*), its very overreaching of its author's limitations makes it historically important.

The work of Stephen Crane (1871–1900) is also experimental, but, unlike Norris and perhaps because his scope was deliberately more restricted, Crane succeeded in producing a few short tales and novels which have the perfection of classics. There is no finer short novel in English than *The Red Badge of Courage* (1895) or short story than "The Open Boat" or "The Blue Hotel." In them the essence of fear is distilled as the basic motive for conduct, and the irrational behavior of men is explained by the ruthless and inevitable action of primitive nature. Because at the crisis in his art Crane commits himself to the new determinism, he can devote his entire creative power to the act of expression; there is no philosophical wavering. Like Norris, he knew the paintings and painters of the impressionist school, and he had doubtless read at least some of the novels of Zola and Tolstoi, although he was inclined to deny all influences. Painting his word pictures with the bright colors and mobile forms of the companion art, he released into expression much of reality of the mind which was unknown to Howells, sensed vaguely by Mark Twain, and recognized only to be tortuously rationalized by Henry James. Somewhere, somehow, Crane had felt the force of analytical psychology before anyone had appeared to formulate its principles. The boy-hero of *The Red Badge of Courage* is swept into battle, away from it, and back to self-conquest by forces deep inside himself over which he has no conscious control, and the strong oiler who should have been the one to survive the catastrophe of "The Open Boat" is the only one to perish. Whether in external nature or in the subconscious, the primitive force of organic life directs the petty actions of individual men.

Diffused in other stories and finally lost in an effort to court the public, Crane's mastery of theme and form in his early and best work was in the tradition of Poe and Hawthorne and Ambrose Bierce rather than in that of Whitman and Norris. As his discipline was derived from art rather than from experience, it did not develop beyond its first sharp distillation, and the forces released so briefly into expression were soon turned inward again to consume the artist himself. Some twenty short stories and one other novel, *Maggie: A Girl of the Streets* (1892), bear the imprint of genius and together provide much of the direction and method of such writers as Hemingway, Faulkner, and others who were not to appear for at least another quarter-century.

The pitfalls of naturalism as well as its powers are apparent in the failures of these two to develop full stature as artists, but they are more fully revealed in the tempestuous career of Jack London (1876–1916), who achieved the popularity that both Norris and Crane struggled for, but, like them, burned himself out with the fire of his own violence. Accepting even more fully than Norris the Nietzschean view of the primitive egotism of man and the ruthless law of survival under which he operates in a Darwinian universe, London was at his best in *The Call of the Wild* (1903), where his hero was animal, uncomplicated by the web of civilization, and free to respond to the forces of nature which could make him whole. When he tried to apply these simple biological laws to the problems of society, as he did in telling his own story in *Martin Eden* (1909), or that of the clash of capital and labor in *The Iron Heel* (1907), the theories underlying his narrative structure revealed too many contradictions to allow a pure art like that of Stephen Crane at his best. The old faith in the perfectibility of man and the new belief in his helplessness before an all-consuming natural law could not exist together; nor could a biological urge to power be reconciled to an almost religious faith in the Marxian doctrine of the supremacy of the social state. By accepting all the new radicalism with uncritical enthusiasm, London put power into his tales but lost control of the forces he had unleashed. In *Martin Eden*, he predicted his own suicide as he successfully analyzed its inescapable causes. Naturalism still was an imperfect instrument of art.

– 5 –

The effort at the turn of the century to remake poetry in the image of science was milder than the similar trend in fiction, and as a result the movement was less dramatic and less immediately influential. When E. C. Stedman assembled *An American Anthology* in 1900, he included the work of such writers as Dickinson, Lanier, Crane, Robinson, and Moody without recognizing in them a movement which was to disturb the idyllic calm of such traditionalists as Aldrich, Stoddard, Taylor, and himself.

The problem is most clearly revealed in the poetry and critical theory of Sidney Lanier (1842–1881), whose *The Science of English Verse* (1880) is the first full acceptance of a change in the theory underlying American poetry after Whitman. Picking up the argument advanced by Poe in his essays on "The Philosophy of Composition" and "The Poetic Principle," Lanier states boldly that "the term 'verse' denotes a set of specifically related sounds." He thus limits his argument, as Poe did not succeed in doing, to the level of technique. Whatever may be said of its meaning, the form of poetry could be reduced to a science (that is, broken down into fixed units that would lend themselves to analysis and classification) by treating it wholly as sound: heard, seen, or imagined. This the art of music had already done in measuring the quantity, quality, pitch, and tone of the sounds with which it deals; by adapting these terms, together with the established system of musical notation, poetry could bring itself into line with physical science.

Lanier was the youngest of the Southern poets who had followed Poe—Simms, Chivers, Timrod—and he was the only one effectively to survive the Civil War. Broken in health by his four months of imprisonment at Point Lookout, and struggling against poverty, he devoted the few years remaining to him after the war to music (he was first flutist of the Peabody Symphony Orchestra of Baltimore), to the study of literature (he became, in 1879, lecturer in English literature at the Johns Hopkins University), and to the writing of poetry (he published his first collection in 1877).

Lanier made himself almost unique among the poets of his day by reaching beyond the influence of the British Romantic poets to the Elizabethans—Sidney, Puttenham, Spenser—for his theory and inspiration in poetry. No better evidence of the limitation of his system could be found than his own later verse which is musically volatile and impressive while lacking in clear-cut images and ideas. Like many another theorist, he disappoints when he tries to practice, but he did more than anyone else of his day to break down the popular verse of the surviving idealists and to prepare for a fresh study of the exacting laws of poetic composition. Later American poets owe him more than they care to admit.

Lanier was not troubled by the philosophical doubts that Darwinian science cast over many poets. His tone of melancholy was personal—a result of his struggle with illness—whereas that of William Vaughn Moody (1869–1910) was rooted in doubt and disillusionment. In his unfinished trilogy *The Masque of Judgment* (1900), *The Fire-Bringer* (1904),

and *The Death of Eve* (1912), this teacher-poet of the new
University of Chicago undertook to set forth in verse-drama
the central problem of humanity: the rebellion of man against
God and the final resolution of mortal conflict in moral idealism. Although in his prose plays *The Great Divide* (1906) and
The Faith Healer (1909) he dealt with problems of his time,
Moody's idealism looked backward rather than forward, and
his call was for a return to the old values and solutions rather
than for an honest confronting of the problems of the world
of science and the machine.

It was rather in Edwin Arlington Robinson (1869–1935)
that the *fin de siècle* found its authentic poetic voice. Heir to
the idealism of Emerson and the skepticism of Dickinson, this
dour New Englander looked about him in his native Gardiner,
Maine, and learned to find poetry in the lives of his fellow
townsmen. His Tilbury Town anticipated by many years the
Winesburg, Ohio, of Sherwood Anderson and the Gopher
Prairie, Minnesota, of Sinclair Lewis as a capsule of human
experience. When *The Torrent and The Night Before* (1896)
was reprinted as *The Children of the Night* in the next year,
Robinson found himself the butt of those critics who believed
with Stedman that ideal beauty and truth were the sole materials of poetry. His quiet rebellion gave to American poetry
an idiom that was in the native grain, and his leadership in the
new movement was immediately assured. His Richard Cory
who had everything but who shot himself, his Luke Havergal
whose ruined life could only "go to the Western gate," and
his Cliff Klingenhagen who won happiness by choosing the
glass of wormwood are but three of a gallery of simple folk
through whom Robinson sought

> "in hate's polluted self-defense
> Throbbing, the pulse, the divine heart of man."

Robinson's inheritance of New England transcendentalism is revealed in his unswerving belief in "the light"; his kinship with the age of doubt in his failure to find the light except in the west, in the setting sun and the twilight. He too looked always toward the western gate. In *The Man Against the Sky* (1916), he stated at once his total reading of life and with it won his place in American poetry. Each man is measured by his own stature against the evening sky, but that he has learned to face death as annihilation is his strength. Without hope, he stands firm in what he knows and has. In simple words and blunt but flowing rhythm, the poet repeated his pragmatic solution to life's riddle until he was heard. Turning to the Arthurian cycle, he stripped it of its traditional romance and gave an honest and realistic version of the loves and doubts and tragedies of *Merlin* (1917), *Lancelot* (1920), and *Tristram* (1927). In longer poems which verge on the melodramatic, he examined in similar vein the dark substratum of modern consciousness: *Cavender's House* (1929), *The Glory of the Nightingales* (1930), and *Matthias at the Door* (1931). Finally, he took the theme of *Dionysus in Doubt* (1925)—that the materialism and standardization of modern life is hostile to the transcendental self—and made of it a drama of complex symbolism in *King Jasper* (1935). With Henry Adams, Robinson rescued from the collapse of nineteenth century idealism his undying faith in humanity and, thus fortified, rode out to meet the dragon of modern scientific determinism.

The literary movement of the nineties had, at the turn

of the century, brought the American face to face with the age of science. As industry herded him from the farms where he was responsible to the weather and the earth into cities where he took his orders from steam and electric power, wheels and cogs, even the average unthinking man was forced to some sort of revaluation of his basic concepts and values.

Twentieth century American literature became a major force in the whole culture of Western Europe because the experience of this change was so much more dramatic in the violence of America's rapid growth than it was elsewhere. Europeans were finally to see in the writings of mid-twentieth century Americans the clear-cut and forceful expression of their own experiences and ideas; but in the 1890's the process of cultural change was not yet completed, the insights for its understanding not yet discovered, and the techniques for its expression in any of the forms of art not yet developed. The *fin de siècle* showed only a hint of what was to come; European literatures—particularly the French and the Russian—were still leading the way.

CHAPTER X

SECOND RENAISSANCE

Dreiser, Frost

SOMETIME between 1910 and 1920 American literature "came of age." The actual moment of maturity might be set at 1912, or 1916, when one or another event could serve as symbol for the putting away of nineteenth century forms, ideas, and habits. A dramatic suddenness in the cultural revolution released the novels of Theodore Dreiser from censorship, provided in *Poetry*, the *Dial*, *Smart Set*, and *Seven Arts*, a ready public for a pent-up flood of experimental poetry and prose, and in the Provincetown, Washington Square, and other semi-amateur groups of players, brought creative drama to Broadway. Finally, and as if to give a single meaning to these apparently unrelated events, a group of "literary radicals," led by Randolph Bourne, Van Wyck Brooks, and H. L. Mencken, celebrated the death of "puritanism" and the birth of a self-conscious critical movement. It was a time of youth and change and promise, the launching of America's second literary renaissance.

These events had a political background, of course. The years 1911–1912 marked the high tide of the Progressive movement in American politics. Of the three Presidential candidates then presenting themselves, two were liberals who waged their campaigns on platforms of radical change in American life. Theodore Roosevelt and Woodrow Wilson were exact opposites as personalities, but as symbols they stood for a common need of the American people; there were few moral, political, or economic ideals upon which they could not agree. They rivaled each other in their attacks upon laissez-faire economy, business monopoly, and political corruption; they outreached each other in their prophecies of revolution unless reforms were brought about by controls and corrections. There was no apparent complacency in the temper of the American people when they elected a Professor of Jurisprudence to their highest political office, and yet underneath their cry for change was the security of the democratic tradition in which they had unswerving faith. In spite of inevitable errors, it would seem that the United States had become a world power, the American experiment had succeeded, and there was missionary work to be done! Woodrow Wilson's doctrine of the "New Freedom," which could be used equally well as an argument for isolation or for a crusade, was the faith of Jefferson writ large and vindicated by more than a century of successful application to a growing and changing people. It fused in the American mind and heart a single concept of nationality which was strong enough to obscure economic inequalities and political disharmonies. And it cultivated self-criticism because only the strong and the confident can afford to look unflinchingly at their own weaknesses.

Literature is likely to come into its own at such moments in history because only in times of fulfillment is life's tragedy safely confronted. Emerson ushered in the first American renaissance by his call for introspection in an epoch of achieved nationality. The second renaissance began when the United

States was about to move as a single people into a distant world war. Then, as Van Wyck Brooks clearly saw, the "pulpy quick" of American life, the "nervous and self-critical vitality," was again "in a strange ferment." The philosophy of naturalism, which science had nurtured, could now become the central drive of a literary movement which had begun in the nineties, had been stalled for more than a decade by the forces of convention and reaction, and now had broken out into the open.

At such a time literary criticism becomes criticism of life. In 1900 E. C. Stedman could write about American poetry as though it were a fragile flower wilting in too rigorous a climate, but the issue was sharper as Van Wyck Brooks defined it in *America's Coming-of-Age* (1915). The cleavage there outlined between the "High-brow" and the "Low-brow" cut through all layers of American culture. Whether it was the Commoner Bryan challenging the "cross of gold" or the pale professors rejecting their times and retreating into the literatures and cultures of the past, the critic found no link between the life of the American mind and that of the American world. Living literature was not acknowledged in colleges, and specialists had little influence in public life, thought Brooks. The time had come for American opinions to come to terms with American facts—a thought to which Fenimore Cooper had given expression almost a century earlier. Brooks called for a critical movement capable once more of dealing with the problem of the literary life in the United States.

His call was answered in force. The critical movement that resulted had three main branches: literary radicalism, neo-humanism, and aestheticism. Brooks in his earlier phase picked up and made more articulate the literary radicalism of his friend Randolph Bourne and of *The Spirit of American Literature* (1913) by John Macy. With *The Wine of the Puritans* (1908), he had opened the campaign against the defenders of Ideality, the survivors of the earlier Puritanism, now reviving a twentieth century "puritanism" of stultifying inhibitions. In *The Ordeal of Mark Twain* (1920) he now studied what happened to the artist who remained in America and submitted to its restrictions of the spirit; in *The Pilgrimage of Henry James* (1925) he explored the fate of the artist who fled. The impasse was insuperable; Brooks himself retired from the battle in 1927, only to emerge again in 1936 with the first of a mellow and untroubled five-volume survey of the literary life in America, *The Flowering of New England*. His personal solution to the problem was to rise above it in order to gain perspective on a rediscovered American literary tradition, half conjectural and half real. The series was completed in 1951 as *Makers and Finders*.

H. L. Mencken, Lewis Mumford, Waldo Frank, Ludwig Lewisohn, Max Eastman, and a host of others shared this mood of literary radicalism without being committed to any one credo of revolt. Each brought his own challenge, each like Brooks finally set himself to solid work on a project which aimed to make more genuine the literary understanding of American life. Mumford surveyed culture in the broadest of terms: architecture, literature, and the technics of business and science. Lewisohn applied the Freudian formula to American literary history, Max Eastman made a brief effort to find a catalytic in Marx, Waldo Frank sought parallels in Latin American history and culture, and H. L. Mencken undertook a definitive study of the American language.

It was this last that, by its solid accomplishment, proved

most thoroughly the validity of the movement. Mencken launched his attacks on all forms of sham in the pages of the *Smart Set* which he edited with George Jean Nathan from 1914 to 1924, and then in the *American Mercury*. Something of the newspaper man survived from his days on the Baltimore *Herald* to help him popularize from Nietzsche and Shaw the challenge of doubt, the faith in biology, and the technique of debunking hypocrisy and provincialism. As a social critic he allowed his skepticism to carry him into a caustic antidemocratic position, but as a literary critic and commentator on contemporary values and mores he was less biased. His *Prejudices* (1919–1927) were tonic to the uncertain radicalism of the day, and his *A Book of Prefaces* (1917) was one of the most direct attacks on American gentility of the many which aided about that time in the requiem for the nineteenth century. By assault on traditional reticence and convention, and by appreciation of Conrad, Huneker, and Dreiser, he did much to release the forces of the new writing. Finally, in *The American Language* (fourth edition, 1936) and its *Supplements* (1945, 1948), he beat the "professors" at their own game with a work of scholarship.

The attack of the literary radicals was forceful, but it could not be long sustained because it was based on no agreed idea, values, or program. That of a smaller group, known as the neohumanists, was more effective because it formulated and preached a limited set of doctrines. With Irving Babbitt's *Literature and the American College* (1908), Brownell's *American Prose Masters* (1909), and the first six volumes of Paul Elmer More's *Shelburne Essays* (1904–1910), it was apparent that here was a defined and organized body of literary thought in which the moral emphasis of the elder idealists was to be preserved, only to be stripped of its sentimentality by an exhaustive scrutiny. In spite of the fact that the two groups were linked for attack by the literary radicals, the neohumanists thought of their movement as antiromantic. Brownell and More were the better critics, but Babbitt defined the position and made it a "school." As his student Norman Foerster later explained in *Toward Standards* (1930), he based his position on the break of the Renaissance humanists with the authority of the Church, but reversed their direction of thought because he found, in the twentieth century, that the threat to human integrity came not from the dogmatism of religion but from that of science. The tendency of the "New Humanism" was therefore away from naturalism and toward moral absolutes. Emerson had come fairly close to the conception of man as a sole creator and judge of his own destiny; Babbitt went the whole way. Although it claimed no specific American heritage, neohumanism was deeply rooted in the traditional American system of values, and Brooks was right in sensing a link between it and colonial Puritanism. In the end, it supplemented rather than undermined the work of the literary radicals when, in 1930, it flared up briefly as a fighting creed, only to be lost in the shifting critical issues of the subsequent decade.

The third branch of the new critical movement is more difficult to define than these two, even though it survived them both. "Aestheticism" is probably its best description because its ultimate American source lay in Poe's choice of "taste" as superior to "pure intellect" or "moral sense," and in his emphasis on "an impression, or effect, to be conveyed" as the main aim of literary art. Alien to the dominant moralistic and nationalistic emphases of the nineteenth century, this view was not stated vigorously again until Henry James based his theory of fiction on "a personal, a direct impression of life." The influence of such impressionistic critics as Anatole France and Walter Pater, however, was not felt in America by any major artist for many years; rather it seeped into the corners of infant urban Bohemias as a mood of mannered decadence which suggested neither its debt to Poe by way of Baudelaire, Verlaine, and Mallarmé, nor its use as preparation for a later and more complex American symbolism. In the essays on music, literature, and art of James G. Huneker, and in the fantasies of James Branch Cabell, this thin thread of pure aestheticism was woven into the coarse fabric of American life during the *fin de siècle* period and the early years of the new century. Its purest statement in Cabell's *Beyond Life* (1919) is an honest defense of romance as escape, for "be it remembered that man alone of animals plays the ape to his dreams"; its academic sanction is found in those idealists who, like Lewis Gates at Harvard and George Edward Woodberry at Columbia, were forced into impressionism by the failure of other sanctions for the life of art. Finally, in J. E. Spingarn's essay on "The New Criticism" (1911), the aesthetic movement in America discovered, in the philosophy of the Italian Croce, a firmer ground for that dispassionate sensibility to life and art which was to provide the foundations for the later structure of American literary criticism.

– 2 –

The vigorous hold that nineteenth century values and standards had upon American consciousness is even more strikingly illustrated in fiction than in criticism. In spite of the new concepts of human motivation that science had intro-

duced, the old romantic plot-romance held firm, particularly
on the popular level of the historical Italian idylls of F. Marion
Crawford and the tales of the old cotton and hill country
South by James Lane Allen, Winston Churchill, and Thomas
Nelson Page. In these novels the significance of the Civil War
seemed to lie mainly in the sad passing of an agrarian and aristocratic way of life; the virtues of Europe to lie in its relics of
a romantic past. Even the serious work of Howells, James,
Crane, Garland, and London could not break into the close-
knit frame of British-American romantic values, built up in a
century of expanding political power and unlimited economic
resources.

The only way open to serious writers of fiction, who saw
their calling as a criticism of life, seemed to be the tentative discussion of a single social issue, usually as the personal problem
of a high-minded individual caught in the cross-currents of
the times. Favorites were the clergyman whose love of humanity overcomes his strict religious code, the industrial leader
who is shocked by the conditions of life among his workers,
the emancipated woman who is bound to an insensitive husband, the artist or architect who is strangled by materialistic
standards of success, the newly rich plain man who is unable
to break into the shabby but proud circles of an older aristocracy, and the strike leader who finds his private life sacrificed
by his devotion to a cause. Howells, James, Adams, and Mark
Twain had all written in this vein; and there were many who
wrote lesser works of the same kind: the antistrike novel, *The
Bread-Winners* (1884) by John Hay; the study of personal
religious crisis, *The Damnation of Theron Ware* (1896) by
Harold Frederic; the analysis of conflicting business and ethical values, *The Common Lot* (1904) by Robert Herrick; and

the story of a woman who seeks happiness in defiance of convention, *The House of Mirth* (1905) by Edith Wharton. More like the plays of Ibsen and Strindberg than like the novels of Hardy, Tolstoi, or Zola, such problem tales as these probably also owe much to an older and more native tradition of psychological fiction as written by Hawthorne and Poe, and through them to ethical codes firmly established in colonial times and reinforced by the democratic doctrine of the integrity of the individual. No one of these writers seemed to feel that the basic structure of American social ethics was seriously threatened. The problem was always that of an individual whose personal values were challenged by social change, but who would survive or fall according to his own ethical courage. Whether the treatment was direct and serious as in E. W. Howe's *The Story of a Country Town* (1883), or was sophisticated and ironic in the manner perfected by Edith Wharton in *The Age of Innocence* (1920), the mode of these novels was a survival from a less troubled past, persistent and productive of interesting if not really important fiction for at least a quarter of a century.

The most distinguished products of this mode were the novels of two Virginia-born women, Ellen Glasgow (1874–1945) and Willa Cather (1876–1947). Glasgow seems very much the senior of the two in spite of the slight difference in their ages, perhaps because she spent most of her life in her native Virginia and immersed herself in the study of its regional characteristics and values. Looking back on the long sequence of quiet but vivacious stories she had told, it seemed to her finally that she had planned and executed a social record of the Commonwealth, "the historical drama of a changing order, and the struggle of an emerging middle class," set behind the many dramas of individual frustration upon which the several novels were focused. At the core of her early work was a rejection of chivalry, both as a pattern of society in the Old South and as a code of masculine superiority. Her radicalism, revealed at once in her first novel, *The Descendant* (1897), and sustained through many variations to her last, *In This Our Life* (1941), was always a mixture of personal and social rejections. The new woman and the New South were integral parts of the same revolt, and the Southern gentlemen who failed to recapture their lost youth were hardly distinguishable from a whole way of life that had vanished with the plantation economy. Dorinda of *Barren Ground* (1925) symbolizes at once the revolt of human fertility against an exhausted soil and the ultimate barrenness of a life in which fortitude had outlived love; and Judge Honeywell's second marriage in *The Romantic Comedians* (1926) stood for the failure of his society's and his own dreams of perennial youth. Combining truth to the simple outside things that Howells had so much appreciated with something like Hawthorne's truth to the human heart, Ellen Glasgow succeeded where others had failed in revealing the social patterns of her times. With a flexible style, capable of almost tragic intensity or comic irony at will, she was able to interpret, out of her own understanding of herself, the shift in values which had so completely altered the society of which she was a part.

The same problem of change found in Willa Cather an even finer artist than it had in Glasgow. The pearl-like quality of her tales gives a deceptive sense of calm and order to her moral restlessness. Her family had early moved from Virginia to the Nebraska town of Red Cloud where she grew up among the wheat fields and the Bohemian immigrants of the still unsettled prairie. Brought thus to terms with the earth, she learned how to give to her portraits of pioneer women a vibrant integrity that seemed effortless because it was pure and primitive. The artist Thea Kronberg of *The Song of the Lark* (1915) and the prairie girl Antonia Shimerda of *My Antonia* (1918) have in common a primitivism that is a moral criticism of society because it is based on unhampered nature. Whereas Glasgow's Dorinda is bound by conventions which she has to overcome in her discovery of new truth about the instinctive level of experience, Cather's women act on their instincts without thought and make of life a noble thing. The world which they create out of their own vigorous and naïve personalities is a world of pioneers, of an escape from the corruption of an effete society left far behind—except for those few who, like Mrs. Forrester of *A Lost Lady* (1923), bring corruption with them. "Lillies that fester," says her youthful admirer, "smell far worse than weeds." In a single character Willa Cather could thus build or destroy a whole system of values. Her naturalism could not control her faith in the human will.

In *The Professor's House* (1925) Cather's criticism by escape became complete. Professor St. Peter's awakening to the lost cities of the canyons has a symbolic value; it is a more nearly complete rejection of life than even his attempted suicides might have been. In him she found the stoical center, born of the quiet of forgotten cities of the prairies and of life no longer lived, that Father Latour of *Death Comes for the Archbishop* (1927) discovers in the passing of his friend Bishop Vaillant and in the preparation for his own death. "It was the Past he was leaving. . . . There was no longer any perspective in his memories." Neither in her further move into the unreal world of *Shadows on the Rock* (1931) nor in her attempted return to her own racial past in the Virginia story *Sapphira and the Slave Girl* (1940) could Cather recapture the sense of reality she had renounced, even though her growing mastery of symbolism opened new ways for others in fiction. Her stories came close to perfection because they dealt with essences of experience and expression, but both life and art escaped her final grasp. More courageous than any of her contemporaries except Dreiser, her one direct contact with the life of her times, when as a young girl she worked for S. S. Mc-Clure and his group of "muckrakers" in New York, never found its way through to her fiction. Instead, she spun a trans-lucent web about her personality and left her criticism of life to be inferred rather than spoken.

There would seem at first to be little connection between these uneasy survivors of the nineteenth century and the first American to win the Nobel Prize for literature, awarded for his uncompromising satire of the materialism of his times. Wharton, Glasgow, and Cather were progressively more and more aware of the deep changes that were taking place in American life, but they sought to meet them by recovering lost personal values; Sinclair Lewis was willing to look coldly at the world in which he found himself, to examine its values rather than his own, and to declare what he found.

The findings were not pretty. The unhappy inhabitants of the dreary town (at least as he saw it) of Sauk Centre, Min-nesota, from whom he escaped to study in the East and to work as a journalist in New York City, had none of the fron-tier glamour of Cather's pioneers. Sinclair Lewis was middle middle-class, and he knew it; he did not view life from an aristocratic or aesthetic distance. When he joined the prophet of socialism Upton Sinclair in his Utopian colony at Helicon Hall, New Jersey, he was meeting rather than escaping from his times. He wanted a workable answer to the problems he saw about him, and he was prepared to ridicule, as did Mencken, the hypocrisy of those who were less honest than he.

His early novels were failures, and it was not until he turned his relentless and cruel gift for satire on his own boyhood home in *Main Street* (1920) that he discovered his natural art. Because he was of it and loved it, Lewis became the complete critic of middle-class American society. An ironic naturalist, he cried out, as had Swift and Mark Twain, against the blindness and hypocrisy that were destroying the simple values of elemental humanity. His portrait of *Babbitt* (1922) added a new word to the American dictionary because it created a symbol of the little man caught up in the success-worship, the materialism, of a city world in an industrial society. Compassion mingled with scorn to reveal the lost humanity in this pathetic victim of the illusions with which he was surrounded. Thereafter, each Lewis character discovered another hole in the mouse trap, usually by sticking his head into it. The medical profession was exposed in *Arrowsmith* (1925), the clerical in *Elmer Gantry* (1927), the mercantile in *The Man Who Knew Coolidge* (1928), and the political in *It Can't Happen Here* (1935). Occasionally, as in George Babbitt, Martin Arrowsmith, and Samuel Dodsworth, of the novel of that name (1929), Lewis's sense of humanity rose above his skepticism and created a memorable and living character, but his normal level was that of the domestic novel of satire, one notch above that of Edith Wharton and Ellen Glasgow because he chose, as they had not, to make the dead level of

American middle-class life his own special province. When he went to Stockholm in 1930 to receive the award as the leading American writer of his time, he brought with him only a sense of the great numbers of better writers than he who made up the literary movement which he had been selected to spearhead. Not the least of the gifts of Sinclair Lewis was this humility which bore eloquent testimony to the sincerity of his work and to his loyalty to the society he had so ruthlessly exposed. It was for the more philosophic naturalists like Dreiser and Sherwood Anderson to give that criticism its roots in the deeper realities of the new age.

– 3 –

No writer who was still bound by the British tradition— Norris or Crane, Glasgow or Lewis—could have brought the movement to a focus as did Theodore Dreiser (1871–1945), son of a poor weaver who had set out from Mayen, Germany, for Dayton, Ohio, in 1844, in search of his fortune. With Dreiser, naturalism in America became one with the movement which had swept through the literatures of central Europe. *Sister Carrie*, published first in 1900 but quickly suppressed, was written in a mood of acquiescence to natural law, in the unstudied language of the lower middle class, and in a form of art wholly derived from the drift and flow of life itself. What Norris and Garland, Crane and London, had consciously striven to achieve, this son of a German peasant immigrant could scarcely avoid. The power was his; all he had to do was to allow it to flow through him and out into expression.

In one sense, all that Dreiser wrote was a single long autobiography. The struggles and conflicts of his parents, his sisters, his brothers, and himself are told in tortuous detail in a series of soul-searching narratives, beginning with the child-hood record *Dawn* (1931), and following through his news-paper days to his maturity as a novelist. Failure had hung heav-ily over his father, "a thin grasshopper of a man, brooding wearily," after the fire which had destroyed his mill and left him with no resources for the support of his growing family. The affectionate, animal-like mother held her many children close to their uncertain home with "a kind of sweetness that never since has anywhere been equaled," but even she could not prevent them from being too soon forced out into the sea of American life. The young dreamer saw his sisters and his brothers drawn in by the currents and tossed on unfriendly shores. One brother, Paul, made a success as a song writer, but the others and the four sisters lived to have their pathetic sto-ries told under other names in a series of "American tragedies" that gave meaning and direction to the new literature. Dreiser wrote of the life he knew after he had brooded over it for years.

The two great drives in all his stories, money and sex, were symbols of succcess or failure as he had known them. An elaborate, theoretical science did not need to tell him that the economic and biological levels of nature provided the strong-est motives for an individual lost in a complex and competitive society. He had seen his father turned into an irascible and brooding old man from too many dependents and not enough money. Prostitution, alcoholism, petty gambling and thievery, and sordid death were on every side of his childhood. The way up and out was obviously through control of these forces, a task which the individual could not hope to accomplish alone. A completely passive acquiescence to natural law was thus early linked in his consciousness with a zeal for social reform, as they had been in the novels of Dostoevski and Zola. The logical inconsistency of the two attitudes caused no philosophical concern for these novelists, for art is not philosophy and need be no more consistent than the experience with which it deals. A goal which must be, and yet cannot be, won is and always has been the crux of great tragedy. In economic and biological necessity Dreiser discovered the modern stage on which the eternal battle between man's will and his destiny could be disclosed and understood. His three helpless and will-less youngsters, Carrie Meeber, Jennie Gerhardt, and Clyde Griffiths are no more victims of their incomprehensible fate than are his three men of power and success, Frank Cowperwood, Eugene Witla, and Solon Barnes. The tragic issue is essentially the same in all, for, in spite of the endless and apparently indiscriminate detail with which Dreiser's pages are filled, the meaning of life was for him simple, deeply moving, and forever the same.

Jennie Gerhardt (1911) and *Sister Carrie* (republished 1912) tell the story in its purest form, with variations. Jennie was Dreiser's own favorite, as she will remain with many of his readers, for it was Jennie's goodness that led to her downfall. Poverty and gentle responsiveness rather than desire for excitement or vice led her to liaisons first with Senator Brander and then with the rich young man Lester Kane. Lester's story, which is here told only through Jennie, was later to become the typical American tragedy of Clyde Griffiths. As the path of opportunity led upward for the one, it led the other to a meaningless morass. When Lester turned to a woman of his own temperament and status, Jennie's gift of life could not be restored to her. Yet it is Jennie and not Lester who survives; the tragic issue is unresolved.

When the critics and moralists swarmed about this book, it was not Jennie's limited promiscuity that worried them; it was the fact that her behavior was condoned rather than condemned. By implication the author had built his story on a morality of omnipotent natural law, on a faith in instinct that transcended man-made values. The very structure of society was challenged; there was cause for alarm. In *Sister Carrie* the violations had been even more flagrant, for the liaisons of the simple country girl, first with a traveling drummer and then with the manager of a "fashionable saloon," had been for her compliant and instinctual nature but rungs on the ladder of success. Carrie was swept upward, Drouet merely moved on to other similar adventures, Hurstwood was caught in crime and pushed downward to poverty and squalor by the same meaningless forces of blood and barter. It was Dreiser himself and not merely Carrie who espoused an anarchic ethic.

These people were the people that Dreiser knew, and he could identify himself with them. The financier Frank Cowperwood (in life, Charles T. Yerkes) on the other hand stood for all that Dreiser did not know, all that he wished for. When the boy Cowperwood watched the lobster in the tank gradually overcome and then eat the helpless squid, he concluded, "He didn't have a chance." The lobster was heavily armed and could feed on the squid, but man was superior to the lobster. "Sure, men lived on men. Look at the slaves." In the financier who could have all the money or the women he desired because of some innate power not given to other men, Dreiser carved out his version of the Nietzschean superman. Three long novels were devoted to his career: *The Financier* (1912), *The Titan* (1914), and *The Stoic* (1947), which repeated the same cycle, first in Philadelphia, then in Chicago, finally in

London. In each, the superman rises by complete ruthlessness and amorality to a peak of power, and then, by overreaching himself, plunges to the depths; but the result is never quite tragic because the destruction of the hero it not total. Each time he seems as triumphant in his shame or death as he was in his moments of heartless victory over the weaker of his fellows. In the end it is his mistress Berenice of *The Stoic*, and not Cowperwood, who discovers the spiritual escape of the *Bhagavad-Gita;* for the lobster, there is no value greater than triumph over the squid.

In *The "Genius"* (1915) and *The Bulwark* (1946), Dreiser explores, through his other two supermen, some of the nonmaterialistic values so lacking in Cowperwood, but without real conviction. Eugene Witla is a painter, but in all other respects he is what the artist Dreiser thought himself, or wished himself, to be. But biography is too closely followed; Witla's career is checkered as Dreiser's had been by a nervous breakdown followed by a long period of business success, during which his art died. His love-life is thwarted by overindulgence, and penitence for the death of his wife brings him to a compromise with life rather than to a solution of its mysteries. Neither Witla nor Dreiser's final hero, the stern and disillusioned old Quaker Solon Barnes of *The Bulwark*, discovers any values higher than a vague and mystic communion with nature to bring him to terms with destiny.

At his best and most authentic, Dreiser was a lusty materialist who turned to modern science for guidance because science in modern terms has most unconditionally accepted life. For this reason the book of his prime, *An American Tragedy* (1925), is both his most representative and his best work. It came after a decade of relative silence, at least as far as fiction was concerned. With the virtual suppression of *The "Genius,"* its author laid aside two unfinished novels, *The Stoic* and *The Bulwark*, and turned to plays, poems, sketches, short stories, and essays. His interest in science was intensified by his readings in biology, from which he developed his theory of "chemisms" as motivation for individual human action; and his concern for human welfare led him deeper into the class struggle and the emerging Socialism and Communism, both at home and abroad. *An American Tragedy*, the most carefully planned of all his novels, reflects both of these interests. The crime upon which the plot centers was one which frequently occurs in American experience—the murder of a young girl by her boy-lover when her pregnancy blocks his way to social and financial success. The actual case of Chester Gillette, who drowned Grace Brown in Big Moose Lake, New York, in July, 1906, was only one of many such incidents in which Dreiser had shown interest, both before and after writing his novel. The newspaper clipping of this case was the immediate provocation to the fictional Clyde Griffiths to commit his crime and to Dreiser to write about it. The record of the trial and execution was spread out in the court reports and printed in the newspapers. All Dreiser had to do was to reconstruct the story behind the record, drawing heavily on his own memories of his young manhood for the circumstances and feelings that could motivate such a crime. His love of humanity and his understanding of the human dilemma here had a worthy subject. The book became the completed tragedy that Dreiser had always hoped to write because in it he had succeeded at last in making the experience he knew stand for the crisis of a society and an era.

The moral crux of the story lay in the problem of human

responsibility. Clyde planned his crime with minute care and carried out the actions leading up to it with a blind and inevitable step-by-step logic, but when the moment came the crime itself was an accident and Clyde was immediately responsible only because he had not saved the drowning Roberta. In order to convict him, the district attorney had to plant the evidence that ought to have been there according to circumstantial logic but was missing. The paradox emphasized Dreiser's conviction that no one really plans his own actions; everything is determined by a complex of internal chemisms and by the forces of social pressure exerted from without. Here is Jennie's story retold with the reasons for a blind acceptance of life now more clearly stated and with the consequences of actions now imposed ruthlessly on the victim. It is also the story of Frank Cowperwood with the film of hero worship removed from the author's eyes. The epic quality so necessary to great tragedy was here achieved because the author had learned how to make his own experience stand for that of a whole society. The financial and social stratification of American civilization was firm enough to prevent Clyde from realizing the goals which were presented to him as the right of every free democratic individual. The "success" formula, so deeply imbedded in American traditions, no longer worked. The code of an expanding frontier society did not apply to the complex and consolidating society of the industrialized twentieth century. What must be, cannot be; the tragic issue was sharp and clear, but it had been developed entirely afresh from a newly formed civilization, without reference to classic norms and rules. Dreiser's art had revealed a total human experience; it was mature and complete.

- 4 -

With Dreiser's success in discovering the formula for the "great American novel," and with the agenda for literary progress now clearly defined by the literary radicals as a return to the sources, the movement of the nineties, which had gone into partial eclipse during the early years of the century, could be said to be fairly relaunched by 1915. Even popular writers of short stories and light fiction like O. Henry, Booth Tarkington, Ring Lardner, Edna Ferber, and a host of others were using the materials of middle and low life, the emphasis on locale, and the reportorial style characteristic of naturalism. America was coming to terms with herself, and her second literary renaissance was moving forward.

In drama and poetry the revival of the creative imagination was even more striking than in criticism and fiction because writers in these forms have greater mechanical difficulties to overcome before they can reach a new public with innovations of thought and style. The break-through was therefore longer delayed and was more sudden when it finally came.

The condition of the American theater in 1910 was not conducive to originality or experimentation on the part of the playwrights. The movement toward naturalism, social criticism, and expressionism which had seized the Continental theater in the plays of Ibsen, Strindberg, and Hauptmann, and had been more mildly reflected in England by Pinero, Shaw, and Barker, had not crossed the Atlantic. The versatile Clyde Fitch, Augustus Thomas, and David Belasco were still turning out comedies and melodramas that would hardly have startled

David Garrick, and the poetic experiments of William Vaughn Moody and Percy MacKaye had difficulty in finding or holding the stage.

The reasons for this situation were largely mechanical. The old local or traveling stock company had by this time been largely superseded by the star system with its emphasis on the actor rather than on the author, its financial control by limited commercial interests, and its concentration on Broadway and on spectacle production. There was no national or experimental theater in America, and the amateur "art theater" had not yet been born. When it did come, about 1915, it came all at once. The "Wharf Theater" in Provincetown, Massachusetts, moved into New York City in the fall of that year after a successful summer in which it had produced several short plays by members of the company, including the then unknown Eugene O'Neill, and some translations of the new and exciting European drama. About the same time, local troupes were setting up community playhouses in Cleveland, Pasadena, Dallas, New Orleans, and on the campuses of Harvard University, the North Dakota Agricultural College, and the Carnegie Institute of Technology at Pittsburgh, Pennsylvania. In New York the Washington Square Players moved uptown with Eugene O'Neill's *The Emperor Jones* and became the Theatre Guild.

Although the policy of these new theater groups was almost evenly divided between the production of the work of native playwrights and that of the more exciting European plays in translation, their resultant influence on American dramatists was highly stimulating. Authors were recognized and rewarded, serious ideas about life in America and life in general could now find immediate expression on the stage in new and flexible dramatic forms. Poets and novelists began to try their hands at plays, and the line between the theater and the creative dramatic arts began to break down. Drama became, for the first time in the United States, a vital form of literary expression, and by 1925–1935, when O'Neill, Maxwell Anderson, Robert E. Sherwood, and Sidney Howard were at the crest of their careers, American plays and playwrights were known and respected throughout the world.

The "little renaissance" in poetry was equally sudden but more immediately productive because poets apparently continue to write whether publication is possible or not. Magazines like *Harper's, Scribner's,* and the *Atlantic* had long used sentimental and conventional verses for "filler," and newspapers could always find space for heartwarming poems at the foot of the editorial page. Richard Hovey, William Vaughn Moody, and Lizette Woodworth Reese were among those who wrote a few memorable verses under such conditions through sheer force of lyric gift; but the genteel poets, Stedman, Stoddard, Gilder, and Aldrich, still were recognized as the controlling group in 1912 when Harriet Monroe of Chicago founded a modest and unimpressive little magazine which she called *Poetry: A Magazine of Verse.* For almost half a century *Poetry* survived financial and temperamental vicissitudes to become perhaps the most influential literary journal, with the possible exception of the *Atlantic,* ever to appear in the United States. As both symbol and fomenter of revolt, it created and abetted an explosive aesthetic release.

Harriet Monroe was not herself primarily an experimenter or thinker. She was merely hospitable to experiment, thought, and feeling. Yet there was hardly a name among the poets who were to gain recognition in the next decade that did not appear at least once in her magazine, and most of them were regular contributors. When the excitement had died down and the literary historian could look back on a record of phenomenal achievement, he could see that *Poetry* had opened the door to two or three major movements in the reborn art. Without closing its pages to the best of the traditionalists, it had, through Ezra Pound, Amy Lowell, and the Imagist group, linked the metaphysical verse of Emerson, Dickinson, and other poets of the nineteenth century to the inarticulate needs of the confused present, and had laid the foundations for an American metaphysical movement which was to develop in full a quarter of a century and more later. But it had also, and more immediately, helped to bring into being a vigorous naturalistic movement in the poetry of Vachel Lindsay, Robert Frost, Edgar Lee Masters, Carl Sandburg, and finally Robinson Jeffers. *The Congo and Other Poems* (1914), *North of Boston* (1914), *Spoon River Anthology* (1915), and *Chicago Poems* (1916) might well have appeared without the opportunity offered by *Poetry* magazine to be heard, but the coincidence of dates is at least suggestive.

The bardic spirit of Walt Whitman returned in the troubadour of Springfield, Illinois. Deeply rooted in the American tradition, Vachel Lindsay (1879–1931) peddled his *Rhymes to Be Traded for Bread* through the Midwest and the Southwest in 1912, singing as few modern minstrels have sung. The melody and sound pictures of the poems of *The Congo* captured the sweeping rhythms of the prairie, the clatter of the city, and the sinuous echoes of a forgotten African jungle. Americans who could not understand what a poem said were caught up in the meaning of pure sound as the towheaded jazz revivalist chanted, shouted, and whispered his lines from the platform of college lecture hall or county fair. Abraham Lincoln stepped out of his grave in Whitman's elegies and walked again, John Brown returned from Paradise to report on the doings of Noah and the Angel Gabriel, Johnny Appleseed prayed on the mountaintop as Lindsay sang "the bold, old songs of heaven and spring." There was as much of religion as of art in his belief in the "gospel of beauty" and in his deliberate use of folk and jazz elements to construct a new kind of native American verse. Apparently endowed with inexhaustible energy and faith in his calling, he shocked his followers in December, 1931, when despair at his "failure" drove him to suicide. He had burned himself out instead of saving his energies for the epic works which were never to be written.

Lindsay's gift to American literature was, like George Gershwin's to music, an awakened sensibility to the folk spirit as a living and continuing force in the creative life. Coming before the general revival of interest in folk ballad, tale, and song, which was to sweep the country in the thirties and forties, he helped more than any other poet to discover native and authentic strains of song. An intense love of the people rather than a political nationalism motivated all of his work, as it did also—in a curiously inverted way—the work of Edgar Lee Masters (1869–1948). The *Spoon River Anthology* was a deliberate turn from imitative and traditional poetry, mainly on classical themes, that this lawyer-poet had written before he discovered the Chicago literary movement in 1912. It was William Marion Reedy, of *Reedy's Mirror*, who suggested that he model on *The Greek Anthology* a group of revealing self-composed epitaphs for the kind of men and women he had known and hated in the small town of Lewistown, Illinois, from which he had come. Sharing with Dreiser a feeling of doom in the thwarted lives of little people and with Lewis a spirit of revolt from the village, Masters wrote one shocking and immortal book, but his later poetry and prose had the heavy and blundering quality of pure naturalism without the sense of the tragic spirit that had lifted Dreiser to greatness, or the ironic perspective that had released the comic spirit of Sinclair Lewis.

It was Carl Sandburg (b. 1878) who succeeded where Lindsay and Masters had pointed the way, the one to the capture of the American folk heritage and the other to a comprehension of the "little people" of the contemporary scene. Sandburg did both, and assumed, as only Whitman had successfully done before him, the role of the American bard. Like most of the other poets of his generation, however, he was recognized only at the age of thirty-eight when he published *Chicago Poems* (1916), the title piece of which had appeared in *Poetry* two years before. The raw brutality and colloquial wisdom of this poem drew immediate attention to the Chicago journalist, the son of a Swedish immigrant and native of Galesburg, Illinois. Surely this was not poetry, this exhortation to the violent city of gunmen and hog-butchers and freight handlers that could fling "magnetic curses" while "laughing as a young man laughs." It was definitely not poetry in the conventional sense in any case. It lacked meter and verse form, even regular rhythm and subtle imagery. A total impression rather than an idea, moral or otherwise, supplied its primary inspiration, and its technique was mainly a massing of direct details in the fashion of Dreiser or of any prose naturalist; but other poems in the book were as gentle as the title poem was rough. In them the fog and the gulls off the lake shore were as vital as the fish crier with his pushcart or the women standing in the doorways. Sandburg once claimed that he owed more to Emily Dickinson than to Whitman, and his kinship with Amy Lowell and the Imagists is not hard to detect. What he owed was a sensitivity to human values and an immediate response to color and form rather than a metaphysical ambiguity. The new poet of the American people was never obscure, never doubtful of the essential values of life as nature presented them. He was ready to accept the tragedy with the comedy of modern experience before either became sharpened to the exclusion of the other. Irony and despair were blended in a spirit of joyous vitality.

From Chicago, Sandburg looked out across the prairie in *Slabs of the Sunburnt West* (1922); he searched for the primitive heart of the people in the fresh legends of childhood, *Rootabaga Stories* (1922); he gathered the folk ballads and songs of all kinds and races of men in *The American Songbag* (1927). Sandburg was perhaps the first of the ballad collectors to recognize that the American folk tradition was distinctive because of, and not in spite of, its heterogeneity. All kinds of people doing all kinds of things could be Americans, for the culture of the new civilization had been shaped by the freedoms that the philosopher-statesmen had so long ago promised. "We hold that all men are endowed by their creator with inherent and inalienable rights." "In the night," echoes Sandburg, "the people march."

In *The People, Yes* (1936) and in the six huge volumes of his biography of Abraham Lincoln (1926–1939), Sandburg rose above the level of the lyric poet of scenes and men to become the epic voice of these generic American people. If his poetry had been largely prose, his prose now was largely poetry as he followed his hero Lincoln from his own Illinois prairie to a sacrificial and symbolic death. Like Whitman, Lindsay, and Masters, Sandburg felt that all of the American spirit that could be captured was embodied and exalted in the giant figure of this man of the people and of the earth. If America was to have an epic, this poet's life of its national hero in rhythmic and impressionistic prose comes as near to supplying the need as does any other single work in prose or verse.

Sandburg's strength lay in the directness of his sensory understanding and in the fresh exuberance of his responses. He set himself to create what Brooks and Mencken had called for: a literature that had its roots in the American tradition and in contemporary American life. One of the few writers of his generation to accept rather than to criticize what he found, his poetry can itself be criticized for sentimentality and lack of subtlety, but his positive contribution in the truths that he discovered and in their memorable expression will leave his work standing when the things he might have criticized are of interest only to the antiquarian. Once more, in his only novel and, next to the *Lincoln* his most ambitious work, *Remembrance Rock* (1948), he attempted to trace the American heritage, this time in a group of people who could defy time and age. Carl Sandburg had defied all "stumbling blocks to truth" throughout his life and was ready, as his fictional Mary Winding had been in 1608, to give the toast "to the storms to come and the stars coming after the storm."

– 5 –

In its excited second coming of age, American poetry seemed almost ready to throw off all connection with the past and with tradition; but the purest poet of the group, Robert Frost (b. 1875), was a conservative as well as an experimenter.

He, together with many younger men and women who shared in the vitality of the movement without accepting its radicalism—Robert Hillyer, Mark Van Doren, Stephen Benét, Elinor Wylie, Edna St. Vincent Millay among them—was ready to prove that the heritage from American formal verse still had its own vitality if shorn of its mannerisms and conventional restraints.

Frost was New England bred if not New England born. His father, a Copperhead politician and newspaperman, had early migrated to California, and the first decade of the poet's life was spent there. When he did return to the home of his ancestors, he came with the zeal of a prodigal son. His life-long hobby of buying New England farms seemed almost a symbol of a passionate need to reestablish his rootage in tough mountain soil. The fervor of the convert brought him to Derry, New Hampshire, in 1900 to rear his family, and he had lost none of it in 1950 when he watched the sunset alone from the porch of the cabin he had built for himself on his latest farm, high in the hills above Ripton, Vermont. His had been a life of devotion to his spiritual inheritance, as well as a shrewd acceptance of the world into which he had been born.

Frost was a twentieth century transcendentalist, a latter-day naturalist. Emerson's faith in the indestructibility of the human soul, for which he had relinquished a less attainable faith in an omnipotent and benevolent God, had by now become in Frost a complete skeptical humanism. Man could safely defy an unreasonable deity if he had first made his peace with nature. With this assurance, he turned to the intimacies of the soil and the people who worked it to learn again the old lesson of the All in Each.

At first his readers thought of him as merely a poet of

nature, and failed to give close attention to his deceptively simple verses. In fact, he had almost lived a life before he had any readers at all. By 1912 he had collected a folder of verses, but had never talked with another poet. Suddenly he sold his farm and took his family to England where association with Ezra Pound and the Soho group gave him heart. Pound was good to him, but Frost soon found that he had no real kinship with the city poets. Again he sought the country, this time in Hertfordshire, where he found more congenial companions in Abercrombie, Brooke, Gibson, and Thomas, but a book of lyrics, *A Boy's Will* (1913), was already on the way, to be followed almost immediately by the conversational narratives of *North of Boston* (1914). In the native grain as was no other modern poet, Frost became overnight the first American maker of verses to be widely read since Longfellow and Whittier. He was soon lectured about in colleges and read in the provinces; he even began to divide his life between lecturing in the colleges himself—starting with Amherst—and tending his farms. Two things he could and would do, observe and teach; his informal poems were the result of a mixture of the two, an ancient formula for lyrics to be loved.

It was possible, of course, to read such poems as "The Tuft of Flowers" or "In Hardwood Groves" as pastoral moralities with no weight other than that of a flitting mood, but there was an intensity in such comments as these on brotherhood and death that held storm warnings for the alert. In "Mending Wall," "The Road Not Taken," and "Birches," Frost's humanism became firm and complete. He had learned to leave his message as an integral part of his observation: the lifting and resetting of the stones that winter frost had rolled from the wall was an act of darkness in itself, as necessary as it was futile; the other road might have made "all the difference" if it had been the one taken; to be set back on earth by the flexing birch was the most satisfying of all possible rewards for the climber. A moment of life involving nature and man in what to most people would be a routine and meaningless act becomes in each of these poems a sharp and complete symbol of truth. The observation, its meaning, and the poetic form in which it is embodied are fused into one; here is perfect art.

Part of the deceptive simplicity of Frost's poems springs from his ear for language tune. A lifelong student of Greek and Latin, he was at heart a classicist and a conservative. With close attention he listened to the clipped New England speech with its falling rhythm and its muffled overtones. In one of his earliest lectures he explained, with the shuffling uneasiness of a schoolboy on declamation day, that there was a difference between the words, "I will put the cat out," and, "Out you go, cat." To him the tone of voice was the beginning of poetry. He would use the iambic meter because it was the most natural one for the English language, but he would spring it and spread it to catch the "speaking tone of voice." Somehow the technique of the dramatic lyric, learned mainly from Browning and already domesticated in the United States by Frost's fellow New Englander E. A. Robinson, came alive in such homely colloquies as "Home Burial," "The Death of the Hired Man," "Two Tramps in Mud Time." So exact was his timing, so alert was his ear, that even the same line—"And miles to go before I sleep"—could mean something entirely different the second time it was said. At its best, Frost's irony is the sharpest of poetic weapons; at its worst it is the forgivable pun of a wise old duffer.

Volume followed volume through these New England

years: *Mountain Interval, West-Running Brook, A Further Range, Steeple Bush,* so even in tone that they could have been, like *Leaves of Grass,* gathered under a single title as a single accumulative work, a book of life. Then personal tragedy struck, much as it had for Mark Twain. Blow after blow swung at the hardwood trunk, but this tree was tough. Robert Frost still stood, and with one more warm but still wry smile he wrote his major work which he had all this time been holding back. Many years before, he had put into a silly little lyric called "Not All There," the capsule of his philosophy of life: Man turned to speak to God and found God wasn't there; God turned to speak to man and found "not over half." To celebrate his seventieth birthday, the half-man turned to God once more and, in the person of Job, flung his challenge at him in *A Masque of Reason.* God replied, in the person of Jonah, in *A Masque of Mercy:* "Nothing can make injustice just but mercy." In such poems the voice of nature is made human and speaks freely with God.

CHAPTER XI

FULL CIRCLE
O'Neill, Hemingway

IN the period between the two world wars, literature in the United States reached a new height of technical perfection and depth of meaning. By 1925 the literary movement of the century had become stabilized, its shape and scope definable. The protests and preachments of the literary radicals and the neohumanists had begun to give way to a criticism that was ready to grapple with specific problems of society, personality, and literary form. Fiction, poetry, and drama threw off their old restraints and plunged into an era of experimentation and self-conscious power such as had never been equaled on the Western continent. Sinclair Lewis, in his Stockholm address of 1930, announced this second "coming of age" as an accomplished fact. His audience, if it wished, could read most of the writings he mentioned in all the languages of Europe. Abroad as well as at home, the new literature of the United States was being recognized as a surprising but undeniable force in Western culture. By 1935 the second renaissance had come to full flower.

The writers who produced most of this literature were not those who had led the revolt. The older group was still active, but most of them were now saying better what they had said before. The year 1925 saw *An American Tragedy,* *Barren Ground,* and *The Professor's House,* and the Pulitzer Prize for poetry at that time was going to Frost, Robinson, and Amy Lowell for volumes that fell short of their best; but the same years also saw the first important experimental work of Scott Fitzgerald, Ernest Hemingway, and their contemporaries. It was a crossroads in time, at which two generations met.

The younger generation of writers, most of whom were born in the final decade of the old century and nurtured in the years when the nation was reaching its maturity as a world power, were quite ready to consider themselves "lost" when they were plunged, at the moment of manhood, into what looked like the collapse of Western civilization. The world they had known, a world in which peace, prosperity and progress had been taken for granted as the evidences of an achieved humanity, was suddenly challenged by barbarities that had supposedly been laid aside for all time. Shocked and dismayed, they first were seized with the spirit of the Crusades and rushed out to set things right, to make the world once more "safe for democracy," to fight "the war to end wars," to care for the wounded, and to arouse the people of Europe against their misguided leaders. Woodrow Wilson led the campaign and provided most of the slogans, but Theodore Dreiser, H. L. Mencken, and the iconoclasts and critics of France, Russia, and England provided their reading. On the surface they appeared to be a company of idealists and reformers, but at heart they knew that the evil they were fighting lay closer to home than they cared to admit.

When the war ceased as suddenly as it had started, these young men looked back to their country only to find that it had suffered the shock but few of the actualities of war, and that its people had profited by war industries and the sense of power and self-righteousness that comes with victory. A second disillusionment then turned them against this insensitive country of theirs, and they took up, with all the enthusiasm they had put into the military crusade, a battle for literary and moral integrity both in America and in themselves. The vigor they had thrown into the driving of the wounded back from the front in Red Cross ambulances, or fighting in the air or in the soggy trenches, they now put into writing. Many—almost a majority—of them rejected the vigorous materialism of post-war prosperity in the United States and returned, after discharge from military service, to Europe, there to haunt the ateliers of Paris, to discuss art rather than politics, and, if one may judge from their own accounts, to waste their disillusioned minds and bodies in drink and dissipation. Even though the pose of decadence did not suit them as well as it had the sad young men of the nineties, the outlook was not promising for a new American literature that could offer solutions to the problems of humanity.

But the literature of power asks rather than answers questions. In the American writers who reached maturity between wars, what at first had seemed an irresponsible flight from reality turned out to be the means toward a realization of their true calling. These young men needed the perspective of distance as well as of time in order to discover new forms of art for the expression of man's dilemma in the twentieth century. The elder writers had posed the problems with which literary art must deal; the younger must learn to write. Whether they stayed abroad or came home and retreated from their society, they slowly taught themselves their art.

Among critics, Malcolm Cowley (b. 1898) and Edmund Wilson (b. 1895) were their best spokesmen. These two must stand for a host of others because they had a clear sense of the literary history of their own times. In Cowley's *Exile's Return* (1934), the experience of a generation of writers is summarized and evaluated. He and his fellows, he tells us, had found that European intellectuals were even more disillusioned than those at home. The burden of inferiority that American writers had traditionally taken for granted as their birthright somehow disappeared—"it was not so much dropped as it leaked away like sand from a bag carried on the shoulder." The realization that America possessed a folklore, new forms of art, and a recognizable national type and civilization gave them the necessary self-confidence. They created the myth of the Lost Generation and set to work to find themselves again. The story, as Cowley tells it, was a pattern of alienation and reintegration. He carries it up only to 1930, but he hints (especially in his revision of 1951) at the meaning of the following decade as well. Exile occupied the decade of the twenties—exile and devotion to art. Reintegration was still to come, and in 1934 the reconstruction of society seemed the natural means for its accomplishment. There were two paths for the artist: either to escape from society into the subjective problems of his own personality or to identify himself with humanity and accept the movements which seemed to promise best for social reform. In either case, there was work at home for the artist to do.

Wilson responded to his times even more fully than did Cowley. When *Axel's Castle* appeared in 1931, the new generation received its testament in art; a decade later, in 1940, *To the Finland Station* provided the formula for its faith in social reform. To Wilson must be credited the most impressive body of literary criticism produced by any one writer of this generation. Combining an immediate but usually accurate comprehension of even a totally new work of art with a firm grounding in historical method, Wilson's complete works, though largely ephemeral in their original inspiration, provided the literary chronicle of the era. He succeeded in producing, in his various reviews and essays, what he himself described to Christian Gauss, his teacher, as a contemporaneous "history of man's ideas and imaginings in the setting of the conditions which shaped them."

Wilson's criticism recognizes three forces operating on the literary mind of his times: symbolism, Freudianism, and Marxism. The first is primarily a concern of art as such; the other two are formulations of personality and of society. If English and American critics had failed to comprehend the work of modern writers, the reason, he explains in the introductory chapter of *Axel's Castle*, might be that they had not recognized a literary revolution which had occurred mainly outside English literature: the symbolist movement as developed in France but represented early in the work of Poe, Hawthorne, Melville, Whitman, and Emerson. Here was an indigenous American literary movement which was shared primarily with the great writers of Continental Europe rather than exclusively with those of Britain. All at once the feeling of American writers that they could command their own place in world literature was validated, the explanation was given. *Axel's Castle* was for this era what Van Wyck Brooks's *America's Coming of Age* had been for the earlier one.

Wilson's attempt to link modern naturalism with an earlier classicism, and symbolism with romanticism, is not altogether successful, but his discovery and definition of symbolism as such elucidates many lesser questions. It was, he points out, a revolt, as the earlier Romantic Movement had been in its first phases, against the objective and conformist demands of scientific rationalism. The poet must find or invent the special language in which to express his personality and feelings, which are different from those of everyone else. The symbols of the symbolists do not stand for broad generalizations, as do, for example, the Cross or the flag; they are private and special metaphors detached from their subjects and designed to convey unique personal feelings. In Yeats, Valéry, Eliot, Proust, Joyce, and Gertrude Stein, Wilson finds the chief exponents of the theory, the makers of modern literature, but he himself is unwilling to accept the divorce of the artist from society which this theory seemed to demand. In his final chapter, he contrasts the renunciation of experience as illustrated in the life-denying hero of Villiers de L'Isle-Adam's *Axel* (1890) with the life of primitive activity as lived by Rimbaud. Neither way would seem satisfactory alone, and yet the twentieth century was forced to a choice. Wilson's book is in effect an angry protest against his times as he is unwilling to accept this impasse either for himself or for literature. Instead of remaining a private language, symbolism, he feels, may come to offer a new and imperfectly understood means of expressing the complicated experiences presented by modern science. One must avoid Axel's castle if one wishes to contribute to the reintegration of modern man and society.

The way was thus open to the influence of Freud, who offered a formula for reevaluating the individual, and to Marx, who seemed to supply a similar instrument for society. Both claimed to wipe away Axel's belief that illusion is superior to reality, and to deal with man in the same scientific terms that man was learning to use in dealing with nature. In the critical essays of *The Triple Thinkers* (1938) and *The Wound and the Bow* (1941), and in his historical study of all branches of socialism, *To the Finland Station* (1940), Wilson explored the sources of these two systems of thought and applied them to literary problems. Without allowing himself to be seriously caught in the webs of dogma that entangled many lesser critics of art and society during these years, he provided the rationale of the American literary movement at its climax. Out of the creative tensions of naturalism-symbolism came the great works of Eugene O'Neill, Ernest Hemingway, Thomas Wolfe, William Faulkner, T. S. Eliot, and all the other once-young men who by 1935 had lived through war and spiritual exile and into an uneasy but dynamic harmony with their times and their country.

– 2 –

When O'Neill's *The Emperor Jones* (1920) moved uptown from Washington Square to Broadway, this modern movement in literature could be said to have reached the American theater. Here was a play on the most urgent of American social problems, that of the Negro, presented as a psychological rather than as a social analysis of the consequences of fear, and expressed in a wholly symbolic medium. Only a few months before, the Provincetown Players had produced his *Beyond the Horizon*, a realistic tragedy of warped lives and hostile nature, and before that, a succession of his shorter plays, most of them at the Wharf Theatre on the tip of Cape Cod. Suddenly—but only after undue delay—America found that it had its first major playwright, as well as a free theater movement similar to that of Europe. O'Neill's success in the realistic and expressionistic drama turned others from the traditions of romantic comedy and melodrama which had for so long bound the American stage, and opened the way for new literary experiments. He was followed in the succeeding years by Susan Glaspell, Maxwell Anderson, Sidney Howard, Elmer Rice, Paul Green, Robert E. Sherwood, Thornton Wilder, Clifford Odets, and a host of others who made the period of the twenties and thirties the high point in the history of American drama.

Strictly speaking, Eugene O'Neill (1888–1953) was not a member of the "lost generation." Not only was he senior by a few years to most of the group, but he did not share their war experience or their exile. Instead, he created his own wander years and moved, in 1920, into full creative productivity, coming to grips immediately with the problem of art in America. Son of an actor and playwright, James O'Neill, he reacted early and violently against such formal education as was offered him at a Catholic boarding school and at Princeton University. Between 1909 and 1914 he tried secretarial, newspaper, and theatrical work at home, but for a large part of the time he was roving the seas, prospecting for gold in Honduras, beachcombing in South America, and working as a seaman on a regular run between Southampton and New York. A physical breakdown led to six months of rest, during which he turned to drama as a medium of expression for the views of life that his varied experiences had begun to develop in him. A year (1914–1915) of work with George Pierce Baker in the 47 Workshop at Harvard confirmed his ambition and laid the foundation of his art. Throughout his career as a serious dramatist, which was uninterrupted until his last long illness, he kept two aims steadily in view: he wrote only for the stage, without being hampered by the conventions of the stage; and he wrote only to explore the human predicament and never solely to entertain. In all these years, but one play, *Ah, Wilderness!* (1933) bears triumphant evidence of what he could have done in lighter vein if he had wished to.

From the start of his career, O'Neill reflected the influences of both the naturalistic and the expressionistic currents in the drama. The similarity of his work to that of Ibsen, Strindberg, Hauptmann, and Chekov gives sufficient evidence of the forces that were feeding his powerful originality, whether he was aware of them or not. Early he discovered the themes of alienation from the land, and its counterpart, the lure and hostility of the sea, and he used them in such naturalistic treatments of frustration as *Beyond the Horizon* (1920), *Anna Christie* (1921), and the one-act plays with which he began his writing. The seaman Yank, who had appeared in both *Bound East for Cardiff* and *The Moon of the Caribbees,* served to lift him from the level of reality into a wholly symbolic play, *The Hairy Ape* (1922). Here Yank is a modern Everyman who denies the moral security of his steady job as a stoker and sets out on a quest to rediscover where he "belongs." Rejected both by the upper class as symbolized in the Fifth Avenue store windows and by the rebellious lower class as represented in the I.W.W., he reverts, as did the "Emperor" Jones, to his own primitive inner nature, only to find that he has also lost mastery of the basic animal passions. The true hairy ape which he releases from a cage in the zoo in order to help him destroy the society that has rejected him turns upon him and crushes him to death.

The theme and motivation of this play are obvious enough to hold an audience in the theater, but at the same time they carry a message which is personal and haunting. In this one excursion into the drama of revolution, O'Neill does not press home the point that here was man in rebellion against the capitalistic and technological society which was oppressing him. It was Yank's own brute nature, at last released wholly from social restraint, that brought his destruction. The crux of the problem was psychological rather than sociological. The dramatist's primary focus, which he maintained throughout his long career, was on what happens to the individual soul when it is lost somewhere between the realms of reality and illusion. The recognition of the subconscious mind and of the dual or multiple levels of motivation, conscious and unconscious, which is so basic a part of modern thinking about human conduct, he presented in a variety of experimental plays through devices which the Greeks had used, and in modern adaptations of the stories of Lazarus, Dionysus, and Oedipus.

In the two major trilogies *Strange Interlude* (1928) and *Mourning Becomes Electra* (1931) O'Neill reached the furthest possibilities of his art. The first of these is wholly modern and naturalistic in conception and technique. The device of the aside is invoked for long passages of introspection in order to tell the story of Nina Leeds as she sees herself and as others see her. The daughter of a New England professor, Nina suddenly finds that her promised conventional life is shattered by the death of her fiancé in the war before their union can be consummated. The sense of guilt which results from her frustration leads her to a variety of sexual experiences through which her full passional nature is revealed. Only O'Neill's absorbing knowledge of the theater and his understanding of individual human beings saves this play from the psychological laboratory and raises it to the level of naturalistic tragedy of

the kind that Dreiser learned to write. Nina is thoroughly convincing as a person, as are her men, and the unresolved final
scene in which she tries but fails to destroy the life of her son
by absorbing him into the complex of her passional needs has
the sense of purged emotions which all true tragedy invokes.

O'Neill tells a similar story in *Mourning Becomes Electra*,
but his naturalism is here modified by the conscious parallel of
his characters, themes, and situations with those of the classical Electra legend used by Aeschylus, Sophocles, and Euripides. In the decay of an old New England family, symbolized
in the "House" of Mannon, he sees repeated the disintegration
of the family of Agamemnon and the self-consuming passions
of the survivors: the wife Clytemnestra (Christine), the daughter Electra (Lavinia), and the son Orestes (Orin). Adultery
and incest become the instruments of destruction and the
symbols of morbid passions that stifle love as the family breaks
apart. Conventional human relations are blighted first by illicit
and then by ingrowing sensual love. The story opens with the
return of the Civil War Brigadier General Ezra Mannon to
his unfaithful wife, his disrupted home, and his son and daughter, already warped by frustration and hate. It closes with the
sister and brother freed from the immediate objects of their
repressions, their parents, but condemned to a life of remorse
and self-consuming guilt. The tragedy is complete in the Aris-
totelian sense, but it is also faithful to the demands of modern
psychological knowledge. The underlying classical legend
serves to universalize a story which might otherwise have
seemed to be merely local and morbid. Again O'Neill had
demonstrated his knowledge of human character and of the
requirements of the theater, and again he had transcended the
clinical and mechanical aspects of his experiment to create a

unified and moving poetic tragedy in prose. Three Pulitzer prizes (1920, 1922, and 1928) and the Nobel Prize in 1936 merely served to emphasize his achievement and his influence, both at home and abroad. In him American drama had come of age.

The impetus of this dynamic personality was immediately felt by other dramatists. Not only did they carry O'Neill's work in symbolic and naturalistic drama to further limits of experimentation, but even the more conventional forms of domestic comedy, historical pageantry, and the social problem play were revitalized. A more mature form of satire gave the comedies of Philip Barry and S. N. Behrman a depth that had been lacking in those of Clyde Fitch and Rachel Crothers, while comedy as such almost disappeared from the social problem plays of Susan Glaspell, Sidney Howard, and Robert Sherwood. Sidney Howard (1891–1939), another product of Baker's 47 Workshop, wrote a series of impressive plays in the mid-twenties, among which *They Knew What They Wanted* (1924) and *The Silver Cord* (1926) combined good theater with probing exploration of human values and passions. The lighter touch of Robert Sherwood's (b. 1896) *The Road to Rome* (1927) developed through the sentimentality of such plays as *Waterloo Bridge* (1930) to a melodrama of frustration in *The Petrified Forest* (1935) and a quietly passionate patriotism in *Abe Lincoln in Illinois* (1938).

Outright social criticism during these years borrowed heavily, as had O'Neill, from German expressionism. Elmer Rice (b. 1892) used this technique in *The Adding Machine* (1923) for an allegory of modern man, but in *Street Scene* (1929) and *Judgment Day* (1934) he gave his direct social protest a more realistic form. His work points in the direction of the Marxian revival of the thirties, but is not as specifically proletarian as *Waiting for Lefty* (1935) and *Golden Boy* (1937) of Clifford Odets or the plays of Albert Maltz. The Federal Theater Project (1936–1939), under the direction of Hallie Flanagan, also used experimental techniques to deal with contemporary problems, but in Thornton Wilder's (b. 1897) *Our Town* (1938) and *The Skin of Our Teeth* (1942) some of the problems of the times are raised from the level of social propaganda to that of more universal human experience through the skillful use of symbolism and fantasy.

It was Maxwell Anderson (b. 1888) who placed next to O'Neill in this dramatic revival. He too sought in Greek legend and in the *Poetics* of Aristotle a guide for the modern playwright. A series of historical plays on the lives of the queens, Elizabeth of England, Mary of Scotland, and Anne Boleyn, taught him some of the principles of classical tragedy, which he also applied to more modern themes and materials. His pioneering war play *What Price Glory?* (1924), which he wrote with Laurence Stallings, reflected a social concern that came out even more forcefully after the Sacco-Vanzetti trial in *Gods of the Lightning* (1928) and *Winterset* (1935). In *Winterset* Anderson most fully succeeded in his life-long ambition to bring poetry again to the stage by using verse to raise the level of intensity in ordinary scenes and incidents. A revenge play, suggestive more of Shakespeare than of Euripides, it transcends the specific social reference of its plot and the ordinariness of its people to create an ennobling tragedy of modern American life.

The coming of the second war in 1939 seemed to bring an end—or at least a major pause—to the renaissance in American drama of the two previous decades. In that year William

Saroyan (b. 1908) reflected the spirit of a new generation and a new time with his symbolic and escapist fantasies *My Heart's in the Highlands* and *The Time of Your Life*, but no new dramatist of serious intent appeared until after 1945. The Theatre Guild and the little theaters continued to produce serious plays, but many of them were revivals or translations. The older playwrights seemed to be exhausted as they turned to other interests. Many of them went to Hollywood to be absorbed by the movie industry, then in its stage of most sensational development; others had died or, like O'Neill, gone into semiretirement. The impetus of the naturalist-symbolist movement in the theater seemed, for the moment at least, to have run its course.

– 3 –

The symbolism of O'Neill, Rice, Anderson, and Saroyan was painted on large canvases with primary colors and sweeping movements. Drama can never, like fiction and poetry, become oversubtle because it is limited by the physical properties of the stage and by the circumstances of production, but in his break with reality and logic in such expressionistic pantomime as the scenes of *The Emperor Jones* and such frank exposures of subconscious processes as the asides of *Strange Interlude*, O'Neill had discovered Axel's castle for himself. His was a deliberate attempt to destroy dramatic conventions in order to free the primitive self-consciousness of man and to trick it into expression through the direct use of fragmented forms, much as the postimpressionistic or cubistic painter uses line and color. His last long play, *The Iceman Cometh*, is not so much a rhapsody on death as it is a pronouncement that illusion is a higher form of consciousness than reality. This is the answer of the symbolist to the demands of the naturalist for a literal record of life.

It was at this point that the influence of Gertrude Stein (1874–1946) on American fiction supplemented that of Theodore Dreiser. Like Dreiser a German-American, Gertrude Stein was unlike him in that she early had the advantages of travel and education. One of the most brilliant students of William James at Radcliffe, she studied the anatomy of the brain in the Johns Hopkins medical school and then applied her scientific knowledge to the arts of painting and writing. After 1902 she lived with her brother in Paris, cultivating her friendships with Matisse, Picasso, and other impressionistic and postimpressionistic painters, and attempted by experiments in words to do what they were attempting in paint. Her *Three Lives* (1909) captured the slow mental processes of three untutored women in a rhythmic and repetitious style that destroyed grammar and syntax in the interest of liberating the single word. Language thus became plastic, and its possibilities infinite. This breakdown of control was exhibited fully in *The Making of Americans* (1925), the most unreadable but perhaps the most influential novel of the era. The profligacy of this experiment in free form was somewhat corrected in later work like her opera *Four Saints in Three Acts* (1934), but she never lost sight of her discovery that art could live in "the complete actual present" by using words out of formal context as the plastic elements of direct expression. Her interest in irrationality and primitivism was a sophisticated escape from reality rather than, as in Dreiser and the more simple naturalists, an effort to track life to its sources.

The influence, whether direct or indirect, of Stein on O'Neill is found in a concern for the primitive consciousness, especially of the Negro, and in the effort to destroy coherence in language and dramatic forms. The same concerns are found in the sketches and short stories of Sherwood Anderson (1876–1941), who had known Carl Sandburg in Chicago and Gertrude Stein in Paris. The "grotesques" of his *Winesburg, Ohio* (1919) were merely portraits of the usual people of a small town, freed of their inhibitions by the artist and allowed to reveal their frustrated selves in spontaneous words. Anderson's interest in the folk of the race track, the Negro of the Delta, and the inhabitants of the village is a revolt against the mechanization of modern life and a seeking for human values in uninhibited sex. Like Henry Adams who came before him and William Faulkner who came later, Anderson believed that women still could supply the secret knowledge that men had lost, that they held the key to the ultimate mysteries. Faulkner knew Anderson in New Orleans and acknowledged a debt to him. A connection between them is immediately suggested by deep-lying similarities in their choice of themes, their picturesque and flowing styles, and their common search for a higher truth in the more primitive kinds of humanity.

When Anderson, in early middle life, closed the door to his own paint factory, deserted his family, and threw himself, as it were, onto life, he performed a symbolic act of renunciation of the modern American world which, to many younger writers, seemed to answer the tragic questions of Dreiser and the ironic criticism of Sinclair Lewis. By accepting illusion and alienation, he opened the road of symbolism in fiction, even though, for the time, he was a lonely traveler on that road.

The revolt of the younger generation was touched off by the semiautobiographical novel of Princeton life, *This Side of Paradise* (1920), by F. Scott Fitzgerald (1896–1940). Fitzgerald had come out of the West—from Lewis's Minnesota—and had served in World War I. Appearing in the same year as *Main Street*, his portrait of the "Jazz Age" was less a satire than a revelation. The background of wealth and privilege and the early personal successes of Amory Blaine in athletics, in friendship, in writing, and in romance are fit preparation for his disillusionment and subsequent abandonment to the search for pleasure, sensation, and forgetfulness. Actually there is more of the pose of hedonistic debauch of an earlier Bohemia inhabited by Oscar Wilde and Swinburne than of postwar cynicism in Blaine's—and Fitzgerald's—somewhat sophomoric abandon. There was as much talk as there was action in the destruction of all accepted moral codes that the Jazz generation threatened. Fitzgerald's own frantic quest for experience, his effort to satisfy his own and his even more neurotic wife's greed for wealth and sensation, and his "crack-up" at an early age are faithfully depicted or anticipated in this first novel. Here, from the inside, is a portrait of the end of one era and the beginning of another.

Fitzgerald's strength—and his weakness—lay in the sincerity of his confession and in the gift of words in which it was expressed. For one brief moment—in his most finished novel, *The Great Gatsby* (1925)—he managed to say what he had to say in a tightly wrought artistic form. This brief tale of the love and death of a fabulously wealthy bootlegger becomes authentic only because it is told, not by Jay Gatsby himself, but by the admiring young cousin of the unhappily married Daisy with whom Gatsby is in hopeless love. The use of a narrator gives Fitzgerald the detachment that his first novel had needed and that his later novels, *Tender Is the*

Night (1934) and the fragment *The Last Tycoon* (1941), also lacked. The story that Nick Carraway has to tell can remain a glamorous mystery because the illusions of which it consists could appear to him as tragedy rather than as the romantic sentimentality they would become in the light of a more rational day. Fitzgerald's success as a popular writer for the magazines and his failure to develop as an artist are reflections of a keen but limited understanding of his own age rather than of moral weaknesses in that age or in himself.

John Dos Passos (b. 1896) was an artist of firmer and perhaps less sensitive texture. In him the revolt of youth, with its attack on the basic institutions of American society, hinted by Lewis and announced by Fitzgerald, really struck out into the open. In an early volume of essays on the art and culture of Spain, *Rosinante to the Road Again* (1922), he presented himself as a student and critic of world society, and his first important novel, *Three Soldiers* (1921), was more significant as a general study of the effects of war on the human personality than as a revelation of individual character. His radical experiments with the language and structure of fiction were undertaken in the spirit of journalism—the effective exposure of social and cultural conditions—rather than as art for its own sake.

Like Hemingway, MacLeish, and many others, a product of the Middle West, Dos Passos shared with them the pattern of Eastern college education, service in Europe in the armed forces or with the Ambulance Corps, and postwar alienation from his times and his country. His *Three Soldiers* was the first of an endless succession of war novels, by many hands, in a realistic vein. Essentially a reporter, he sought in the civilization of Spain, Russia, and Mexico—the current centers of social revolution—the meaning of alienation and its answer. His novels were interspersed, throughout his career, with reports on his travels, like *In All Countries* (1934), and with tracts on political and social theory, like his study of Jefferson (1954); and in all of his better fiction the core meaning is derived from a political or economic problem. Squarely in the polemic tradition which can be traced back through Howells and Mark Twain to Cooper and Paulding, Dos Passos drew upon his knowledge of architecture for his sense of structure and on his studies of language and symbol for his variety of fictional technique. In his work that aspect of naturalism which depended upon the criticism of society found its most effective expression in the art of fiction because he went to school to Henry James as well as to Theodore Dreiser.

Manhattan Transfer (1925) was his first really experimental novel. Using the panoramic view which became his trade-mark, he told the sordid story of a group of inhabitants of New York City and of their confused and often morbid relationships. His plot centers on the city itself rather than on any individual, and his theme is social deterioration and decadence. There are Marxist implications in his attack on the capitalistic system in its every aspect, but his social philosophy is not doctrinaire as was that of some of his contemporaries; for this reason his work has outlived the many novels on similar themes of the period 1925–1939.

The trilogy *U.S.A.* (1938) is composed of *The 42nd Parallel* (1930), *1919* (1932), and *The Big Money* (1936). Again using the panoramic method to survey, in this case, the whole range of contemporary civilization in the United States, he applied it in a more systematic and complex fashion.

His main stream of action involves the lives of a selected few characters whose stories are told much more fully and consistently than in the earlier novel. This solid core of fiction is then seen from several points of view outside itself: the "Newsreel," which uses newspaper headlines to shout at the social awareness of the times; the "Camera Eye," which reflects the subjective level of the author's reactions, often totally irrelevant to the event, by a stream-of-consciousness method; and the thumbnail biographies of prominent people —Ford, Debs, Roosevelt, Morgan, and others—which offer contrast and parallel to the meaner lives of the fictional characters. These various components are woven together by a system of staggered episodic fragments, with the effect of immediate confusion but over-all unity of impression. Technically one of the most ambitious novels of its time, *U.S.A.* succeeds in achieving its main objective with sufficient force to hold together its diverse elements and to give a single and powerful total impression.

The second trilogy, *District of Columbia* (1953), is less unified than the first because Dos Passos had turned from attack to defense. By now he had accepted a more native democratic loyalty, and from this base he launched diatribes against the three political systems that seemed to him to threaten those principles: Communism in *Adventures of a Young Man* (1939), Fascism in *Number One* (1943), and the New Deal in *The Grand Design* (1949). Largely abandoning his panoramic method, he now used a more conventional technique and a more conservative social philosophy. Although it can be argued that he had not substantially altered his political and social views, the objects of his attack were so different in the 1940's from those of the 1930's and his methods in the second work so much less experimental than in the first that many of his critics have dismissed him as an exciting revolutionist turned tame conservative. Time alone can discover the unity of purpose in his best writing, both as artist and as social critic, and reaffirm his position in the tradition of social criticism in American fiction.

- 4 -

Dos Passos sought to resolve the central conflict of modern living in terms of society as a whole, Thomas Wolfe (1900–1938) confronted the same conflict within a single human soul—himself. Wolfe was even more free of dogma or doctrine than was Dos Passos, but he depended, as did his fellow naturalist, upon the most modern knowledge in his field of interest: for him, psychology. Whereas Dos Passos looked outward to the panorama of moving and changing life that passed before him, Wolfe looked inward and tried to capture, through observation and memory, the essence of its meaning for the artist within him. A realist in his approach to his material, he was a master symbolist in its expression. The sensory impression received through a voracious sensibility had to be paralleled, detail for detail, by subjective reaction and consequent meaning. Substituting the modern view of man and nature for the idealism of the transcendentalists, he revived their organic theory of art and developed a symbolism which bears a close relationship to that of Emerson, Melville, and Whitman. His confusions were those of the naturalistic view of the universe dictated by modern science; his illuminations were those of American aesthetic experience at its best.

It is impossible to separate Thomas Wolfe the writer

from Eugene Gant and George Webber, the two protagonists of his fiction. The life of his major character is always entangled in the life of its creator and it always derives its power directly from the imagination as the events of experience are reviewed within the creator's mind. Wolfe seems constantly to have tortured himself in his efforts to get his art outside his personality and to find in aesthetic objectivity the meaning of his experience, but it is perhaps fortunate that he did not succeed. His was not the way of a deliberate artist like Faulkner or Eliot. Once wholly outside himself, Wolfe would probably have lost his vision; he could no longer have commanded its unfolding. In the novels in which he thought he had succeeded, he achieved only a philosophical objectivity —only a command of ideas, not of sensation—and these novels are correspondingly weaker than the earlier ones. His art was one with his genius, organic and spontaneous rather than calculated and controlled.

The tendency of all naturalists to write long and detailed autobiographies has given us a remarkably full knowledge of just who Wolfe was, of the events and experiences of his life, and of what he was trying to make of it. In addition to his self-revealing novels, he has left many letters to his mother and others and a long essay, *The Story of a Novel* (1936). The parallel of fact and fiction begins with the birth of Gant-Webber-Wolfe in the hill-entombed town of Altamont, Old Catawba (Asheville, North Carolina), the son of a tempestuous giant of a stonecutter from the North and a repressed but equally violent Southern mother. It proceeds to his schooling, his early loves and hesitant friendships, his stormy family relationships and his romantic dreams, his further education in the University at Pulpit Hill (Chapel Hill), and his final revolt and departure from his mountain prison, first in spirit and then in fact, for the North and a writer's career.

The theme of this epic is that of escape, its failure, and the effort to return "home." The cycle of one man's life is therefore the symbol of the basic human cycle from womb to tomb, and the quest for freedom from this earthbound fate is the struggle for identification with the father rather than with the mother. Borrowing freely from the system of symbols offered by psychoanalysis, but putting them to his own use, Wolfe proceeds then to describe his rise and fall in alternate hope and despair.

Eugene Gant is the protagonist of two novels: *Look Homeward, Angel* (1929) and *Of Time and the River* (1935). The first tells the story from birth to the moment of departure for Harvard to learn the art of playwriting at Baker's 47 Workshop, which Wolfe attended in 1920–1922; the second carries him through this experience and on to the wander year in France. As a detailed study of childhood and adolescence, it suggests the romantic *Weltschmerz* of Carlyle, Rousseau, and Goethe. Eugene suffers his own *Sturm und Drang*, his own everlasting nay and yea. His lack of control of these feelings is reflected in the torrent of words that pours from his creative pen, sometimes startling and deeply moving, sometimes revolting in their meaningless rhetoric. It is reported that when Thomas Wolfe once submitted a manuscript to Maxwell Perkins, the editor at Scribner's, he brought it to the publisher's office in a truck; when Perkins had finished the task of cutting and editing he returned it to his rooms in a taxi. Of such tall tales is the legend of the gargantuan Wolfe made. Anecdote heaps upon anecdote as though he were a Paul Bunyan of the pen.

Whatever the cause—Perkins, Wolfe, or the inherent form of the material itself—his first novel has a much tighter internal unity than has any of its three and a half successors. The mother-father complex is understood and constantly present in a series of symbols: the encircling hills and the angel of death, the river and the train, and the recurring trio of a stone, a leaf, a door. "Which of us is not forever a stranger and alone?" asks Wolfe, and Eugene answers with the wailing cry, "O lost, and by the wind grieved, ghost, come back again!" In the death of his brother Ben, his longing to lose himself in another living human being was once and forever thrown back, unanswered, upon him: you can't go home again. "It had grown dark. The withered leaves were shaking." This was his realization of dawning maturity, and the novel was done.

Young people in general read this story with avid interest because the experience of adolescence is here so fully and accurately realized, and then they read on into its successors, only to discover that what seemed like the unity of life revealed through art is lost again. *Of Time and the River* opens with the account of the train trip north, an episode which might well have served as an introduction and background for subsequent events but which runs on to the length of a short novel in itself. Success had freed Wolfe from some of the authority of his editor, with a resulting disproportion of material and feeling. To those who like their Wolfe straight, this is an advantage; but the novel also lacks a compelling central theme. Neither the friendship with Starwick, the love of Ann—"strong, grand, and tender"—nor the recapture of his childhood memories was sufficient theme to hold his spiritual wanderings to their course.

Wolfe realized his failure and told of his reaction to it in the subsequent novels, now in the person of another alter ego, George Webber. In the front matter of his second novel he had allowed his publisher to announce a series of six in all, which were to deal with Eugene and with the Gant and Pentland families from 1791 to 1933. Of these, he there tells us, "the first four have now been written and the first two published." But *The October Fair* (*1925–1928*) and *The Hills Beyond Pentland* (*1838–1922*), if actually written at that time, must have been in unfinished and confused condition. At all events, when a third and fourth novel finally did appear they bore little resemblance to the implications of this announcement.

Meanwhile Wolfe had quarreled with Perkins and had moved his trunk of manuscripts and his loyalty to Harper's editor, Edward C. Aswell. The painful story is told by Wolfe himself in his final novel and has been retold and discussed many times since then. The rights and wrongs of the issue are blotted out by Wolfe's illness and death before the next volume could be issued by his new publisher. Aswell became the sponsor of George Webber and his two books: *The Web and the Rock* (1939) and *You Can't Go Home Again* (1940). *The Hills Beyond* (1941) is a collection of fragments. These volumes completed Wolfe's published work except for a collection of short stories and another of the lyric passages from his novels, printed as verse.

In the opening of *The Web and the Rock*, a renamed Eugene Gant, now less gangling and more compact in appearance but still huge and awkward, steps off the boat from Europe in the person of George Webber and takes up the life of a writer and teacher in New York and Brooklyn. His job as instructor in English composition at the fictionalized Washington Square College helps him to tide over the period until the publication of his first novel (about his own youth in North Carolina). His emotional life is soon centered on Esther Jack, the wife of a successful and indulgent businessman, and herself a scene designer in the new theater movement. The novel follows the course of this stormy love almost to the final parting. For Wolfe it is more than the courting of an attractive woman—it is first his absorption and then his rejection of the city as a place of refuge—for Esther is the voice of his needed but unwanted maturity. The events once more are but symbols of his inner quest, even though they are recounted with such detailed and literal truth that the mystic quality which carried the earlier novels is here lost for long pages. Wolfe's newly discovered objectivity which he prized so highly had merely robbed him of some of his emotional and rhetorical power, but when he allows the story to seize him and write itself in the old manner his power returns. The green sorcery of that "final, fatal and ruinous April" when he parts from Esther conquers him with hate as well as love. After the storm, he finds that again he can utter his "wild goat-cry of pain and joy and ecstasy." With that he remembers through his pain the hills that he had left.

You Can't Go Home Again is Webber's—and Wolfe's—final renunciation of the North Carolina part of his past also. A less unified novel than its predecessor, it contains more of the old Wolfe because, in his friendships with Sinclair Lewis and Maxwell Perkins, he gives of himself with his recaptured ego-centric abandon. In the end it is America itself that he turns to as the foreboding of early death seizes him: "To find a land more kind than home, more large than earth—"

Wolfe never quite grew up in the ordinary sense because

he rejected all that Esther Jack and Maxwell Perkins and the city had to offer him. In short, he successfully fought off his own completed maturity; but his loss was also a gain. By holding on to youth to the end, he realized the unquenchable hunger and thirst of life, and his faith in the power of words to resolve the conflicts of mind and heart made it imperative for him to reveal all of himself—and with himself, humankind—more fully than has any other modern American novelist. He was by his inescapable nature the spontaneous, organic artist of America that Whitman had struggled to become.

– 5 –

The contrasting violences in Dos Passos' denunciation of society and Wolfe's revelation of the inner self are fused and quieted in the short stories and novels of Ernest Hemingway (b. 1898) by a mastery of the art of fiction. Here was an artist whose control of his medium reached from the most profound levels of meaning to the uppermost limits of conscious style and language. In one sense Hemingway was more limited in scope than most of his contemporaries, for he had but a single theme —how man may meet death in a world stripped of all values except that of intensity. But in the larger sense he was, with the possible exceptions of Faulkner and Eliot, the most nearly universal of them all, for in this one image of stoic courage, repeated in all the moods and ages of man from Nick Adams of *in our time* (1924) to the fisherman of *The Old Man and the Sea* (1952), he made up in depth for what he lacks in range.

Awareness of death by violence came to him in the hunting trips with his father in the woods of northern Michigan; and of the complex of civilized society in his journalistic days in Kansas City. Like many other young idealists of his generation, he chose the American Ambulance Corps for his war experience, and he reported rather than fought his battles. The Hemingway hero of the early novels, battle-scarred either mentally or physically, is but the symbol of the writer who deserted after the peace to join the expatriate group in Paris. Gertrude Stein appreciated nevertheless how real the desertion was when she christened the whole generation in his person with the adjective "lost." O lost, and by the wind grieved, ghost . . .

Hemingway's break with his own past and with the civilization he had left behind in the prosperous land of his birth was complete in a sense in which Wolfe's was only partial. The stoic impersonality of his first hero, his alter ego, is in sharp contrast to the emotional self-abandon and self-pity of the young Eugene Gant. Nick Adams is only present to the stories collected as *in our time*—ironically, a time in which there is no peace—as the boy who observes and learns from the stupidities and sordid violence of a succession of intimate human episodes. Here was a new kind of short story, plotless and episodic, stripped of emotion and chary of language, but bound into a tight and powerful sequence by a receptive and recording sensibility.

Nick disappears in the later work, for Hemingway learned how as author to be that recording personality. By this means he could write of his heroes with a detachment as cool and impersonal as that of the soul regarding its useless body on the morning after death. It is this special quality that distinguishes all of Hemingway's best work; and out of it he created a symbolism and a language that many have attempted to imitate—always without success. His trick of dispassionate compression is not a technical device; it is the essential part of his attitude toward life.

Just what the influence of Gertrude Stein meant to him as an artist would be difficult to determine. Perhaps it was only the new conception of the power and use of language, which was coming from James Joyce and the international Paris group in general, that freed Hemingway from the conventions of fiction which otherwise might have hampered him. From them he might have learned the value of the word and phrase as immediate symbols of intense, momentary, and highly personal experience rather than as instruments disciplined by normative grammar and rhetoric. With a born sense of inner discipline that most of his contemporaries lacked, Hemingway followed in this path and created a new and distinctive style for his special message.

The expatriate group of *The Sun Also Rises* takes its stand squarely on the principle of an alienation from society that had been forced upon it by the circumstances of the times. His war injury and his resulting impotence make Jake Barnes the symbol of his own and his creator's generation. Others in the story are less obviously cut off from normal experience and distracted by violent substitutes. Lady Brett Astley's final cry, "We could have had such a damned good time together," is set in so low a key that the reader almost fails to realize that here is the whole meaning of the story. The normal world was already a world of the might-have-been. Now it was only a good time—a phrase capable of interpretation on any level from the highest to the lowest—it was intensity alone that they were seeking and that they found fleetingly in frantic love-making, in death in the bull ring, in Martini after Martini. Fitzgerald's jazz was now providing the accompaniment for a macabre dance of death. Nihilism was complete.

So total a denial of values could seem to have only one

outcome: this writer would write no more. But Hemingway denied the denial. Ruthless probing to the depths of the human predicament had discovered an unsuspected rock bottom. The will to live was there, and beyond it, as Faulkner was later to assert so defiantly in his Nobel Prize address, the will to prevail. On this base an art could be built.

To the readers of that day, Hemingway's next novel, *A Farewell to Arms* (1929), seemed only another farewell to everything. The symbolic alienation of the Caporetto desertion is not healed by the intensity of Catherine's love and flight. With her death Frederic Henry, the new Hemingway Everyman, is left in a strange land, alone and without direction. Wounded and haunted by his own inadequacy, he had known love and death; bound to the level plain, he had finally discovered and had sought the mountains. Even though he might never learn to climb, he could not now die by his own hand. Hemingway heroes do not commit suicide even though they know how to face death when the moment comes.

A later generation of critics would discover how central this story was to Hemingway's vision, how all his other writings were but an expansion or a contraction of the theme here so simply stated. Whether he himself recognized this fact or not, he now rested from storytelling for almost a decade. When he had returned from his African safaris and from his books on bull fighting and on big-game hunting, he was ready to provide for his hero the social frame so lacking in all the early stories. The insensitive Harry Morgan of *To Have and Have Not* (1937) finally learns in his private bootlegging war with the Federal Government that one man alone cannot survive; and, in the Spanish Revolution, Hemingway experienced for himself this revelation. Robert Jordan of *For Whom the*

Bell Tolls (1940) differs from Frederic Henry only in his recognition of the truth of the preaching of the poet John Donne, quoted at the start of the novel: "No man is an island, entire of itself." The critics who saw in this book merely a tract for the Loyalist cause were not reading Hemingway. For him now there were two parties to every alienation: the man and his society. His canvas was larger, his theme the same.

It is hardly likely that this novel represented an awakened social consciousness, an overdue conversion of the most subjective and individualistic of American writers to a doctrinaire commitment. As the Communist and Fascist powers poured support into this dress rehearsal for the great conflict, idealists of all countries were drawn to one side or the other, and the Loyalist cause seemed hardly distinguishable from that of democracy. Jordan fights for that cause, but his is a private war. He is forever at odds with the Spanish guerrillas with whom he hides out in the mountain cave while waiting for the moment to come when he may blow up his bridge and so fulfill his destiny. Political theories and programs have little to do with the motives of Pilar, the earth woman, who commands her weakling mate Pablo; and it is in the intense and physical love for a woman of his kind rather than in self-sacrifice for a cause that Jordan finds his reasons for life and for death. The stupidity and suspicions of both parties to the political conflict cancel out any immediate social significance to Jordan's sacrifice. He loves Maria, he blows up his bridge, he meets a meaningless death in flight; but he has heard the bell toll and he can die thinking, "One thing well done can make—"

In several of his short stories, Hemingway's meaning is even clearer, his symbols more daring, his language sharper, and his plot more compressed. Perhaps the central symbol is to be found in "The Snows of Kilimanjaro" (1936). In such earlier stories as "The Killers" (1927), or even in the more fully developed "The Short Happy Life of Francis Macomber" (1936), death is confronted with varying degrees of indifference or courage, but in "The Snows of Kilimanjaro" both levels, that of symbol and that of reality, are fully developed. The sordidness of his personal affair with the woman who is tending him is intensified by the wounded man's memories of happier days as he lies in the hot sun of the African plain to wait for his leg to fester and poison his system. On this level, his only hope is the possibility of a rescue by air; but there is a frozen leopard close to the western summit of the snow-capped and towering Kilimanjaro. "No one has explained what the leopard was seeking at that altitude." No one need explain why the plane, bearing him finally to his dream of safety and health, suddenly turned left to head for the unbelievably white square head of the mountain.

In the novel of his maturity—a part of his proposed master work—Hemingway took the same turn. There is little of reality left in *The Old Man and the Sea* (1952), even though there was a last pathetic effort to retell his soldier story once more in *Across the River and into the Trees* (1950). The old fisherman is a Christian symbol used to reveal a pagan truth. He and his marlin are never much other than man and nature in their final and unresolved conflict. Both are triumphant, for the old man "gets" his fish even though he is not allowed to have it. "I do not care who kills who," he says when the battle is in its final stages; but in the end he could sleep and dream of lions—or perhaps, leopards. An era had found a literary voice for its skepticism and its faith.

CHAPTER XII

THE USES OF MEMORY
Eliot, Faulkner

THERE is a law in physics which proposes for every force an equal but opposite force; thus nature retains her equilibrium. In literary history some such law seems to supply for every dynamic or romantic movement an equal and countermovement toward standards, forms, restraints. The literary movement which flowered in the United States in the twenties and thirties was no exception; it carried within it the seeds of reaction. Even before 1920, T. S. Eliot was calling for the depersonalization of poetry and the recognition of an ideal order in art. He and a few others were ready to apply the lash to unruly American authors and to bring them into line.

Some of these authors heeded the warning and applied sufficient discipline to their impulses to create *The Great Gatsby, Winterset, Mourning Becomes Electra, A Farewell to Arms*, and the lyrics of Robert Frost. Others, like Dreiser, Lewis, Sandburg, and Wolfe, were unreconstructed. The organic theory of art, which had always been so essential a part of the American tradition in literature, kept the floodgates open to free exploration of meaning and form and to the unhampered expression of emotion and thought. Romantic naturalism in the twentieth century had developed a large and dynamic symbolism in O'Neill and Wolfe, as an earlier romanticism had in Melville and Emerson; and, for the second time in American literary history, there was a major renaissance.

By 1935 the movement had reached its climax. The outbreak of the Second World War within a few years probably deferred the reaction for at least a decade, but by 1945 the counterrevolutionary movement was exerting its full force as a balance and corrective. The aesthetic school of criticism led the way in this reaction. Some years elapsed before those associated in this movement came to be generally known as "New Critics." In its formative stages the movement was distinguished by its turn away from the artist and his problems, historical or otherwise, to the work of art. Because poetry is recognized as the "purest" form of literary art, and therefore most subject to discipline and most nearly akin to the arts of music and painting, aesthetic criticism turned first to a new study of its aims and methods. Sidney Lanier had led in this direction by his early effort to make a science of English verse on the principles of music and of physics, and the neo-Bohemians like J. G. Huneker, who had helped to split the cocoon of nineteenth century "puritanism," identified poetry with the impressionist movements in both music and painting and therefore made it subject to the same controls as these kindred arts. But the process of working out a systematic discipline for it was slow. "The anarchy of impressionism," said Spingarn, "is a temporary haven and not a home. . . . We must substitute the conception of the critic as thinker." With his formulation of an aesthetic position based mainly on the work of Croce, in his lecture on "The New Criticism" (1910), he gave the aesthetic movement a name and a clear direction.

Spingarn is not always accepted by the later "New Critics" as one of their number because he stopped short of applying the principles he had formulated. Wholly a theorist, he never himself became the critic he had called for. He therefore remained, like Kenneth Burke (*Counter-Statement*, 1931) and a number of others, a shaper of the new movement rather than a contributor to it. The work of developing an aesthetic discipline through the close study of works of art was left to such practicing poets as Ezra Pound (b. 1885). Pound's contributions to critical thinking and practice were eclectic and sporadic, but they were also original, courageous, and effective. In his early connection with Amy Lowell and the Imagists of *Poetry* magazine, and in his association with the international group that gathered in the Paris studio of Gertrude and Leo Stein, in the alleys of Soho, and on Italian shores, Pound preached a purer form of devotion to the religion of taste than did any of his American contemporaries. From T. E. Hulme in England and Rémy de Gourmont in France he learned that it might be possible to erect into law the direct impressions received from art. Searching widely in unexplored or forgotten literatures—Provençal, Elizabethan, Chinese—and experimenting with every new fad or method that he or his friends could devise, he succeeded finally in bringing criticism into close relationship once more with poetry, both made and in the making. Erratic as his own work was, both in poetry and in critical prose, Pound became for T. S. Eliot and others of the aesthetic group the yeast that leavened their art. Critical ideas which he threw out in an apparently careless gesture of defiance were later assembled and ordered by the cooler Eliot into an aesthetic harmony; and the method which he developed for his *Hugh Selwyn Mauberley* (1920) and for his project of one hundred *Cantos* (1925, and later) was explained by the philosopher-poet and applied in *The Waste Land* and others of his poems with far greater technical proficiency and poetic depth than the "master" himself could command.

Of lesser formalist poet-critics there were many. John Crowe Ransom (b. 1888) was the sponsor of a group at Vanderbilt University in the twenties who called themselves the Fugitives and who sought in a revival of Southern agrarianism to create in life a world as pure as the world of poetry they had envisioned. Perfection in the way a mathematical equation is perfect became their ideal. To achieve it, they turned to a restudy of language and imagery under the incentive of the British I. A. Richards who had proposed a form of "practical" criticism, the analysis of meaning as actually conveyed by the poem to the reader rather than as intended by the author. A new analytical criticism followed the development of this analytical poetry, a criticism at once impressionistic in its sanctions and scientific in its methods. Debate and discussion, formulation of theory and application to verse, went on steadily through the twenties and thirties as the movement became nation-wide. Then suddenly, in 1945, it became apparent that America had a strong, entrenched, and authoritarian body of literary critics, most of whom were accomplished writers of verse, but that American poetry had no new voice.

– 2 –

Thomas Stearns Eliot (b. 1888) was the dominant figure of this reactionary movement and of his literary era. Born in St. Louis and educated at Harvard, the Sorbonne, and Oxford, he was scarcely thirty years old when he thrust himself into the center of the literary scene with a small volume of poetry,

Prufrock and Other Observations (1917), and a prose collection, *The Sacred Wood: Essays on Poetry and Criticism* (1920). Then an unknown bank clerk in London, he became within a very few years the acknowledged leader of the younger poets both in Britain and in the United States, and as editor of the *Criterion* he was soon looked to by friend and foe alike as the giver of laws and the arbiter of taste in the new poetry and criticism. The body of commentary on his ideas, his achievements, and his "dictatorship" accumulated far faster than did the carefully wrought poetry and critical prose that he parsimoniously offered to his public. By 1925 he was admittedly the leading poet and critic of both the land of his birth and that of his adoption.

The roots of Eliot's thought and art lay deep in the British-American tradition. The Eliot family had produced, among other distinguished New Englanders, a Harvard president and a Congregational clergyman who had shared with one of Hawthorne's ancestors the duties of a juror at the Salem witchcraft trials. The poet's grandfather had gone West after graduating from Harvard Divinity School and had become a founder and chancellor of Washington University. His father was a prominent St. Louis industrialist, and his mother, a poet and biographer herself, was descended from one of the first settlers of the Bay Colony. When T. S. Eliot entered Harvard in 1906, he was completing for himself a familiar cycle in American frontier experience: the return to the East in a later generation of a pioneering Western family. But Eliot reversed the frontier movement in more than the physical sense. He retreated into his art, and later into his religion, building a house for his soul with the care of a hibernating caterpillar that knows of the beauty to be revealed.

The St. Louis of Eliot's youth shared with Chicago the role of capital of the newly awakened Midwest. It not only harbored a vigorous young university, but had libraries, publishers and periodicals. Of the periodicals, perhaps the best known was the *Journal of Speculative Philosophy*, edited by William Torrey Harris who had been associated with Bronson Alcott in the Concord School of Philosophy and who had carried Concord idealism to St. Louis in 1857. Paul Elmer More, also from St. Louis, returned to teach after studying at Harvard; and it was in St. Louis that Dreiser began his newspaper career. Which of these influences were felt by the young Eliot no biographer has as yet disclosed, although More remembered teaching Eliot's brother in the University School; but there may well be a connection between them and Eliot's acknowledged kinship with Irving Babbitt and the neohumanist movement in the early phases of his thinking. The groundwork of his criticism was a thorough training in philosophy.

This philosophical foundation probably accounts for the tone of authority which his critical pronouncements carry through inconsistencies, contradictions, growth, and change. The mixture of quiet irony with firm conviction in each of his statements allowed for a flexibility of thought and feeling without sacrifice of assurance. His readers heard at once in his criticism the voice of a man who had thought his way through his problems and was giving them the mature results of that thinking, however tentative or skeptical his conclusions at that moment might be. In *The Sacred Wood* he offered the problem which is perhaps the cornerstone of his critical thinking: the relationship between tradition and individual talent, of the new work of art to the existing order of art masterworks, of the present to the past and the past to the present and the future.

Two correlated problems were immediately evident: the relationship between the poet and the poem before, during, and after the act of creation, and the need for a reversal of the historical process so that the insights of the present might throw their illumination upon the past. These few problems and their variations provide the themes of Eliot's best poetry from *Prufrock* to *Four Quartets* and of his criticism throughout his career. They guide his reading and his writing.

The searcher is often thought of as a romantic merely by that fact alone, but the objects of Eliot's search were order, form, and discipline. No one was surprised, therefore, when he announced in *For Lancelot Andrewes* (1928) that he was a royalist in politics, a classicist in literature, and an Anglo-Catholic in religion. Later attempts on his part to avoid the dogmatic consequences of this profession of faith did not change its essential accuracy. Here was an exploring, growing, changing reactionary on a well directed and meaningful search for values which both he personally and his times felt that they had lost. His leadership was assured to the extent of his genius and his energies, both of which were as striking as those of any writer of his day. His most germinal work was done in the twenties; his influence on contemporary literature became paramount in the forties. Meanwhile he had turned to a third phase of his creative activity, the drama, leaving the small volumes of poetry and criticism virtually completed: *Collected Poems, 1909–1935* (1936), *Selected Essays, 1917–1932* (1932, revised 1934 and 1950), and *The Complete Poems and Plays* (1952).

Eliot's poetry, both lyric and dramatic, is a series of experiments toward achieving the kind of art he describes in his criticism. He tells us that the immediate inspiration for his earliest verses was Jules Laforgue, that from him he learned both wit and visual imagery. The debt is of course broader than this, for the method of the French symbolist movement is indigenous to his poetry from the start, and behind that, the method of the English metaphysical poets of the seventeenth century, notably Jonson, Milton, Marvell, and Donne. This is the method that Emerson and Emily Dickinson had also striven to recapture, for both of them, like Eliot, rejected the nineteenth century British romantic poets to study with the early metaphysicals; Emerson with George Herbert and Emily Dickinson with Sir Thomas Browne. There is something about the liberalized Puritan conscience—even as early as the colonial American poet Edward Taylor—which is thus drawn to violent symbolism as a means of escaping from a disturbed emotional condition into a more impersonal if not yet a quite codified moral and aesthetic order. Eliot was thus squarely in the American literary tradition even though he could not accept modern American life; and he revealed himself as a moralist even though his road to moral realization lay through art; an art that led directly into theology, without an engagement with ethics as such.

The earlier poetry—through *The Waste Land* (1922)—reveals the violence of this method and, at its best, achieves its desired objectivity. Myth, as man's permanent record of his experience, must be recaptured and used as a measure of contemporary events and personal emotions. Broad-bottomed Sweeney, Burbank with a Baedeker, the impotent J. Alfred Prufrock, are characters in a comedy, drawn from contemporary life, high and low, but representative, each in his way, of modern man's incompetence to deal directly with his condition. Memories such as these are awakened in the opening passages of *The Waste Land* only to be at once associated with memories drawn from the legend of the Holy Grail, from Ecclesiastes, from an early and blighted romance of the poet, from Shakespeare's *The Tempest,* and from Baudelaire. Scraps of experience are thus assembled in what at first seems merely a meaningless potpourri until the poem settles down to its primary task, an aesthetic exploration of the meaning of the sterility of modern life. Because it is an exploration rather than an exposition, *The Waste Land* has escaped those who would find in it an intellectual order and outcome. This poem contains no answers, but the question it asks—"Shall I at least set my lands in order?"—may imply almost any answer that the reader wishes. At the base of its structure lie the four elements—earth, air, fire, and water—and in the foreground, used as a means of tying the action together, are the various vegetation or fertility myths with their sexual implications and their haunting reiterations of the themes of birth, love, and death. But the strength of the poem lies in its shock of perspective achieved simultaneously on a number of levels of sensibility so that a quick understanding is virtually impossible for the most careful reader; but the rewards of re-reading are great. Eliot has gone far beyond the limitations of the symbolist who uses his art as a private world of escape for himself only. He starts with his private world and draws, without apology or explanation, upon his reading and experience in such a way that his special clusters of symbols are erected into worlds of escape for others as well as himself. The difference between his work and that of lesser poets who are merely obscure is not at once apparent because such a poem as *The Waste Land* does not immediately reveal its underlying philosophy. The difference between it and the *Cantos* of Ezra Pound, for example—two poems of equal scope which employ almost identical methods—is that Eliot's poem has the firm base in human integrity which Pound early rejected and never recaptured.

Much might be made of two developments in Eliot's progress as an artist: of his shift from purely aesthetic to theological-aesthetic materials and methods, and of his increasing interest in dramatic rather than lyric poetry as a medium. These changes were not as abrupt as they might appear, for the early poetry was an examination of what is essentially a theological problem (the relationship of modern man to a deity who seems to have forgotten him) in an essentially dramatic form (the projection of personal experience into a set of symbolic and representative characters and events).

Ash Wednesday (1930) marks the shift from concern for modern man, with his sense of personal futility and of social waste, to a concern for the tradition of Christianity as a symbolic system of human values. This is a psalm neither of life nor of death, but of mystic acquiescence. With its echoes of Anglican ritualistic chants and sermons, it provides the needed transition from pagan to Christian fatalism. *The Rock* (1934) and *Murder in the Cathedral* (1935), a poetic tragedy on the death of Thomas à Becket, Archbishop of Canterbury, are, in a sense, occasional pieces, written to celebrate events in the life of the Church, but they carry the poet further along his now chosen path by the return of poetic drama to the church ritual in which it originated.

Four Quartets (1943), comprising the separate poems "Burnt Norton," "East Coker," "The Dry Salvages," and "Little Gidding," is the major work in nondramatic poetry of Eliot's maturity. Each of the poems suggests by its title that its theme is located in time and place, but the poetic movement spreads backward and forward across the two intersecting planes of experience, slowly identifying the personal with the universal, change with eternity, multiplicity with unity, dismay with peace. The only progression in the four poems is a growth (which is a recapitulation of his own) from the rose garden of remembered desire in the first part to the flame of a love that destroys and redeems in the last. The end of all searching is to return at last to the point of starting and to know it for the first time. The thought is a simple one, familiar to all mystics, particularly to Christians, and much of the symbolism is that of the Christian tradition: the rose, the garden, the dove, the flame. The method is still that of *The Waste Land*, the achievement of a sense of the universal by mingling the past with the present, the serene with the harsh, the real with myth; but the process is now a blending rather than a mixing, harmony rather than dissonance, soft outlines rather than sharp edges, vague impressions rather than clear images.

In a later essay on "The Three Voices of Poetry," Eliot distinguishes between the voice of the poet talking to himself, the voice of the poet addressing an audience, and the voice of the poet saying only what he can say in the person of an imagined character. Perhaps this is only a new way of stating the differences between lyric, epic, and dramatic poetry, but, as always, it is in Eliot a discovery drawn from his own efforts and achievements. Most of his early poetry was semilyric, semidramatic, but (with the exceptions of the choruses in *The Rock* and in *Murder in the Cathedral*) not quite firmly in the middle group. In *Four Quartets* the dramatic element was eliminated and the poet struck his purest lyric note in the elegiac form.

At the same time he was turning to a personal dramatic idiom. Eliot himself early pointed out that modern verse drama could not be written either in blank verse or in heroic couplets; it would have to find a new form "devised out of colloquial speech." When he was finally ready to undertake a social drama, *The Family Reunion* (1939), he had become more obviously British. What he produced was a modern British version of the Orestes theme, at about the time that both O'Neill and Maxwell Anderson were experimenting with the same kind of material in America. There was no vestige of his American past in this study of a family's introverted obsessions; nor was there any in the later plays of a similar kind, *The Cocktail Party* (1949) and *The Confidential Clerk* (1954), in which colloquial speech is raised to poetry in four-stress uneven rhythm as an instrument for discussing contemporary psychological problems against a background of Christian myth.

T. S. Eliot grew old gracefully and, in his maturer years, developed an art which was as suitable to the mild skepticism of age as the early poetry, written for himself, was an expression of the urgencies of youth. Here was a literary artist who did not forget to grow, even though he never took a step without first measuring the length of his journey to within a millimeter.

Eliot's associates and followers in the classical movement started their thinking where he did, with the concept of the artist as the maker of something projected wholly outside himself and subject to laws of order and form derived from the nature of art itself. Of the poets in this group, Archibald MacLeish, Hart Crane, Wallace Stevens, Marianne Moore, and William Carlos Williams were far more American than he because they remained at home or returned, devoting themselves to practical pursuits while writing poetry of sheer beauty of rhythm and imagery; but most of their verses finally created a realm for themselves beyond time and place.

The two exceptions were Archibald MacLeish (b. 1892) and Hart Crane (1899–1932), both of whom began in poetry under the strong influence of Eliot, but did not follow him into the further reaches of his conservatism. *The Hamlet of A. MacLeish* (1928) was almost the testament of a Prufrock, but with *Conquistador* (1932) and *Frescoes for Mr. Rockefeller's City* (1933) MacLeish completely reversed his ideas on the relationship between art and society. From being one of Cowley's "exiles," he became a leader in the movement to recover an American political and literary tradition in harmony with the modern age. Experiments with radio plays and collective journalism in *Fortune* magazine stretched and strained his poetic art almost into greatness, but his *Collected Poems, 1917–1952*, contains the miscellaneous works of a gifted singer rather than the epic he seemed to promise. The same combination of strains left the far more perceptive Hart Crane an early suicide, and his poem *The Bridge* (1930) an exalted vision. If Walt Whitman had been called back to answer the nihilism of Eliot's *The Waste Land*, but had been given an insufficiently rugged sensibility, he might have produced something like the "dynamic and eloquent document" that Crane attempted. In *The Bridge* Crane sought an American tradition of unity and faith in a complex of symbols from Columbus to Brooklyn Bridge, but the poem remained an expression of a brilliant and confused personality rather than of a united people. The aging Frost and Sandburg were still the bardic singers of the day.

– 3 –

Fiction and drama turned to classicism more slowly and reluctantly than did poetry and criticism; in some degree even avoiding its extremes completely. The generation of novelists who became prominent in the thirties, in addition to Wolfe and Hemingway, included James T. Farrell, John Steinbeck, Erskine Caldwell, and William Faulkner. Naturalists all in their primary inspiration, these men also developed in varying degrees the possibilities of symbolism and moved generally in the direction that Sherwood Anderson rather than Dreiser had indicated, toward fantasy and away from literal realism. At first unnoticed, the silvery laughter of the comic spirit began to be heard above the voices of tragedy, corruption, and death, with which their work was most concerned. As the theme of illusion which had so obsessed O'Neill came more and more to supplant that of reality, their art grew increasingly self-conscious and objective. From the most realistic of them all (Farrell) to the most symbolic and purely aesthetic (Faulkner) there is progress in technical virtuosity and philosophical depth. American fiction, like American poetry and drama, reached its highest point of achievement in the equilibrium of conflicting forces that characterized the mid-thirties, rather than in either extreme.

The novels of James T. Farrell (b. 1904) are examples of the persistence of naturalism in American fiction during an era when main currents were moving in a contrary direction. In intention and method the trilogy *Studs Lonigan* (1935) might almost have been the work of Dreiser himself, for in it Farrell merely retells, with minor alterations, the life of a childhood friend in Chicago's South Side. The character

Danny O'Neill represents the author in the story, and it is Danny's story in that Farrell was interested in the arrogance and power of Studs mainly because Danny idealized him as the hero of his Irish-Catholic world and was deeply moved by his failure and death. The tragedy was ready-made, and a literal recording preserved a sense of unity and resolution which is lacking in the subsequent novels about Danny himself and about a second alter ego, Bernard Clare (Carr) who, like Wolfe's George Webber, goes to New York and becomes a writer of fiction.

The world of reality begins to recede in the novels of John Steinbeck (b. 1902). Perhaps one reason is that the scene moves to the California coast where the impossible seems to thrive in the literary products of the Salinas Valley, as well as in its fantastic orchards, vineyards, and religious sects. Another reason may have been the mingling of Irish and German blood which produced the romantic tale *Cup of Gold* (1929) and the pseudo-realistic studies of the people of an isolated valley, *The Pastures of Heaven* (1932). Steinbeck's own basic attitude was a comic detachment which allowed him to mingle social concern with good-humored laughter at the irresponsibility of his paisanos. Even the lilt of Irish-English prose is in the tales of the carefree inhabitants of *Tortilla Flat* (1935), followed almost immediately by the plight of migratory workers in the orchards, *In Dubious Battle* (1936); and the two elements of fantasy and reality were mingled inseparably in *Of Mice and Men* (1937), a short novel written with an eye to both stage and movie adaptation. So far, Steinbeck had refused to be typed; his study of the friendship of the lumpish Lannie and his faithful George is believable as a revelation of warped personality at the same time that it is symbolic of man's eternal longing to return to the land.

The level on which Steinbeck's art finally settled was that of the primitive; in this he proved to be in the richest American literary tradition. He was interested in the animal motivation underlying human conduct, and with its aid he created a world of unreality with which he could offset that of the ugly world he knew. He was at his best when he succeeded in maintaining a contrapuntal interplay between these two worlds by the use of a larger symbolism, in the fashion of O'Neill rather than of Eliot. The balance between these worlds was so precarious that failure followed success, and success failure, throughout his literary career, sometimes even in the same work. *Grapes of Wrath* (1939) is epic in its recognition of the plight of American migratory workers—specifically, the "Okies," driven westward by the industrialization of their Oklahoma farms—as but one more symbolic event in man's eternal search for the promised land. A tract against social injustice, which aroused vigorous protest and defense from those who thought of it only as fictionalized propaganda, it remained, after the controversy had died down, an American epic, a culminating expression of the spiritual and material forces that had discovered and settled a continent.

In his later massive work, *East of Eden* (1952), Steinbeck used the same primitive base for his study of evil, to symbolize the regenerative power of earth in allowing a choice between good and evil to each of the furthest descendants of Adam. "Nearly everything I have is in it," Steinbeck wrote to his friend Covici, and, he might have added, nearly everything that America has as well. The daring mixtures of comedy and tragedy, myth and reality, that crowd these pages give them a richness of texture which can excuse their inequalities of feeling and form. Actually more at home in such comic studies of character as the inimitable *Cannery Row* (1945) and its less happy sequel *Sweet Thursday* (1954), he will perhaps be remembered longer for the amoral and happily incongruous "Doc" and his friends than for Tom Joad or Adam Trask, who had undertaken to measure their experiences with the moral issues of this world against universal truths. For Steinbeck had dared, as had Thoreau, to drive life "into a corner, and reduce it to its lowest terms, and, if it proved to be mean, why then to get the whole and genuine meanness of it."

The distinction between reality and illusion is even harder to make in the novels and short stories of William Faulkner (b. 1897) because he shared Steinbeck's concern for social justice, his faith in the primitive as the seat of truth, and his mixture of moral earnestness with sardonic humor; but he seemed, more successfully than any of his contemporaries, to approach his material as the "objective correlative" of experience, and to preserve his integrity as an artist. Illusion was for him a complete and separate state of being from which he could view his other and real being objectively and with emotional freedom. To unsympathetic readers he seemed a mere sensationalist, trafficking in perversion for its own sake, and many linked him with his Southern contemporary in fiction of the "hard-boiled school," Erskine Caldwell (b. 1903). It is characteristic of the two men that Caldwell protested his artistic sincerity in his early stories, *Tobacco Road* (1932), *God's Little Acre* (1933), and *Trouble in July* (1940), only to lapse into repetitive sensationalism in the later ones, while Faulkner professed sensationalism in the preface to *Sanctuary*

(1931) and then made the story one of the principal stones in the larger edifice of his art. Almost from the start of his career, Faulkner showed an aching sensibility to the confusion and loss of values of men in his time. This, coupled with a confidence in his art that allowed him to live his own life in his own way, enabled him to write a series of books which were all parts of each other because they were parts of a steady aesthetic vision.

The publication, in 1946, of Malcolm Cowley's introduction to *The Portable Faulkner* turned public recognition upon him, and the award of the 1949 Nobel Prize (in 1950), an honor which would have seemed to many to be violently misplaced only a few years before, was by then an overdue acknowledgment of world fame. Faulkner left Mississippi long enough to go to Stockholm and back (as he had earlier to Hollywood and back when the movie industry thought it needed his assistance), but he made it clear that he had work to do at home and that these events were interruptions. The same spirit of humility, fatalism, and seeming innocence characterized his every act except that of writing, where he was quietly at home and busy.

Just where and how he acquired the manner of his early work is hard to discover as we know little about his reading and education. His own family, who appear under the name of Sartoris in his novels, were active in local politics and business in and around Oxford, Mississippi, for several generations, but they were "new people" set apart from the decayed gentility symbolized in the Comptons or the migrant tenant farmers known as the Snopes. Except for a colorful great-grandfather who took time out from business speculations to write *Rapid Ramblings in Europe* and *The White Rose of Memphis*, there seem to have been few literary or intellectual influences in Faulkner's background, although there was apparently some artistic talent in his mother's family.

Contrary to common impression, it was not until his third novel, *Sartoris* (1929), that Faulkner began to make use of his Mississippi background and racial memory as material for his saga of society. His first, *Soldiers' Pay* (1926), draws on his experience as an aviator in the Canadian and British air services during the First World War and tells of the effects of a horribly wounded soldier on his family and friends when he returns to normal society in his Georgia home. The theme, strangely reminiscent of Stephen Crane's "The Monster," suggests the traumatic experience which underlies his fascination for the abnormal and the grotesque; just as *Mosquitoes* (1927), a satiric novel on New Orleans, with its plotless assembly of witless sophisticates, suggests the escape from horror into sardonic humor that became characteristic of Faulkner's mature work. This was during the time that he was working on a newspaper in New Orleans and knew Sherwood Anderson, whose love of things deeply American and broadly human was probably the most shaping of the literary influences he had felt so far. Perhaps it was Anderson too who taught him the technique of indirection, the slipping from direct narration into a kind of stream-of-consciousness in which turbulence of thought and feeling could flow directly into words and reveal themselves by the trick of obscuring fact and action. Committed to a rhetorical style which he later learned to control, Faulkner showed little evidence in these

early novels of his ability to use his love of words imagina-
tively—almost fantastically—on the actual life that he so fully
understood.

In *Sartoris* he finally accepted the life he knew, with all
its distortions and horrors, because he was a part of it and he
loved it. And in *The Sound and the Fury* (1929) he became
wholly the naturalist in his basic thinking. This is a tale first
told by Benjy Compton, a born idiot, capable of receiving
from life only sense impressions, blending them into a flow of
sensory responses. Benjy's brothers Quentin and Jason and
his sister Caddy were, if not idiots, at least human beings so
warped by temperament and circumstance that conventional
morality no longer could give them control over destiny. The
tale—which is finally Quentin's, as the most sensitive, the
most intelligent, the most human of them, and the most like
Faulkner himself—is told by the merged personality of the
Compton brothers, speaking in turns. It has also by now become the tale of the South, for Faulkner has added another
level to his art, that of formal concern for society as such. An
intricate web of recollection, this complex novel signifies
nothing—and everything.

There is probably no angrier book in all literature, yet
in a later novel Quentin is made to say, in answer to the question, in the iron New England dark, of his Harvard room-
mate: Why do you hate the South? "I don't hate it. . . . I
don't. . . . I don't hate it." For Quentin was Faulkner's second alter ego, more removed from himself and from reality
than his returned aviator could ever have been, a creation of
fiction in whom and through whom he could express his love
for the South and his despair at the folly of man. With this
novel Faulkner really began his Yoknapatawpha Chronicle,

the history—told by snatches and flashbacks in interweaving novels and short stories—of the town of "Jefferson" (Oxford on the map), Mississippi, in "Yoknapatawpha" (Lafayette) County, and of all that stretched out from it, backward and forward, in time and space. In spite of actuality, Jefferson was a complete creation of fiction, and William Faulkner was its "sole owner and proprietor." With no more distortion of fact than Dreiser or Farrell used in telling of their memories of childhood and youth, or Wolfe put into the character of Eugene Gant or the town of Altamont, Faulkner had created a realm of fancy over which his imagination had control and about which he knew, from firsthand experience, every detail. The material was real, the aesthetic control absolute. He had moved into this realm in some of his early stories and in *Sartoris;* with *The Sound and the Fury* it took over his imagination.

Faulkner's French readers at once associated him with Poe, but his later American critics have perhaps more accurately linked him with Hawthorne and James. Like Poe he encouraged myths about himself to conform to the public notion of the author of his tales, and like Poe he threw himself into the horror and violence of his creations. But he lacked the elementary quality of Poe's thought and style. His aesthetic detachment was more nearly complete and his themes and characters more complex. In these respects he suggests the art of fiction as taught by James and such later European novelists as Joyce and Proust; but his brooding sense of guilt, first fully realized in Quentin, has in it more of the renegade Calvinist conscience of Hawthorne than of the complexes of Freud. His efforts to recapture the past in order to explore the hidden secrets of man are surely in the tradition of Melville and of the customs inspector of Salem. New England and the Deep South held almost identical meanings for the twentieth century American author: equally they symbolized the failure of a Utopian dream for man, the decline and corruption of an overidealized democratic culture. In the moment of its power and achievement, a nation no longer young could afford to recapture its childhood dreams and to meditate upon the essential tragedy of life as rediscovered in its own past.

As I Lay Dying (1930) was Faulkner's own favorite among his novels, at least when it was written. An absurd story, it does not bear retelling except as Faulkner wrote it—in a six-week burst of energy while on night-shift in a power plant. The journey of her mourning husband and assorted children to Jefferson with the corpse of Addie Bundren is discussed from the viewpoint of each of the participants with the curious mixture of reminiscent monologue and omniscient author-insight that had by now become Faulkner's characteristic style.

The difference between this tale and its more notorious successor, *Sanctuary,* is not so great as either Faulkner or his readers have proposed. The author's assurance that here he was deliberately writing a potboiler to attract attention needs more than a grain of salt. The story of Temple Drake and Popeye has more plot and more detail of horrible event than most of Faulkner's stories, but the scene is Yoknapatawpha, the characters are people of the Chronicle, and the theme is perhaps as much that of the rape of the South by impotent Northern industrialism as it is of a weak and corrupt girl by a diseased gangster. A far lesser novel than its successors, *Sanctuary* fitted into the over-all scheme of Faulkner's work as it was now developing even though it did, as he says he hoped it would, serve to broaden his public and to prepare for the critical acceptance which came in the next few years.

Those years were Faulkner's Waste Land, explored and discovered and revealed. They brought forth most of his best work, for now he had reached that moment of delicate equilibrium when his vision was completed, his art sure, and his solutions to man's dilemma not yet articulated. Two novels, *Light in August* (1932) and *Absalom, Absalom!* (1936); two shorter tales, *Pylon* (1935) and *The Wild Palms* (1939); and two collections of short stories, *These 13* (1931) and *The Unvanquished* (1938), are chief among the works that fill these overflowing years. It was Faulkner's great period as it was the richest period in America's literary history—for, at the same time, O'Neill and Maxwell Anderson were offering their major plays; Robinson, Frost, Sandburg, and Eliot were writing their more philosophical poems; and Hemingway, Wolfe and Dos Passos were publishing their most ambitious fiction.

It would be a mistake to try to read back into Faulkner's novels and short stories of this period the explicit concern with morality and with the cause of the South that is found in his later work, but it would be equally a mistake to see them, as early criticism did with few exceptions, as morbid studies of human degeneracy, lacking in both ethical and social conscience. Joe Christmas, the central character in *Light in August*, is surely as dehumanized as any human being could become, and the obvious Christian reference of his name is direct irony, used not maliciously but with a deep sense of tragedy. As symbol he is modern man stripped of his humanity by the rigidities of both religion and economics. It is thus possible to read the novel as an ironic allegory of sin as created within the Protestant Church and without (as some later critics did), or as an epitome of the plight of the South. It was probably both of these, and far more, to its author because his messages were not yet intellectualized. The sense of a work of art creating itself is present throughout.

In like manner, the reading of *Absalom, Absalom!* as merely a study of the failure of the South to reestablish its economic and social stability is to limit a work which is also an allegory of man's search for his soul in despite of his own narrow egotism. Thomas Sutpen is the instrument of revenge against those whose weaknesses had destroyed the Old South, but his effort to establish his own racial line backfires when he cannot produce an heir that is sure of race and free of sin. Quentin Compton, who tells most of the story, is fascinated by Sutpen's failure because he sees in it a mirror for his own problems and for those of the South, but he finds in it no solutions. Faulkner is here using all the instruments of a now fully matured art to reveal the range of life as he has observed it and meditated upon it.

When these stories and the many shorter ones of the same period are brought together, the problem with which Faulkner is primarily concerned becomes apparent. In every one there is presented, in a symbolic guise, the fury and dismay that result when the biologic life force comes into conflict with mechanism. This is the central theme of thoughtful American literature from Henry Adams to T. S. Eliot. Faulkner's special power lies in his ability to reveal the fury rather than merely to discuss the conflict.

With the economic and social overtones of *The Hamlet* (1940), a folk comedy mainly about the Snopes family, the voice of the reformer became more explicit in Faulkner's work. There now came a change which was generally welcomed by the critics because the author, in spite of an even more involved style, seemed to be willing to help in revealing the intended meanings of his work. The allegory of the Bear in *Go Down Moses* (1942) is perplexing because Faulkner's own attitude toward the wilderness theme is not consistent in the two versions of the story, but there is no doubt that he is proposing in both the answer of the primitive to the complexities of humanity. Old Ben is more symbol than fact, but whether he should be destroyed as a bear or reverenced as a god is not altogether clear.

With *Intruder in the Dust* (1948), meaning became message, and with *A Fable* (1954) it became allegory. Breaking at last from absorption in the Jefferson Chronicle, Faulkner here returned to his earlier theme of the soldier and the wound of war. Point for point, the triumph and death of the corporal who brings about the false armistice of 1918 is paralleled with the passion of Christ; yet his power is limited as that of Christ was not, and the tone of the allegory contains too much irony to permit it to be accepted, even in its noblest passages, as pure Christian doctrine. Once more, comedy is mixed with tragedy, irony with faith, to reveal the essential humanity of man rather than to preach formal solutions to the impasse which man's stupidity has created. Faulkner had developed in late life a more intellectualized art form, but he was still, first and last, an artist.

It is not so easy to define the classical elements in Faulkner's work as it is in Eliot's. Almost entirely self-educated, he did not have the foundation in systematic philosophy upon which the poet's control of his medium was based. His ability to detach himself from his natural material and to view it at will with tragic seriousness or sardonic irony seems to have been instinctive rather than planned. His power over language and symbol were likewise spontaneous. But when he is compared to Wolfe or Steinbeck or Caldwell, the presence of a conscious and controlled aesthetic is apparent. Once he had discovered his special mission—to reveal the saga of the South as a modern epic of the fall and corruption of man—he never wavered. The discovery by his critics of his technical mastery over material and form was probably as much of a surprise to him as it was to them; but the mastery was nevertheless there. In him, as earlier in Hawthorne, the tragic depths of American experience had been ruthlessly probed by an artist who instinctively knew what he was doing and how to do it. His originality and skill became apparent only when his imitators and critics made them so by less subtle means than were his. Then it also became apparent that America's second literary renaissance had reached and passed its meridian.

– 4 –

Faulkner's turn to religious allegory was not an isolated event. Hemingway's Old Man was in many ways a fisher of men, Robert Frost's Masques of Reason and Mercy used the stories of Job and Jonah, O'Neill's Iceman was but Death demanding his reckoning, and T. S. Eliot's late verse tragicomedies were all thinly disguised religious debates. After 1945 leading writers of the older generation were preparing to face something larger than their own individual deaths; there was the unmistakable tone of Judgment Day for an era in their common symbolism and skeptical otherworldliness.

Perhaps the discovery of atomic power was a decisive force in shaping the temper of the times into a conservative mold, dulling the edges of individual aggressiveness, instilling fear where hope had been, stressing the need for strong national government and international cooperation to erect bulwarks against impending doom, and inciting a religious revival. Perhaps, on the other hand, something less unique in human history had happened, for the period of revolution that had swept Western Europe for two centuries had burned itself out, and the era of American history that had civilized a continent was over. Every action has a reaction, every rise a fall, every radical movement an ultimate conservatism. The cultural equilibrium that had produced in the United States an original and vital literary movement in the previous half-century could not be expected to continue indefinitely and without change.

Critics and literary historians who predicted a fresh impulse to come from the generation returning in 1945 from the Second World War were therefore disappointed. Their error lay in the shortsighted notion that as the first war had produced a lost generation and a literary revival, a second war would repeat and produce another. Sober second thought brought the realization that the generation of the fifties was, in training and temperament, almost the reverse of that of the twenties. It had nothing to revolt against except revolt. Born into a world which apparently was already falling apart, it was not interested in destructive attacks upon any rigid systems of value or forms of expression. The revolt of the lost generation had been all too successful. Mere survival now dictated constructive effort or resignation to fate.

To accentuate this trend toward conservatism, many of the older critics and writers were teaching the arts of poetry, drama, and fiction in the universities, and others were held up as models for imitation. Henry James, Hemingway, and Faulkner supplied the standards for fiction, Eliot for poetry, O'Neill for drama. A feeling had grown up that there are right ways and wrong ways of shaping style and structure and fixed standards and methods by which a work of art might be examined and judged. Summer conferences spread from coast to coast, giving employment and a fee to critics and writers and providing them with a forum and a following. At the same time professionalism was once more taking over popular literature as mass production in radio, television, movies, and paper-back books enormously increased the available public for literature but discouraged careful and thoughtful reading. Thus, as popular taste tended to become standardized on one level, cultism and retreat into esoteric forms and modes tended to standardize cultivated taste on another. Writers who attempted to strike out in their own directions were pulled toward one of these norms or the other. The split between the "High-brow" and the "Low-brow" that Van Wyck Brooks had deplored in the late nineteenth century writers seemed to be opening once more. F. O. Matthiessen wrote just before his death in 1950, "American poetry in these years furnished the most serious evidence of cleavage between what we have learned to call mass civilization and minority culture." To a somewhat lesser degree the same thing might be said of fiction and drama. Conformity had seized the mass; convention had taken a firmer hold on the culture.

If the cyclic theory of literary history is valid, and if the contemporary period is one of reaction against the burst of creative energy which had provided a second renaissance in American literary history, members of the younger generation of 1950 were faced with the choice of carrying reaction further or providing some kind of new revolt. If the latter, the nature of the revolt had not by then been clearly declared. There was as much new and vibrant writing as any historian could ask for, but the voices of the new writers seemed to be calling for values, standards, and security rather than for further upheaval and change. They seemed older and wiser than their elders, but many of them were confused as to whether they should supply the demands of the mass public or of those masters of style and form who were now dictating standards of propriety and correctness. With a fuller knowledge of human nature and society at their command than almost any previous literary generation in America had had, and with a larger public than any literary generation at any time or place had ever known, they seemed at the mid-point of the century to be waiting for a leadership that could point direction.

INDEX